THE KING'S FRIENDS

THE COMPOSITION AND MOTIVES OF
THE AMERICAN LOYALIST CLAIMANTS

by Wallace Brown

BROWN UNIVERSITY PRESS
PROVIDENCE, RHODE ISLAND · 1965

PREFACE

IN THE United States, Bancroftian interpretations of the American Revolution, which de-emphasize social conflict within the colonies, apparently neglect the Tories or Loyalists. (I am thinking of such scholars as Edmund Morgan and Robert E. Brown.) In Great Britain the Loyalists, perhaps an embarrassment to the Whig school of historiography,[1] have been snubbed, just as they often were as refugees at the time. Only in Canada, where many emigrated and where they were officially designated the United Empire Loyalists, with the right to use the letters U.E. after their names, are they remembered and even venerated as founding fathers. Yet contemporary Americans such as Washington, Franklin, and John Adams were well, even painfully, aware of the Tory problem.

In December, 1815, Adams wrote to Dr. Jedidiah Morse concerning the Tories and the Revolution. Adams, convinced that Toryism was mainly the result of greed and bribery, gave several examples from his native Massachusetts and continued, "Where is the historian who can and will travel through the United States, and investigate all the similar intrigues in each of them for the same purpose? Yet without this, the real history of the United States, and especially of their revolution, never can be written."[2]

Adams had no doubt of the great importance and strength of the Tories; yet the only serious general study of them is sixty years old[3] and needs replacing. Admittedly, ever since 1847, when Lorenzo Sabine published the first edition of his *American Loyalists*, the Tories have been written about with sympathy; some useful state and local works have appeared, and there is a recent, informative book on Loyalist political thought.[4] But several colonies lack monographs, and many questions remain to be answered. What were the over-all social and economic effects of the Tory exile and loss of property? How many émigrés returned? What was the connection between Federalism and Loyalism? These are but a few.

This study aims somewhat at what John Adams had in mind. Primarily it seeks to answer two simple questions: who were the Loyalists and why were they loyal? (Some light, it is hoped, will also be thrown on such other matters as the suffering of the Loyalists, their political philosophy, and the reasons for their failure.) I have not traveled physically through the United States as the former president suggested, but have journeyed metaphorically through time and space investigating the "intrigues" in each state chiefly by means of the remaining records of the claims commission set up by the British government to indemnify American Loyalists for losses caused by the Revolution.

The first thirteen chapters deal with each of the colonies in turn, from New Hampshire to Georgia. Statistical tables upon which a good deal of each chapter rests (and an explanation of these tables) are found in an appendix beginning on page 287. A final chapter draws some conclusions for the colonies as a whole. The statistical tables drawn from an analysis of 2,908 white claimants (that is, those Loyalists who submitted claims for losses to the British) do not pretend to provide the basis for complete answers to questions about the Loyalists. The tables do represent, however, a hitherto largely untapped source for a work of this kind, and will in the future, it is hoped, be either confirmed or refuted

Preface

by more detailed local studies, of which (with some notable exceptions) there is a dearth.

A note on terms: The words Loyalist, Loyalism, Tory, and Toryism are impossible to define precisely. This book is based mainly on a study of Loyalist claimants, who are not synonymous with all the Loyalists, and it must be stressed that the conclusions drawn here about Loyalism are, strictly speaking, only valid for that segment of Loyalism represented by the claimants. However, the claimants are a useful and sometimes representative sample,[5] and in the absence of conflicting evidence the conclusions made about them can frequently be cautiously extended to the Loyalists in general.

The spelling, punctuation, and syntax of all quotations from manuscripts remain the same as the original with such usual exceptions as the expansion of unfamiliar abbreviations and the lowering of superior letters. Square brackets indicate any additions, and *sic* has been used sparingly, only where confusion might arise.

I am very grateful to the Royal Society, Burlington House, London, W.1, for permission to quote from two letters in the Blagden Collection. The Society retains the copyright and all rights to these letters. Quotations from Crown-copyright records in the Public Record Office appear by permission of the Controller of Her Majesty's Stationery Office.

There remains the pleasant duty of thanking some of the individuals who have helped me. This book began as a Ph.D. thesis at the University of California at Berkeley under the supervision of Professor Carl Bridenbaugh and was completed under Professor Robert L. Middlekauff. To these two gentlemen I owe most. I also wish to thank Professors Norman S. Grabo, L. H. Harper, and Brooke

Preface

Hindle, who read the manuscript at the thesis stage. More recently, Professor Bridenbaugh has rendered me further valuable services. All the errors and shortcomings remain my own responsibility. The History Department and the staff of the library of the University of California were very good to me when I was a graduate student. A Woodrow Wilson Traveling Fellowship enabled me to visit the eastern United States in August, 1963, and a Canada Council Grant-in-Aid helped me to England in August, 1964. (Some other fruits of these two visits will appear in future works.) I undertook the final preparation of the book fortunately as a member of two congenial universities, first the University of Alberta, Edmonton, and now Brown University.

Finally I record various kinds of help, direct and indirect, from the following: Mrs. Charlotte Brown, Dr. and Mrs. A. B. Brown, Mrs. Roberta Bridenbaugh, Mr. Grant Dugdale and the staff of the Brown University Press, Mrs. Erich Müller, Dr. G. D. Ramsay, the late Mr. C. O. Mackley, and Mrs. Barbara Moore.

TABLE OF CONTENTS

Contents

MAPS

PHILADELPHIA, August 30, 1776.
Spent the evening with Messrs. Brewer and Buchannan.
Both *Sgnik Sdneirf*.   —Nicholas Cresswell, *Journal*

I. NEW HAMPSHIRE

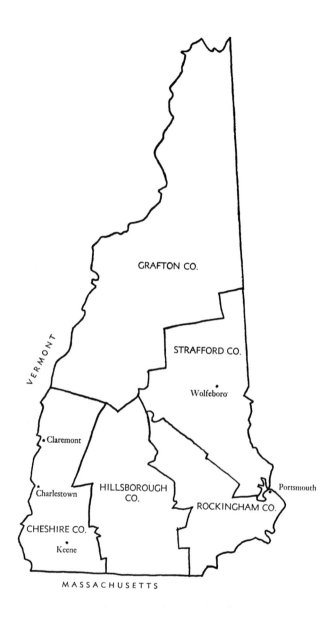

GRAFTON CO.

STRAFFORD CO.

VERMONT

Wolfeboro

Claremont

HILLSBOROUGH
CO.

Charlestown

Portsmouth

ROCKINGHAM CO.

CHESHIRE CO.

Keene

MASSACHUSETTS

NEW HAMPSHIRE

IN NOVEMBER, 1778, the New Hampshire Assembly passed an act of banishment against seventy-six Loyalists, all of whom had left the state.[1] Only eighteen of these are found among the claimants who later went before the British claims commissioners, but the seventy-six are the core of New Hampshire Loyalism and an analysis of them is valuable.

Only two pieces of information are given in the act, occupation and residence. The breakdown is as follows:

Occupation

Governor	1
Gentlemen or esquires	29[a]
Major	1
Physicians	4
Minister	1
Merchants	8
Traders	5
Ropemaker	1
Printer	1
Postrider	1
Yeomen	19

Residence

ROCKINGHAM COUNTY

Portsmouth	33
Pembroke	1
Exeter	1
Concord	1
Newmarket	2
Londonderry	6

HILLSBOROUGH COUNTY

Merrimack	1
Hollis	3
Dunbarton	6

Amherst	2
New Ipswich	1
Francestown	1
Peterborough	1
CHESHIRE COUNTY	
Keene	5
Packersfield	1
Alstead	2
Winchester	1
Rindge	1
Charlestown	4
Claremont	1
Hinsdale	2

ᵃNo further information is given. They were probably holders of landed estates.

The banishment act was followed shortly by a confiscation act which included twenty-five names mentioned in the earlier act plus three more. Confiscation seems to have been the fate reserved for particularly active Loyalists who had actually joined the British armed forces or at least fled to the British lines. They had, as the act put it, "to the utmost of their power aided, abetted and assisted" the enemies of New Hampshire.[2]

There is no reason to quarrel with the Loyalist who told the claims commissioners that Portsmouth was the least disaffected part of New Hampshire.[3] General John Sullivan indicated a certain Loyalist strength in a letter to Washington, dated Portsmouth, October 29, 1775. He complained of the lack of defenses there: ". . . in short, not a moment's defence could be made, or annoyance given to the enemy. . . . That infernal crew of Tories, who have . . . endeavoured to prevent fortifying this harbour, walk the streets here with impunity, and will, with a sneer, tell the people in the

[4]

streets that all our liberty-poles will soon be converted into gallows." [4]

The tables[5] support the evidence of contemporaries that New Hampshire Loyalism was focused in this town, which, with a population of 4,590 in 1775, was easily the major urban center in the colony.[6] Twenty (or 53 per cent) of the claimants whose residence is known were from Portsmouth, as were thirty-three (nearly half) of the seventy-six New Hampshire Loyalists banished in 1778. Otherwise, the claimants were scattered generally around the three southern counties, Cheshire, Hillsborough, and, on the coast, Rockingham (a fact again emphasized by the banishment act). Grafton County, with no claimants or banished inhabitants, and Stafford County, with one claimant and no banished inhabitants, were extremely weak Loyalist areas.

There is a strong indication that New Hampshire Loyalism was weighted towards wealth and position, particularly official position. Eleven out of twenty-five claimants put in for more than £2,000 in losses; the largest single occupational category is that of royal office-holder with fifteen out of a known thirty-nine claimants,[7] and if the five professional men are added, over one-half of the occupations are accounted for. A fairly strong contingent of farmers and commercial people completes the picture of Loyalism. A look at the seventy-six banished Loyalists gives a fairly similar impression. Twenty-nine gentlemen or esquires (probably owners of landed estates) are recorded (this figure includes at least four royal office-holders); there are six professional men, fifteen connected with commerce, and nineteen farmers.

The sparse figures reveal three times as many native-born claimants as British immigrants. Fifty per cent served the

British either in the armed forces or in some other official position, a high percentage indicating active involvement.

Portsmouth, the center of New Hampshire Loyalism, requires further discussion. A glance at the seventeen Portsmouth claimants reveals that the great majority were American born, nearly all were wealthy (only one was not a gentleman),[8] and eight, or nearly half, were royal office-holders, the town, of course, being the site of the royal administration. Only two claimants were known to be merchants.

In January, 1777, fifteen inhabitants of Portsmouth (several of them leading ones) were arrested as Loyalists, but twelve were released on bond, and one of them, James Sheafe, became a United States senator from New Hampshire in 1801.[9] The indications are that even in Portsmouth it was apathy rather than Loyalism which was strong, the adamant Loyalists being mainly office-holders.

The Loyalists were undoubtedly weak in general throughout New Hampshire. Forty-two claimants are recorded, 0.06 per cent (one of the lowest percentages)[10] of the population of 77,053.[11]

As with every colony, it is impossible to say accurately what fraction of the total Loyalists the claimants represent. Otis G. Hammond, an early historian of the New Hampshire Loyalists, concluded that at the most he had discovered 200 men for whom there was "record evidence of guilt or suspicion of Royalist tendencies," but even some of these were falsely accused.[12]

Samuel Hale, a Portsmouth lawyer, claimed that one-third of the New Hampshire people "for a long time retained their Loyalty" but at the same time modified his statement by admitting that "the people in general . . . were rebels" and that by the end of 1774 "no honest Man could keep any further semblance of being with the people." [13]

The weakness of New Hampshire Loyalists is suggested by the comparative mildness of their treatment. In January, 1777, the House of Representatives was willing to give all who wished three months in which to leave freely with their families, during which time they could sell their property.[14] Admittedly this action by the legislature was followed in 1778 by the harsher acts of banishment and confiscation mentioned above. No indication of persecution is found among the evidence of the claims commissioners, a fact which supports Hammond's statement: "It is to the credit of the people of New Hampshire that persecution of the Royalists never reached the extreme, never the loss of life or permanent physical injury to any human being. There were no serious riots." [15] Two New Hampshire counter-feiters were executed, but this happened in Connecticut.[16] Simon Baxter, having been legally indicted for passing counterfeit money, was kept for an hour on the gallows with a rope around his neck, but this was not really perse-cution by the standards of the day. However, he was later beaten by a mob.[17] When the war ended New Hampshire quickly allowed Loyalists to return—a strong indication of a lack of bitterness, in turn a sign of weak Loyalism.[18]

During the Stamp Act crisis there was mob action in Portsmouth, although George Meserve, the stamp collector and later a claimant, was actually forced to resign by a Boston mob when he returned from England with his new appointment in his pocket. However, it is clear that the act was generally detested in New Hampshire. Only one claim-ant, Bartholomew Stavers, a stage driver, refers to this period, explaining his early desertion of New Hampshire in

November, 1774, by the fact that he had been "obnoxious ever since the Stamp Act."[19] There is evidence that New Hampshire was, as A. M. Schlesinger has put it, "a laggard in entering into extra-legal organization" during the years 1765–1775, and no delegates were sent to the Stamp Act Congress, but this is not evidence of any real Loyalist strength, any more than Rhode Island's spotty record is. It rather illustrates each colony's "orneriness."[20]

From the British point of view far too many New Hampshire people stayed neutral, even among segments of the population from which strong loyalty might be expected. For example, Leo Hubbard, who had held the position of surveyor and searcher of the royal customs at Portsmouth, which netted him £200 a year, claimed temporary support after the war though he admitted that he had submitted to the rebel government and remained in New Hampshire, where he was, in 1785, one of the judges of the supreme court. (No decision on this rather insolent claim is recorded.)[21]

In October, 1774, Governor Wentworth sent New Hampshire carpenters to Boston to help General Gage, who could get none there. Austin Middleton, one of those involved, was later arrested for his suspected Loyalism, but he went on to represent his locality at the convention held to consider the federal Constitution, and was then elected to the House of Representatives.[22]

Joshua Atherton, a wealthy native of Portsmouth, chief justice of New Hampshire and uncle of Governor Wentworth, might be expected to be a natural Loyalist. He did refuse to sign the Association because of his oath of allegiance, and he was involved in passing counterfeit money for the British, but in the long run he managed to remain neutral and did not attract animosity. Breed Batcheller, a merchant and a major in the Queen's Rangers, is perhaps New Hampshire's only example of a vigorous and notorious (from the Whig point of view) Loyalist. But Hammond concludes that Batcheller was only following his economic interests and his ferocious stubborn nature.[23]

A good illustration of the weak and equivocal nature of New Hampshire Loyalism is the behavior of the Anglicans. As often happened in the north, there was an Anglican tinge to Loyalism; the large group of office-holders must have been members of the church, as was Governor Wentworth, but it is significant that no Anglican clergyman submitted a claim. Anglicans in fact were usually at best merely neutral in New Hampshire, a strong indication of the sorry state of the Tory movement there.

There were two Anglican churches in the colony, Trinity Church, Claremont, and Queen's Chapel, Portsmouth. The rector of Queen's Chapel, Arthur Browne, was an "absolute neutral" and was never suspected of Loyalism in spite of his daughter's marriage to Robert Rogers, a prominent Loyalist. (The marriage was dissolved during the war.) The Reverend Ranna Cossitt, of Claremont, was arrested in 1775 together with Samuel Cole, the local schoolmaster and catechist, and many other Anglicans. As a contemporary, Colonel John Peters, wrote, Cossitt and Cole "had more insults than any of the loyalists because they had been servants of the Society [i.e. the Society for the Propagation of the Gospel] which, under pretense (as the rebels say) of propagating religion, had propagated loyalty, in opposition to the liberties of America." Cossitt claimed, "It is an affront if people don't call me a Tory," and he managed to officiate in his parish throughout the war, apparently even continuing to pray for the king. But the notable facts are that Cossitt did *stay*, and neither he nor Cole worked actively against the Whigs.[24]

This and the discovery of a swamp called "Tory Hole," which was one of a series of hiding places for Loyalists en route between New York and Canada, gave Claremont a strongly loyal reputation. In March, 1784, forty-eight Claremont families, claiming Anglicanism and unbroken loyalty to the king, petitioned Haldimand, governor of Quebec, for asylum. But it was at best a passive loyalty which had aided the British and the active Loyalists not one whit. Thus it comes as no surprise that only one claimant gave his residence as Claremont, and that no one from the town is mentioned in the banishment act.[25]

New Hampshire was, of course, overwhelmingly Nonconformist and generally Congregational. Every indication is that Nonconformist pastors and flocks were Patriot almost to a man. The act of banishment does contain the name of the Reverend John Morrison, a Presbyterian minister, but he turns out to be the exception which proves the rule. This wild-living Scot was ordained minister of Peterborough in 1766 and suspended in 1772, having shown himself "dangerous alike as the companion of either sex." He later joined the American army but the day after Bunker Hill deserted to the British, with whom he continued until his death from dissipation at Charleston, South Carolina, in 1782. His son, apparently the antithesis of his father in his personal habits and all else, not surprisingly chose the Patriot side.[26]

New Hampshire Loyalists were an uninspiring group. Apart from the Loyalists mentioned in this chapter, the bulk of New Hampshire's somewhat mediocre talent was

New Hampshire

Patriot; one can mention such men as Meshech Weare, a Harvard graduate and chairman of the committee of safety; John Langdon and William Whipple, leading merchants; General John Sullivan; John Wentworth, the governor's cousin; Dr. John Giddinge; and the Reverend Jeremy Belknap, a prominent Congregational minister, to name a few at random.

Very few political leaders, apart from Governor John Wentworth, put in claims as Loyalists. Only two members of the council, Daniel Rindge (the governor's uncle) and George Boyd (his claim was considered fraudulent and himself a rebel), are found among the claimants, but three others, Theodore Atkinson (the governor's uncle by marriage), George Jaffrey (related by marriage to the governor), and Peter Gilman, were certainly Tories of one kind or another. At least two council members were not loyal: John Phillips and the governor's father, Mark Hunking Wentworth, who was neutral at best, having been chairman of the Portsmouth committee of safety which in 1774 criticized the governor for sending carpenters to General Gage. No member of the House of Representatives put in a claim.[27]

Governor John Wentworth, a New England blue blood if ever there was one, is generally agreed to have been a very competent and popular governor, but he was unable to use his position to rally a Loyalist party. In 1774 he rapidly discovered that he could expect little support from the Assembly, or from anybody else for that matter. When a mob disarmed Fort William and Henry in Portsmouth harbor on October 14 and took away the gunpowder, he obtained support from only four council members, two justices, a sheriff, his private secretary Thomas Mac-

[11]

donough, and Benning Wentworth, his eighteen-year-old brother-in-law and cousin. The revenue officers were not to be found, but "chose to shrink in safety from the storm," as Wentworth put it. Some weeks later he found it impossible to arrest the ringleaders, adding, "No jail would hold them long, and no jury would find them guilty." While a provincial congress was meeting at Exeter, the legal Assembly at Portsmouth proved itself opposed to the governor in a quarrel which focused on the election of Captain John Fenton to a constituency newly created by Wentworth at Plymouth. In January, 1775, fifty-nine persons signed an association at Portsmouth to defend themselves and the governor. The signatories were mainly relatives of the governor (as many as fifteen), office-holders, rich landowners, and merchants, and the whole movement proved to be a fiasco.[28] By June, 1775, it was clear Wentworth could get nowhere, even with the legal Assembly, and on the 13th he fled with his family to H.M.S. "Scarborough" and eventually to Boston in August.[29]

New Hampshire did produce two well-known Loyalists, Benjamin Thompson (later Count Rumford), and Robert Rogers, but both are perhaps exceptions that prove the rule of Tory weakness in New Hampshire. Young Thompson, a future scientist of note and a native of Woburn, Massachusetts, arrived in New Hampshire only a few years before the Revolution began, and was virtually forced into the Loyalist camp because of local jealousies and his failure to get his rank of major in the militia recognized in Washington's army. The flamboyant Rogers did not spend any time in New Hampshire after 1761, as his adventurous and dissipated career took him to South Carolina, Detroit, England, Michilimackinac, and possibly Algiers. He too at first attempted to join the Patriots, and after the defeat of his regiment, the Queen's American Rangers, at White Plains, his military reputation, based on his exploits during the Seven Years War, vanished permanently. It is interesting to recall that Thompson was invited back to the United States in 1799 to set up the military academy at West Point, although he was unable to accept the appointment.

New Hampshire counterfeiters have already been mentioned in connection with the persecution of the Loyalists,[30] and the colony seems to have had a somewhat notable counterfeit operation.[31] Several claimants were involved, but the most important was the leader, Colonel Stephen Holland, of whom a later governor of New Hampshire wrote, "Damn him . . . I hope to see him hanged. He has done more damage than ten thousand men could have done."[32] Holland, an Irish veteran of the Seven Years War, had been persuaded by Governor Wentworth to remain in New Hampshire and organize the dissemination of the counterfeit money, which he did until discovered in 1777. It is typical of New Hampshire that even involvement in this activity was not necessarily a final commitment to Loyalism. Joshua Atherton, a member of the group, later became a United States senator.

There is little to be said about the motives of New Hampshire Loyalists. The self-interest of the largest group, the royal office-holders, is obvious. Then there is a group of rich conservatives often connected with Wentworth's political clique. A hint about possible reasons for the Loyalism of at least one merchant is found in the memorial of Woodbury Langdon, of Portsmouth (from whom no claim is extant), who mentioned supplying blankets in 1774 to General Gage in Boston.[33]

The few remaining Loyalists must have acted from combinations of personal considerations. The claims testimony tells almost nothing. For example, why should John Stinson, born in New Hampshire and educated by his uncle, the American general John Stark, go over to the British after an early period of service with the Americans?[34] (The Stark family was very much divided. The general's brother, William, who died in 1782, and for whom no claim is found, was a Loyalist and engaged in passing counterfeit money in New Hampshire. His motive seems to have been personal resentment at being passed over for the colonelcy of a rebel regiment.)[35] Split families illustrate the personal nature of Loyalism, and as Woodbury Langdon remarked with reference to his rebel brother, "such a differance [*sic*] of sentiment between the nearest relations is far from being an uncommon circumstance in this unhappy civil war..."[36]

More understandable are Loyalists who were immigrants from Great Britain, especially if they were former professional soldiers who had served the crown during the Seven Years War. His previous service probably explains why Captain John Fenton remained steadfast although it was claimed that "he was offer'd any Command but Mr. Washington's" by the Americans.[37]

The Reverend Ranna Cossitt (not a claimant) gave a hint (at least in the first part of his statement) of what was probably in the minds of numerous Tories and potential Tories throughout the colonies when he said, "I verily believe the British troops will overcome by the greatness of their power and the justice of their cause."[38] Samuel Hale expected the war to be "short," and Robert Fowle, the official printer at Portsmouth, wrote in 1783, "I never once conceived it possible—the Rebels could so far carry their

Point as it seems they have . . ."³⁹ New Hampshire was the only colony or state (even including Vermont) which was not invaded by British troops. Had Portsmouth been held for a length of time, had a powerful army been present in the back country, New Hampshire Loyalism might have been dramatically stronger. As it was, it seems that New England traditions of religious and political self-government allied to pure self-interest kept Loyalism at a weak embryonic stage.

II. MASSACHUSETTS

VERMONT   NEW HAMPSHIRE

LINCOLN CO.

CUMBERLAND CO.

YORK CO.

PENOBSCOT
AREA

• Falmouth

• Newbury

ESSEX CO.

MIDDLESEX CO.   Salem
                 • Marblehead

BERKSHIRE CO.   HAMPSHIRE CO.   WORCESTER CO.   SUFFOLK CO.
                                                   • Charlestown
                                                   • Boston
                                  • Worcester   Cambridge   MASSACHUSETTS
                                                                BAY

                                  NORFOLK CO.
                                                 PLYMOUTH
                                                 CO.
CONNECTICUT   Taunton   • Middleboro
                                   • BRISTOL CO.

                            RHODE ISLAND   BARNSTABLE CO.

MASSACHUSETTS

MASSACHUSETTS is an outstanding example of a colony where the cleavage between potential or future Whigs and Loyalists developed early. The first clear issue was the Stamp Act. The whole executive clique, in particular Governor Bernard and Thomas Hutchinson, received an irreversible blow to their prestige owing to the brilliant exploitation of the situation by James Otis and his followers. It is only natural to expect royal officials and Church of England clergymen[1] to take the British side at that time, but several claimants who belonged to neither of these groups mention the act as a turning point. Probably they would all agree with John Adams that they were a mere "handful"; many future Loyalists like Daniel Leonard opposed the act. This point was made by Thomas Robie, a hardware dealer, who claimed to be the only man in Marblehead to dissent from the opposition to the act. George Deblois and Thomas Knight, two Boston merchants, dated their Toryism from this time, while the following became "obnoxious," as most of them termed it, for their various actions: William Warden, a Boston hairdresser; James Barrick, who patrolled the streets in the governor's company of cadets; David Ingersoll, a barrister and member of the Assembly; Edward Stow, a Boston trader "mobbed and Libelled ever since the Stamp Act"; Richard Saltonstall, who had defended Castle William where the stamped papers were lodged; and Timothy Ruggles, a distinguished citizen and one of three delegates to the Stamp Act congress, where "when he saw how violent they were he dissented from their measures," a position which brought a reprimand, but did not prevent his re-election to the lower house.² But Henry Hulton, a Boston customs official, later recalled that "since the Stamp Act affair many gentlemen of property and liberal minds have been left out of the Council and Assembly, and more violent and less informed people brought in."³

From 1765 on, the chief political problems of the day—such as "rescinding," the Captain Preston trial, the non-importation movement, the tea question, support of Hutchinson and Gage—served further to divide Massachusetts society into Whigs and Tories.

In June, 1768, Governor Bernard, at Hillsborough's behest, required the House of Representatives to rescind the resolution which led to the famous Massachusetts circular letter following the Townshend duties. Ninety-two voted against the governor, only seventeen (including five claimants) in favor. They were known as "Rescinders." William Brown reported to the commissioners that by "this action he instantly lost the confidence of his constituents," as did Peter Frye of Salem. Dr. John Calef, of Ipswich, also mentioned the subsequent decline of his practice. But this was not always the case. Josiah Edson (a Loyalist who died too soon to claim) was re-elected for Bridgewater in spite of being a "Rescinder."⁴

Involvement in the trial of Captain Preston following the "Boston Massacre" of March, 1770, is mentioned by several claimants as the occasion which made them particularly "obnoxious": Robert Auchmuty and Sampson Salter Blowers for defending the officer; Gilbert Deblois for helping to weed out of the jury those of "violent principles"; William Hill, whose house was tarred, and James Barrick, whose livelihood as a ropemaker declined when Hancock and others withdrew their business, for serving on the jury;

Newton Prince, a pastry cook, for giving evidence; and Daniel Silsby for undisclosed services for Governor Hutchinson.[5]

Failure to keep the non-importation agreement created trouble for at least twelve claimants who refer directly to it, and several others were involved in the East India Company's attempt to sell tea, including two of Governor Hutchinson's sons, Elisha and Thomas, who were consignees. In 1774, following the Tea Party, two events, the departure of Governor Hutchinson and the arrival of his replacement, General Gage, provided an opportunity for those with Loyalist leanings to stand up and be counted. Both governors were "addressed" in writing, and the signing of one or more of the various petitions of support marked one as an "addresser" and of suspect patriotism. Seventy-two claimants helped speed Hutchinson on his way, and fifty-eight welcomed Gage.[6] Gage's military rule, of course, was followed by the first bloodshed at Lexington in April, 1775, the siege of Boston, and finally the permanent British evacuation in March, 1776.

Now to examine the structure of Massachusetts Loyalism as revealed by the statistical tables.[7] Seventy-three per cent of the claimants were American born. Even the immigrants tended to be long established; about three-fifths had arrived before 1763. The Scots, with fourteen claimants, were easily the largest group of "foreigners." There was little immigration, so this small number does not indicate that the Scots were generally Whig. Rather the opposite; Governor Hutchinson wrote that the Scots in Boston "were almost without exception good Subjects." So probably were the rest of the British too.[8]

Boston was the stronghold with well over half (52.5

per cent) of the known claimants, a fact accentuated by
the eighteen further claimants from the nearby towns of
Brookline, Dorchester, Roxbury, Cambridge, and Charlestown, not to mention many claimants from towns only
slightly further afield. Loyalism was largely a seaboard
phenomenon; Essex, Middlesex, Suffolk, Plymouth, Bristol,
and Nantucket Counties were the homes of 223, or about
75 per cent, of the claimants, a proportion increased if the
thirty-six Maine claimants (from Lincoln and Cumberland
Counties), thirty-two of whom lived in the Falmouth (now
Portland) and Penobscot areas, are considered. Worcester
County, a central county, supplied twenty-four claimants
and the two western counties, Hampshire and Berkshire, a
mere ten. One must note also, at the eastern extreme, that
Barnstable County produced not a single one.

The geographical distribution comes as no surprise when
the occupations of the Loyalists are examined.[9] The largest
category is merchants, with 106 of a known 302. Add the
remaining commercial group, and the total is 149, almost
half.[10] The mercantile element becomes a majority because
at least fourteen of the royal office-holders were also merchants on the side.

As Schlesinger has amply demonstrated, the Boston merchants took the continental lead in the imperial struggle
after 1763.[11] But finally they discovered that they had raised
a Frankenstein's monster. Miss Ann Hulton, the sister of
the customs man, anticipated Schlesinger's thesis when she
wrote, on July 25, 1770, that New York merchants had
broken the non-importation agreements "and tho' 90 out of
a 100 of the Merchants and traders here, want to do the
same, yet they are terrified to submit to [the] Tyranny of
the Power they first set up . . ."[12]

Massachusetts

A minority of the Massachusetts merchants, in particular the Bostonians, were the backbone of Loyalism in the colony; but they were only a fraction of the trading community, and a smaller fraction went into exile.[13] One has only to bring to mind John Hancock, William Molineaux, and Thomas Cushing to recall that many leading Whigs were merchants. A typical contemporary English remark was the dubbing of Boston as the "Dunkirk of America," with reference to the smuggling trade.[14] However, the Loyalist claims records are replete with names of wealthy, important merchants and such business families as the Deblois, the Coffins, the Ervings, the McMasters, the Clarkes, the Lloyds, and the Winslows.

After the mercantile element the next biggest category is the royal officials (mostly customs men) with sixty-four or over one-fifth of the claimants. The next group is professional men with about 17 per cent of the claimants. Doctors, lawyers, and Anglican clergymen comprised the bulk of these. This large number of doctors and lawyers tends to confirm the assertion by modern scholars that a majority of each was loyal.[15] The merchants, royal officials, and professional men were naturally concentrated in Boston, the administrative and commercial metropolis. A few more were scattered among the other seacoast towns. The rural element, farmers and landowners, contains only about 11 per cent, another indication of the weakness of Loyalism in the interior. Representatives of most occupations are found among the claimants, but there is a manifest commercial and, to a lesser extent, office-holding side to Massachusetts Loyalism. The point is emphasized by the fact that although the bulk of the population lived on the land, farmers make up the smallest group of Loyalists.

The King's Friends

The amounts of the claims show a wide economic scale; 129 were for £2,000 or less, 108 for more. Great wealth is represented by the twenty-one claims for over £10,000, yet fifty-one claims were for £500 or less. Of course, a tiny proportion of the Massachusetts population, Whig or Tory, was worth £10,000 compared to that worth £500, and similarly more people were worth under £2,000 than over, so Loyalism was weighted considerably towards wealth, although persons at all economic levels were found within the movement. An analysis of the claimants for £500 or less does not reveal a distribution strikingly different from the claimants as a whole except in one particular: while the majority were still native-born Americans with twenty-three claimants, the foreign-born are close behind with sixteen. This suggests that the native-born, humble Loyalist was quite a rarity.

It has been asserted that most of the royal officials in Lincoln County (the Kennebec region of Maine) were Whig, and that the bulk of the Loyalists there were poor parishioners of the Reverend Jacob Bailey, the local missionary of the Society for the Propagation of the Gospel. As far as it goes, the claims record supports this view; of the twenty-two claimants only three are royal officials, and of the nineteen whose claims are known, eleven asked for £500 or less and fifteen for £1,000 or less. It must be added that Lincoln County was proverbially poor.[16]

In spite of this predominance of poor claimants in Lincoln County, the typical Massachusetts Loyalist was a native-born, quite wealthy Boston merchant, royal official, or professional man.

But figures and generalizations give no idea of the quality of Massachusetts Tories. To begin with, the fact that 153, nearly half the claimants, served in the armed forces or in some other official capacity indicates that they were active. Most of these served in the Associated Loyalists, formed during the British occupation, but Massachusetts claimants also contributed to such regiments as DeLancey's, the King's American Dragoons, and the Loyal North British Volunteers. Edward Winslow, a Harvard lawyer from a distinguished family, was master-muster general, and Ward Chipman, of similar background, his deputy throughout the war. Yet Massachusetts produced no outstanding Loyalist soldier. Brigadier General Timothy Ruggles raised the King's American Dragoons, but apparently saw no action. The colony's Loyalists included a wealth of talent ranging from Thomas Hutchinson, the outstanding governor and historian, to Daniel Leonard, the Loyalist writer, to Isaac Clemens, a Boston engraver and silversmith, who counterfeited two million pounds sterling in paper money to "distress" the rebels.[17]

Colonial political leadership was by no means unanimously Whig. Discounting mandamus councilors, twelve claimants had been representatives at the General Court, and three had been councilors. In addition, a further seventeen claimants had held local offices, four as selectmen, ten as justices of the peace, two as sheriffs, and one as a locally appointed superintendant of Indian affairs. Of the justices of the supreme court probably only William Cushing was a genuine Whig. As governor (until 1774 when he had to leave following the tea incident), Thomas Hutchinson, of course, held a royal appointment. But until 1766, when he was dropped from the council, he had been held in sufficient confidence to be elected regularly to public office for nearly three decades. Hutchinson's uncompromising, inexpedient attitude and actions as governor, however, weakened the Loyalist party and provided the radicals with much unwonted fuel.[18]

The great majority of Harvard graduates were certainly not Loyalists, and many of the revolutionary leaders, such as the two Adamses, were its alumni. The college was generally a Whig force. But fifty-nine claimants, over one in five, were Harvard graduates, and, of course, many other Harvard men were Loyalists but not claimants. The *Harvard Graduate Magazine* of 1905 listed 199 Harvard Loyalists, who had graduated between 1714 and 1774. This is nearly one-sixth of the total of 1,219 graduates of the period who were alive in 1774. Massachusetts Loyalists stand out even more as an educated group when it is remembered that other claimants were graduates of other colleges; in particular there were a few from Yale and several from England.[19] In short the claimants contained a notable proportion (over one-fifth) of college graduates, and Harvard, although predominantly Whig, produced a significant minority of Loyalists.

Only two schoolteachers were claimants, including Richard Holland, a teacher of the Indians at Freetown for the Society for the Propagation of the Gospel. The Anglican cleric Robert Boucher Nickolls, who also taught school, told the commissioners he was the only one of the profession to teach the union of the colonies with England. Nickolls exaggerated. John Lovell, master of the Boston Latin School, although he did not always succeed in proselytizing (his pupils included Samuel Adams and John Hancock), was certainly a Loyalist, but died too soon to submit a claim.[20]

The Church of England was an important element in

Massachusetts Loyalism. Forty-six claimants (including nine of the clergy) specifically mention their Anglicanism. No other religious affiliation is recorded except in isolated cases. Most of the lay claimants stand out as rich Boston merchants or royal officials (claiming more than £2,000) who attended one of the three Anglican churches, Christ, Trinity, or King's Chapel. Of the nine claimant ministers six were American and three British (one of whom had been in America since early childhood).

A witness laconically informed the commissioners that a person "being a Church of England man [was] more suspected to be a Tory." An Anglican claimant, the Reverend William Clark, wrote years after the event in 1803 when he had returned to his native land: "Never man lived more peaceably and quiet; never man meddled less with politics, or was better friend to Civil and religious liberty than myself. But all would not do. I received a small salary from an Incorporated Society in England, (not from the Government). '*Hinc illae Lachrymae!*' This was my crime."[21]

Fear of the Anglican church was not altogether unreasonable. The Reverend Mr. Clark quoted above was not as innocent as he made out. Twenty years earlier, in pressing his claims, he declared that he had suffered eleven months of imprisonment for sheltering Loyalists. The history of the agitations after 1763 shows the Anglican church in the vanguard of the pro-British forces. In particular, the possibility of the introduction of a bishop had been agitating the northern colonies especially for some years.[22]

The Reverend Henry Caner, the rector of King's Chapel, told the commissioners that he had written several pamphlets in favor of Parliament's authority, and that in 1761 and 1767 he had appealed for an American bishop. In 1767 the Reverend William Walter also joined in the petition. Walter had also condemned the mob violence against Andrew Oliver, the stamp distributor, at which time he became "obnoxious." As in Connecticut, there is evidence of Anglican proselytizing success, which increased Congregational dread. Three claimants, the Reverend Joshua Wingate Weeks, the Reverend John Wiswall, and the Reverend Mather Byles, Jr., were converted Congregational ministers, and the Reverend Henry Caner had graduated from Yale in 1724. Wiswall had been a Congregational minister at Falmouth, Maine, before going over to the Episcopal system with much of his congregation "from the conviction that the Church [of England] was apostolic and the British constitution more beneficial to the rights of mankind than the republican system of New England." [23]

Several Anglican laymen also stand out in the troubles which followed 1763. For example, George Deblois, a member of a prominent family of Huguenot origin, took the British side as early as the Stamp Act; so did David Ingersoll (a fairly unusual stance for a lay or non-office-holding Loyalist). He said he could seldom walk the streets without meeting insult from the "Republicans." A mob destroyed the property of Ebenezer Cutler, a Groton Anglican, when he ignored the non-importation agreements. Henry Barnes of Marlboro was advertised as an enemy in 1769 for opposing the agreements and was obliged to go into temporary exile. Gilbert Deblois, a warden of King's Chapel, similarly opposed non-importation and aided Captain Preston during the celebrated trial. Dr. John Jeffries, later the first man to cross the English Channel by balloon, lost part of his practice when he gave evidence in favor of Captain Preston. John Erving, another warden

Massachusetts

of Trinity Church, signed the Boston Memorial, and was mobbed at the time of the "Liberty" affair.[24]

The Anglicans were a minority; most people in Massachusetts were Congregationalists, and most Congregationalists were Patriot. Not all, however: six claimants specifically reveal themselves as Congregationalists, including two most distinguished Loyalists, Chief Justice Peter Oliver and Brigadier General Timothy Ruggles. Only one Congregational minister figures in the claims testimony, the Reverend Dr. Mather Byles, Sr. (whose son of the same name went over to the Anglican church); two claimants, Martin Gay and William Bowes, were sons of dissenting ministers. Two recent writers on western Massachusetts agree that a noticeable minority of Congregational ministers were Tory, but none seems to have become unpopular enough to be forced into exile.[25]

Some minor sects did not follow the Whiggish lead of the Congregationalists. Five claimants, including Isaac Winslow, are recorded as Sandemanians, a sect founded by Robert Sandeman, who arrived in Boston from Glasgow in 1764. This group was almost unanimously Tory, as was the branch in Connecticut. Why this should be is not clear, but it may be the result of a minority of heretics seeking protection against the predominant Congregationalist church. This was apparently the case with the Baptists of Ashfield, although there are no claimants from the town. Ezra Stiles noted that most New England Baptists were "cool" to the Whig cause and reported that one prominent Baptist feared that the sect would be "crushed" by a victory of Congregationalists in the north and Anglicans in the south.[26]

Female Loyalists, in their own right, are no more regularly found in the claims commission testimony than they are found in any other spheres of life in the eighteenth century. Quite a few do crop up, but usually as widows, Loyalist claimants only through their marriages. Of the women Loyalists *per se* perhaps the most interesting is Dorcas Griffiths, who followed the one profession which has never been closed, the oldest one. Mrs. Griffiths, a native of Boston, received a Loyalist pension in London for a time. Thomas Flucker, the disapproving former secretary of Massachusetts, told the commissioners that the lady, who kept a huckster's shop on Hancock's wharf, lived as a "Common prostitute and bred her Daughter in the same way, She was kep'd by the famous Handcock [*sic*] and when he turned her off, she lived with Capt. Johnson." Mrs. Griffiths, alas, is not a very uplifting example of Loyalism for her sex; principle was clearly not involved because, following the well-worn cliché, she changed her viewpoint as she changed lovers. The Captain Johnson mentioned was a Royal Marine officer, wounded at Bunker Hill, who was nursed and conquered by the enterprising woman.[27]

More sterling service was given by Ann Greenleaf and Margaret Draper. The former reported carrying letters and intelligence for the British, until forced to flee. Mrs. Draper, whose grandfather, father, and husband had been provincial printers in Massachusetts, carried on the business, splitting away from her late husband Richard's partner, the Whig John Boyle, in 1774, and maintaining the *Massachusetts Gazette and Boston Weekly Newsletter* as a pro-British organ under Gage's patronage. But these are two rare examples. Woman's role was usually between the sheets, behind the scenes, or at least behind the parlor curtains. The younger Peter Oliver wrote from Boston in December,

Massachusetts

1775, to Elisha Hutchinson in London, "Your wife braves it
out; by the last accounts from her in Sept. she is President of
Club composed of 8 ladies. They meet over a tea table once
or twice a week, in opposition to the Rebells. They keep up
their spirits strangely . . ." [28]

Discussions of Massachusetts Loyalism often revolve
around this question: Did it matter whether the Massachusetts Loyalists stayed or left? Was their exile akin to the
flight of the Huguenots from seventeenth-century France?

As for western Massachusetts, the tables make it clear
that Loyalism was a negligible movement, and therefore
the question hardly arises. In the central county of Worcester numbers were small—only 250 Tories were the subject
of official action, and only thirty-five estates were confiscated out of a population of 30,000. But several leading
families were involved; the Ruggleses of Hardwick, Colonel John Murray of Rutland, and at Worcester James
Putnam and the Chandler family.[29] A recent historian of
the Massachusetts countryside states that it made no difference to local history whether the Loyalists remained or
fled, but even he admits that they were generally the better-
educated people.[30] Henry Hulton ventured into the back
parts of Massachusetts in May, 1771, found that "the spirit
of equality prevails throughout . . . and they have no notion
of rank or distinction in society." He also noted a general
absence of civilization, law, and order, and was obviously
convinced that control from Boston, far less London, was
a vain hope there.[31]

As for the eastern seaboard, the question of what would
have happened if the Loyalists had not fled is probably
unanswerable. What is clear is that eastern Massachusetts
lost a tremendous amount of talent, whatever the effects of

[31]

the loss might be.[32] This loss is illustrated by a partial listing of the distinguished claimants.

The following were leading figures, usually from distinguished families: John Coffin, John Chandler, Samuel Curwen, George Erving, Thomas Flucker, secretary of the province, Dr. Sylvester Gardiner, Colonel Thomas Goldthwaite, Francis Green, Benjamin Hallowell, Colonel Elisha Jones, Chief Justice Peter Oliver, Lieutenant-Governor Thomas Oliver, Sir William Pepperell and some of his Sparhawk kin, Timothy Ruggles, Colonel Richard Saltonstall, John Vassall, Francis Waldo, Abijah Willard, and Edward Winslow. Some notable lawyer claimants were Robert Auchmuty, Sampson Salter Blowers, Daniel Leonard ("Massachusettensis"), James Putnam, whose pupil was John Adams, and Jonathan Sewall, solicitor-general and attorney-general. Doctors included John Jeffries, who gave the first anatomy lectures in Boston and was a pioneer balloonist, and William Lee Perkins, who delivered the first medical lectures in Massachusetts. Among the leading merchants are found Jolley Allen and the Deblois family.[33] To these can be added outstanding Loyalists who were not claimants, such as Thomas Hutchinson, John Lovell, John Mein, the Scottish printer, the Reverend Jacob Bailey, the native-born poet and writer, and the fine artist, John Singleton Copley.[34]

It is difficult to quarrel with the statement that there is "scarcely a name of distinction which is not found in" the pages of the claims commissioners, or Moses C. Tyler's assertion concerning the banishment act of September, 1778, that it reads "almost like a beadroll of the oldest and noblest families concerned in the founding and upbuilding of New England civilization."[35]

The exile of a very few of the leading Loyalists was not

permanent—for example, Dr. William Paine returned to Boston to become a founder of the American Antiquarian Society, and Francis Green returned to pioneer the education of deaf mutes—but in general Massachusetts' loss was Canada's and Britain's gain. The Massachusetts Loyalists, although not top in numbers, led all other colonies in quality. It seems incredible that their going could have made no difference to the new state.[36] However, if the Loyalists were talented, the Patriots were more so; the Tories could not match such figures as John Adams, Samuel Adams, James Otis, and Josiah Quincy.

Three hundred and thirteen Massachusetts claimants are analyzed, but the total must be increased to 319 by the addition of six claimants for whom there is no information. This is approximately 0.11 per cent of the white population of 292,022 in 1776.[37] The percentage is low, but it is the highest of all the New England colonies. The percentage for Boston alone is 0.98, a startling figure, nearly four times the proportion for Philadelphia.

The Loyalists were an impotent minority in Massachusetts. This assertion is borne out by the familiar successful record of the Whigs there and by the testimony of contemporaries. Richard Lechmere's letters of 1774 make clear his belief that "the friends of government" were outnumbered and could never "be restor'd to the good opinion and confidence of the people, nor do I think they will be in safety at any time hereafter if the troops should be withdrawn." In the same year Ann Hulton reported that the Tories were "intimidated and overpowered by Numbers." At the time of Lexington Walter Barrell estimated the enemies of Britain "as not short of four to one," probably a considerable underestimate.[38]

But if the Massachusetts Tories were proved impotent, they nevertheless felt the brunt of persecution earlier and more forcefully than in any other colony. This helps confirm that Loyalism was comparatively strong there, or at least that the Whigs were powerful and well organized and had a certain fear of their opponents. Violence (referred to below) began at the time of the Stamp Act and became a permanent feature of the times.

Two claimants mention being tarred and feathered—David Ingersoll and Jonathan Malcolm, a tidesman, who asserted he was the first Loyalist to suffer this fate in the whole of America. The time was early 1774. Ann Hulton has left a vivid account of the incident which is worth quoting to illustrate the cruelty which was possible in the colony:

. . . he was stript Stark naked, one of the severest cold nights this Winter, his body covered all over with Tar, then with feathers, his arm dislocated in tearing off his cloaths, he was dragged in a Cart with thousands attending, some beating him with clubs and Knocking him out of the Cart then in again. They gave him several severe whippings, at different parts of the Town. This Spectacle of horror and sportive cruelty was exhibited for about five hours.[39]

According to the testimony before the claims commissioners, at least two Loyalists were executed in Massachusetts. Jane Hilding told how her husband John, who returned to Boston after the convention of Saratoga, was caught trying to steal a boat in order to sail to Rhode Island and was executed along with another Loyalist called Armstrong. The above examples represent the extremes. Massachusetts Loyalists suffered many fates. Edward Stow recalled, "my House [was] bedaubed with Excrement and

Massachusetts

Feathers May 14th. 1770, repeated July 5th. 1770 and repeated again with Blubber Oil and Feathers July 9th. 1770."
Later a mob broke into his house, and he was struck with
a piece of wood. A mob burned Peter Frye's house in
Salem in October, 1774. Daniel Dunbar noted being ridden
on a "sharp rail" in 1775. The wife of Edward Brinley
(not a claimant), preparing to have a baby at Roxbury, was
accompanied by "a guard of Rebels always in her room, who
treated her with great rudeness and indecency, exposing her
to the view of their banditti, as a sight 'See a tory woman'
and striped her and her Children of all their Linen and
Cloths." [40]

Such mob action was accompanied by the legal steps of
oaths, banishment, and confiscation of property,[41] but Massachusetts rapidly repealed the laws against the Tories after
the war.[42] After the opening years of fighting passions
seemed to have cooled considerably. This is because of the
success of the Patriots, the withdrawal of the British from
Boston in 1776, and the absence of civil war, that great in-
ducer of cruelty. Further it is very noticeable how many
claimants indicated that they were already resident in Massachusetts, or finally did return there or occasionally to some
other state; ten of those claiming in Nova Scotia and twenty-
three in London. Ward Chipman wrote in his diary on his
return to Boston in 1783, "We immediately found how
groundless our fears had been of meeting with anything unpleasant or disagreeable and determined to visit all our
friends publickly in the morning." [43] In England in November, 1783, Samuel Curwen wrote that Captain Nathaniel
West brought "a message from the principal merchants and
citizens of Salem, proposing and encouraging my return," a
request to which Curwen soon acceded.[44]

The Loyalists were strongest in Boston, yet a minority. In February, 1774, Richard Lechmere wrote of Boston after the Tea Party: "You can have no idea of the miserable scituation [*sic*] the town is in, nobody dare speak their sentiments for fear of being tarr'd and feather'd, or perhaps worse treated." It was not a case of a ruthless minority terrorizing the majority. Only about 1,100 Tories left Boston with Sir William Howe on St. Patrick's Day, 1776. Of these 105 were from outside Boston. Boston's population of 16,000 in 1775 dropped dramatically to 3,500 in 1776, a vivid indication of the dislike of the British garrison.[45]

But the presence of British troops had been a stimulus and a temptation. Many merchants, shopkeepers, and artisans mention trading with troops, so that they were obliged to leave at the evacuation. This does not of course mean that all who did business with the British were Loyalists only by the accident of economic interest, but no doubt some were.

The preceding review of some of the political issues which helped to define many Tories and the account of the structure of Massachusetts Loyalism deal only obliquely with the tangled questions of motives. What caused the loyalty of the Massachusetts claimants? The motives of a large proportion of claimants are basically self-explanatory as in the other colonies: the British elements' loyalty to the home country; the conservative inclinations of the rich; the self-interest of the royal officials—it was partly a case of the "ins" (Hutchinson, the Olivers) versus the "outs" (the two Adamses, Otis); the interests of such groups of professional men as those lawyers who thrived on official patronage; the natural allegiance and minority fears of the Anglicans.

Occasionally officers or officials mention their oaths to the king which, although generally taken seriously, probably merely bolstered an existing disposition to Loyalism. John Gallison (not a claimant), while protesting his devotion to the liberties of Massachusetts and the rights of Englishmen, told the town of Marblehead in January, 1775, that he would not resign his military commission because he could not see how he "or any other officer is to Be absolved from an Oath." [46]

The dread of trade disruption and the temptation to deal with the British armed forces, which swayed the commercial element, were made acute by the occupation of Boston. Trade with the British occurred at all levels: Mary Brown, a versatile fruiteress, made many hundred dozen shirts for the troops; William Hill, a Boston baker, made bread for them; Abijah Willard supplied provisions; John Coffin turned his distillery and sugar house into a barracks. [47] Ann Hulton wrote in July, 1774, that those "well disposed towards Government" were so "more from interest than principle it's to be feared, as there are few willing to acknowledge the Authority of Parliament." [48] On the other hand a Loyalist such as Governor Hutchinson sincerely saw himself as a Massachusetts patriot struggling to save the credulous population from the blandishments of a few fanatics. [49] Similarly, Chief Justice Peter Oliver considered the Revolution in his native state to be the work of a few ignoble demagogues. [50]

The Loyalism of the Reverend Mather Byles, unique among Congregational ministers, is to be explained in a similar way. Byles was socially and temperamentally very close to the royal officials and is said to have remarked to a companion while watching the funeral of the victims of the "Boston Massacre," "They call me a brainless Tory; but tell me, my young friend, which is better—to be ruled by one tyrant three thousand miles away, or by three thousand tyrants not a mile away?"[51] It is notable that Byles does call the king a tyrant.

To tackle the problem from the other side, the extreme weakness of Loyalism in the west is explained by the absence of any sectional split before the Revolution, general apathy towards the issues (until Samuel Adams stirred the area up for the Whigs over the question of the Coercive Acts), an absence of any widespread self-interest in the imperial link, and the dislike of absentee Tory proprietors.[52]

In 1815 John Adams explained his view of the motives of the Loyalists throughout the colonies by quoting examples from Massachusetts. He began by stating that the Tory party barely existed in 1765 but grew formidable during the following decade. The reason for this conversion of so many "real or pretended Americans," he believed, was usually greed and vanity. William Brattle (who died too soon to submit a claim) was seduced by Jonathan Sewall and by appointment as brigadier general in the militia; Daniel Leonard, whose weakness for ostentatious luxury was perceived by "the two sagacious spirits, Hutchinson and Sewall," was courted and flattered by the governor "with the ardor of a lover"; Samuel Quincy's Achilles' heel, jealousy of his more successful Patriot brother, Josiah Quincy, Jr., was similarly spotted by the fiendish pair, who accordingly "applied their magic arts" and had him appointed solicitor-general; William Brown's price was the post of judge of the superior court; Harrison Gray apparently simply drifted into Loyalism through weakness of mind when his "oracle" Dr. Mayhew died in 1766. Adams held that these examples were well known, but typical, and could be repeated in Massachusetts and the other colonies.[53]

This opinion does not have to be accepted whole, but John Adams' view of the Revolution can never be ignored. (Adams was obviously baffled by the Loyalism of his close friends and could only explain it in crudely materialistic terms.)

Lee N. Newcomer argues that kinship was one of the strongest determining factors in western Massachusetts and notes such Tory families as the Williamses of Hatfield, the Partridge family of Hampshire County, and John Murray's family in Rutland. In Worcester the three leading families, the Putnams, the Paines, and the Chandlers, were all Tory and interrelated. In Petersham the Whig schoolmaster Ensign Man opposed the Loyalist minister, the Reverend Aaron Whitney, but upon marrying Whitney's daughter, Man, like many a one before and since, gave up the battle and became a Tory.[54]

The point about family relationship can be extended to the whole of Massachusetts (and indeed to all the colonies). In Boston one thinks of such powerful Loyalist families as the Hutchinsons, the Olivers, the Deblois, the Winslows. But at least seventeen claimants were members of split families. For example, George Inman joined the British army, as he put it, "contrary to the wishes of my Connections and friends," and of his rich father Ralph, who remained in Boston, "neuter in the Dispute"; Dr. John Jeffries' father, David, the treasurer of Massachusetts, was a strong Patriot; two of John Lovell's sons were loyal, but a third was a member of the Continental Congress; Colonel Richard Saltonstall's brother, Dr. Nathaniel, was a Whig.[55]

The fissure extended to business, professional, and social levels. Benjamin Davis broke with his brother in the haberdashery business over the signing of the non-importation agreement. James Putnam, under whom John Adams had studied law, was a claimant. As mentioned above, Adams lamented the loss of three lawyers among his "most intimate friends" who became Loyalists, Jonathan Sewall, Daniel Leonard (both claimants), and Samuel Quincy, attributing their seduction from liberty to the "Jesuit" Governor Hutchinson.[56]

Many well-read Americans were led to a reverence for the British political system which, if they did not approve of every act of the government (often just the reverse), made them loath to take any action which might upset it. Examples abound in all colonies, and Thomas Hutchinson is a prime Massachusetts case.[57] However, a much less-known figure, Samuel Fitch, a Boston lawyer, can be quoted. He told the claims commissioners that "having been led from the course of his reading to the particular study of the principles and history of the British constitution, he early imbibed a strong predilection in favour of a system of government which he considered as the most perfect that human wisdom had ever adopted . . ."[58]

In the last analysis Loyalism was often a state of mind, an emotional commitment. On the morning of the battle of Lexington Joshua Loring hastened to join the British, remarking to a friend, "I have always eaten the King's bread, and always intend to."[59] Even John Adams hinted as much when he wrote somewhat priggishly to his wife in April, 1776, concerning Samuel Quincy's allegedly greedy Loyalism, "But let us take warning, and give it to our children. Whenever vanity and gaiety, a love of pomp and dress, furniture, equipage, buildings, great company, expensive diversions and elegant entertainments get the better of the principles of men or women, there is no knowing where

Massachusetts

they will stop, nor into what evils, natural, moral or political they will lead us." [60]

Thomas Darnforth expressed himself nicely when he stated that his "loyalty arose from natural temper, from education and from expectations." The "expectations," which John Adams would have seized upon, was the promise of Lord Dartmouth in 1773 that Darnforth would fill the first vacancy of a suitable office in America.[61]

In conclusion it is fitting to consider two female Loyalists who were not claimants, or even exiles. Probably only Massachusetts could have produced such ardent Patriots as James Otis and Samuel Adams, or such dyed-in-the-wool Tories as the Byles sisters, Catherine and Mary. In them flowed the distinguished blood of the Mathers and the Cottons. They dwelt in Boston with their father, Mather Byles, the poetry-writing Congregational minister and Tory punster (he dubbed the sentry posted over him his "observe-a-Tory"), who died in 1788 in poverty and disgrace, having been deprived in 1776 of the church he had held for forty-three years. It is significant that Byles's son had become an Anglican and fled to Halifax, Nova Scotia. In the years after the Revolution the sisters carried on, maintaining their home on Nassau Street (now Tremont) as a kind of Loyalist museum with themselves as the chief exhibits. (They also had a chair which belonged to their grandfather, Lieutenant-Governor Tailer, on which they would seat Republican guests and then ask if the guests could sit comfortably under the crown, pointing to a carved crown in the center of the chair.)

Among their souvenirs and royal portraits, the sisters, sipping "loyal tea," relived the festivities of the Boston siege when Earl Percy and Lord Howe visited them, berated the "Yankeys," and corresponded with their far-flung Loyalist relatives. (Catherine even wrote to George IV on his accession assuring him of continued loyalty.) In 1835 the authorities removed part of their house to make way for a street. The sisters were pained, but hardly surprised. It was simply "one of the consequences of living in a Republic." When they died they made sure that their property found its way out of the United States to more congenial loyal resting places.[62]

III. RHODE ISLAND

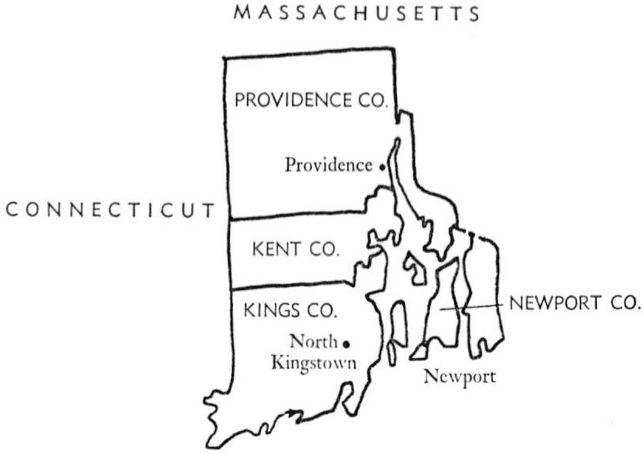

MASSACHUSETTS

PROVIDENCE CO.

Providence •

CONNECTICUT

KENT CO.

KINGS CO.

North •
Kingstown

Newport

NEWPORT CO.

RHODE ISLAND

LOYALISM in Rhode Island was not diffuse; it was concentrated both geographically and within particular ranks of society. Forty-four, almost all, of the forty-nine claimants whose residences are known lived in Newport, and none lived in Providence. Fifty-eight per cent of Rhode Island claimants were connected with commerce, and if the office-holders and professional men are added, 80 per cent are accounted for. About half claimed for sums in excess of £2,000; there was little lower-class and no mass support for Loyalism. More than 63 per cent were native born, doubtless reflecting the comparatively small immigration to New England, and especially to Rhode Island.

The Newport Loyalists, the nucleus of the party, have similar characteristics; the vast majority were merchants or connected with commerce, were American born, and were wealthy (only two claimed for less than £500).

Newport was the only real center of Loyalism in Rhode Island. In December, 1776, a colonial newspaper reported the landing of British troops at Newport under the command of Sir Peter Parker. "We hear the enemy's troops were escorted into Newport by a set of well-known infamous Tories, who have long infested that town . . ."[1] Earlier, in July, 1775, Governor Cooke complained of the Newport Loyalists that "nothing can be said or done in the colony that they have immediate intelligence of it," adding that with the exodus of Patriots from the town the Tories "will have the Rule there soon."[2] In July, 1776, the Patriot Colonel Lippitt tendered the test oath to eighty suspected inhabitants of Newport, but all but three refused it.[3]

Loyalism was undoubtedly feeble in the Rhode Island hinterland. For example, when Thomas Vernon, Richard Beale, John Nicoll, and Nicholas Lechmere refused the test oath of June, 1776, Rhode Island officials felt secure in removing them to Glocester, the third-ranking and most northerly town in Rhode Island. Vernon's diary for July, 1776, makes it clear that he was living in a strongly Whig area. He remarked that women, very unusually, were pulling flax, and that farm work was falling behind. "The reason is plain that there are not people left to do the necessary work." Rhode Island had five regiments at that time. The next month he recounted that a female weaver of the area refused to supply him with handkerchiefs, fearing "that if the people of the town knew it, the consequences might be injurious to her and her family . . ."[4] Only five claimants are positively identified as having lived in the interior.

But even in Newport the Loyalists were a minority. A newspaper reported that when General Charles Lee arrived at Newport in December, 1776, to tender the oath of fidelity to "a number of obnoxious persons," only three Loyalists, Joseph Wanton, Jr., Nicholas Lechmere, and Richard Beale, were principled enough to refuse it. The latter two, both customs officers, were then sent to Providence under guard.[5] When the British evacuated Newport a mere fifty Tories went with them,[6] a small proportion of Newport's population of 5,299 in 1776. Further, one year earlier, 1775, the population had been 11,000. It had halved at the prospect of a British invasion, a fact which suggests that Newport Tories were a minority.[7] Many years ago Henry E. Turner argued, with some force, that the history of anti-British riots at Newport, from the Stamp Act crisis in 1765 to the sinking of the "Liberty" in 1769, suggests that patriotism was strong there.[8]

Rhode Island

Some of the claims commission testimony supports Turner. John Watson, a Newport merchant, returned from trading at New York in October, 1774, to be met by a mob which "threatened to pull him to pieces if he did not damn the King and Lord North which he was compell'd to do." In July, 1776, another Newport mob used the threat of tar and feathers to make him sign the test and promise to help the Americans.[9] Mathew Robinson, another Newport trader, from the first branded as "a Rank Torey," suffered several indignities, including the pulling down of his fences by a "multitude . . . under colour of laying out a Highway," climaxed in 1781 when, after "a New England Saint" charged that Robinson "drank the King's Health, and damn'd the Congress and call'd them damn'd Rebels and Presbyterians," he was imprisoned without examination "against their own Bill of Rights." [10]

There are records of fifty-four Rhode Island claimants, but the total is increased to fifty-five by one claimant for whom there is no information. This is 0.1 per cent of the white population in 1776,[11] one of the middling percentages.

In summary, Rhode Island Loyalists were numerically quite weak, quite wealthy, centered almost exclusively in Newport, generally native born, and connected with commerce, although a substantial sprinkling of farmers, professional men, and office-holders must be noted.

The conclusion that Rhode Island Loyalists were fairly insignificant is bolstered by the mere five claimants who mention examples of real persecution beyond the usual confiscation, imprisonment, and banishment. Mathew Robinson suffered several times at the hands of a mob; Isaac Lawton was "publickly carted" for supporting the British; Moses Hart, a Jew, reported the murder of a loyal uncle in 1780; John Watson was mobbed in 1774 and 1776; but the most remarkable story was Ebenezer Slocum's concerning his parents. His father, Charles Slocum, was killed by a mob in 1778, and his mother was later pilloried, her ears cut off, and both cheeks branded. The reason for this possibly uniquely ferocious treatment of a woman was that she had passed counterfeit money, or as she told the commissioners, "She paid the notes for Rent." [12] Another claimant, Charles Dudley, collector of customs for Rhode Island, was so severely attacked by unknown assailants in 1771 that he was not expected to recover. His office and English birth are sufficient to explain the attack and the lack of sympathy he received.[13]

Finally, although it can hardly be called real persecution, the case of Elizabeth Gray should be mentioned. After her Loyalist husband died in prison in Providence, she "still persevered to Serve her King and Country," resulting in her trial for her life as a traitor and imprisonment for ten months in Boston "in a Dismal Dungeon" for delivering a letter to General Burgoyne.[14]

The confiscation of Loyalist property was generally measured and moderate, over half the confiscated property actually belonged to Bostonians, and little action was taken to prevent the return of the Tories after the war. John Andrews told the commissioners that he had been back to Rhode Island to collect debts "which he has done to a very considerable Amount." [15]

The clue to the extreme weakness of Loyalism in Rhode Island may be that, like Virginia, the colony had been for a long time virtually a self-governing republic. As early as 1704 the chief justice of New York wrote that in Rhode Island "they did all things as if they were out of the dominions of the crown." [16] Whatever its faults, the colonial charter served the new state as a constitution until 1843! In northern rural Rhode Island the exiled Newport Loyalist, Thomas Vernon, realized, as did many Loyalists in other colonies, that the bulk of the people had acquired definite views on the rights and wrongs of the Revolution, which, however uninformed, were unshakable. He recorded with genuine sincerity, "Our landlord inclined much to talk of liberty and the times. . . . It is amazing what false and erroneous opinions and ideas these people have entertained, and what is worse is that it is impossible for the human mind to undeceive them, such is their prejudice." [17]

Rhode Island entered the Revolution remarkably united. There are claims records from no member of either house of the legislative Assembly, nor do any claimants mention holding local offices such as that of justice of the peace. This is not surprising from what is known of Rhode Island history at that time. The choosing of sides was first forced on the Assembly in April, 1775, shortly after the fight at Concord, when it was proposed to raise an army of observation consisting of 1,500 men. In the lower house only four Newport deputies voted negatively; in the upper house only the governor, the deputy governor, and two assistants took a similar stand. On May 4, 1776, the legislature ended the colony's allegiance to George III with only six deputies (probably from Newport) dissenting, while in July of the same year one vote was cast against independence. [18]

The flavor of Rhode Island Loyalism can be had by considering some of the leading Newport Loyalists. In June, 1776, the Rhode Island Assembly passed a test act by which Tories would be singled out if they refused to subscribe. It is not known how many refused, but the five earliest and most notorious, Thomas Vernon, Richard Beale,

John Nicoll, Nicholas Lechmere, and Walter Chaloner, were all from Newport.[19] Vernon, a native Rhode Islander, was register of the court of admiralty and postmaster of Newport; Beale, Nicoll, and Lechmere were customs officials, and Chaloner was sheriff of Newport County. Only the three customs men are found among the claimants. All five were paroled to Glocester in the north, but Chaloner did not actually go.

Other leading Newport Loyalists were two doctors, Halliburton and Hunter (for whom there is a claim), and the Brenton family. The Brentons, members of an old colonial family, were the owners of Brenton's Point from which Benjamin Brenton supplied British men-of-war in Newport harbor. Captain Jahleel Brenton, a brother of Benjamin, who served thirty-seven years in the Royal Navy, claimed losses of over £4,000.[20]

Whatever its exact strength, the concentration of Loyalism at Newport demands an explanation. It is tempting to put it down to the British occupation between December, 1776, and October, 1779. This must certainly have been a stimulus—the British were successful in organizing the "Loyal Newport Associators," possibly consisting of three companies[21]—but Newport's Loyalist leanings were strongly apparent long before the British arrived, as the preceding paragraphs suggest. Conversely, the utter lack of Loyalism at Providence poses a problem, and again the fact that it was never occupied is not sufficient answer. Providence, of course, was a rival town and thus inclined to take an opposite course to Newport's on principle. Geography probably played a part. Newport was in an exposed island position and was the usual stopping place for the Royal Navy, while Providence lay to the north, at the head of Narragansett

Bay. But something of a mystery remains. The best approach is to accept the fact that Rhode Islanders were basically Whigs and concentrate on explaining the odd men out, the Newport Loyalists.

The Newport merchants were the nucleus of Rhode Island Loyalism, and, as with so many colonial merchants, fear for their trade within the British Empire must have influenced their Tory stand. James Frost told of his trade with Quebec before the war. Also, the temptation of trade with the British services when the troubles first began compromised many. This may well have been the case with claimant Elizabeth Ivey, whose parents kept the "Sign of the Royal Oak" where they entertained the British troops.[22] An agent for a British trading firm, George Rome, told the commissioners that he sent provisions to Sir James Wallace's army in 1774 and 1775, but "asked if he did it for profit He evades giving an Answer." Newport merchants, including the Brenton family, certainly traded with the Royal Navy and the army at Boston.[23] However, the Providence merchants were all Patriots, and the twelve Newport merchants who put in claims were clearly a minority of the trading community there. Schlesinger notes the fact that Rhode Island in general and Newport in particular proved "refractory" over non-importation in 1769 and the years following, but not apparently because of Loyalist leanings. In 1775 the Continental Association was well enforced all over Rhode Island, even at Newport. He also points out that John Maudsley, subsequently a Tory (and a claimant), was a Son of Liberty in 1770.[24]

Newport was the center of the English administration, the customs, and the court of vice-admiralty. Rhode Island office-holders, like their breed in general, seem to have been mainly loyal. This is not surprising, since several must have had unpleasant memories of various riots such as that over the "Gaspee." The five claimants who were office-holders (four in the customs, one a judge of vice-admiralty) all apparently lived in Newport; one, Augustus Johnston, had had the misfortune to be appointed stamp master in 1765, and two, John Nicoll and Nicholas Lechmere, had to take refuge on board the "Cygnet," a man-of-war, during the Stamp Act riots.[25]

Newport was the governor's seat, and throughout the colonies there is a close connection between the governor's power, patronage, and personality, and Loyalism. At the crucial period Joseph Wanton was governor. He had been governor since 1769, the fourth of his family to hold the position. He was re-elected just before the news of Concord and then suspended and finally deposed by the legislature after he opposed the setting up of a Rhode Island army of observation in April, 1775. Previously Wanton had been a moderate Whig. He had first become governor at the time of the sinking of the "Liberty"; he took the colony's side in that dispute, as he did over the "Gaspee" affair. After his fall from power he was left alone, and most of his heirs received their property.[26] He did not leave Newport when the British evacuated, staying on until his death in 1780. His sons were more Tory than he. By the time the claims were made Joseph, Jr. was dead, but the other son, William, claimed joint losses of £18,000.

Even William Wanton admitted that he had taken the rebel oath, and accordingly the commissioners gave him a moderate annual allowance because of the "Speck in that Loyalty which destroys all its Lustre."[27] Because of his behavior, the governor's loyalty was also not unflecked from the British point of view and this partly explains the weakness of the Tories in Rhode Island.

The Loyalist tradition in Newport was stimulated by a somewhat shadowy body called the Newport Junto, which appeared in 1764. The Junto deprecated opposition to the Sugar and Stamp Acts and petitioned the king to revoke the charter, which they considered left too much power with the people and too little with the king and Parliament. The Junto (which had up to twenty members), led by Martin Howard, Jr., an Anglican lawyer and pamphleteer, included Dr. Thomas Moffat, George Rome, an English merchant, and several royal office-holders, among others.[28] Significantly, these leaders were foreign born, Anglicans, outside the two main Rhode Island factions (the forces of Ward and the forces of Hopkins), and never got any substantial support. Such was the case during the Stamp Act troubles. Even the stamp distributor, Augustus Johnston, although he later became a Loyalist, was no friend of the Junto; rather he was a popular member of the Hopkins faction and had been elected attorney-general since 1758. Like several other distributors he got his fingers unexpectedly burnt. Howard and Moffat fled the colony permanently during the stamp riots, but Rome continued at Newport and finally put in a claim as a Rhode Island Loyalist.

There was a religious side to Newport Loyalism. As far back as 1761 Anglicanism had been associated with the attack on the Rhode Island charter. The Wanton family was Anglican, Governor Wanton being a devoted member of Trinity Church, Newport, the minister of which, George Bissett, took the Loyalist side. Thomas Vernon was a warden of Trinity; the Brenton family attended; Lynn Martin, a native-born merchant, claimed the loss of a pew there. The royal officials were *ipso facto* members of the Church of England; for example, Charles Dudley, the Rhode Island collector, who was the son of a west-country clergyman. However, before the Revolution Anglicanism was no bar to political success, as is illustrated by Governor Wanton's career, and also that of James Honeyman, the son of a rector of Trinity Church, who was elected to such offices as attorney-general and senator. But it is significant that neither of the colony's two leading politicians, Samuel Ward and Stephen Hopkins, was an Anglican.[29]

Another religious group, the Jews, deserves brief mention. It is certain that the Newport Jews, who had contributed so much to the town's well-being, left during the Revolution and did not return at the end of the war. It has been suggested that none of the Jews were Tories, but two, Jacob Hart and his son Moses, who had left Newport with the British army, put forward claims. The loyalty of the family seems to have been outstanding, if the murder of Jacob's brother as a Loyalist in 1780 is any indication.[30]

With the exception of the Wanton family none of Rhode Island's chief political leaders were Loyalists, and it is of great import that both leaders of Rhode Island's two factions, Ward and Hopkins, were sent as delegates to the First Continental Congress. However, Loyalism did have an important effect on Rhode Island politics. In 1774, Joseph Wanton, Jr.'s political career ended, and he lost his seat in the Assembly because of his Toryism. His father, the nominee of Hopkins' faction for several years, was re-elected governor in 1775 in spite of being charged with Toryism. His subsequent behavior proved the charge not unfounded, and the result was the end of the Hopkins regime and the return to power of Samuel Ward and his cronies.[31]

To sum up, Newport Loyalism was the result of several factors: the early influence of the Newport Junto, the influence of royal office-holders and the British administration, trade considerations, the town's vulnerability to sea attack, and finally to some extent the military occupation.

Explain the motives of the office-holders and the merchants of Newport and you have largely explained Rhode Island Loyalism. However, nine farmers put in claims. This is a small figure in itself, but it is 20 per cent of the claimants, and a larger group than the office-holders. Farmers made up the bulk of the Rhode Island population and these nine claimants clearly represent a tiny minority. A reading of their testimony reveals nothing about possible motives. Seven were certainly natives of Rhode Island and an eighth probably was; only three could be called rich (i.e. claimed more than £3,000; another five each claimed less than £700). Their motives for loyalty were presumably very personal in each case. Of the six whose residences are known, two lived in Newport, a fact which may be connected with their politics, while five lived in Kings County (three in North Kingstown). There seems to be no way to explain this apparent little knot of Loyalist strength in North Kingstown.[32]

To recapitulate, the claims would indicate that Rhode Island Loyalists were a small, quite well-to-do minority, chiefly Newporters. They produced no outstanding writer (save perhaps Martin Howard),[33] or soldier, or politician (except possibly Joseph Wanton). They were a rather mediocre collection.

IV. CONNECTICUT

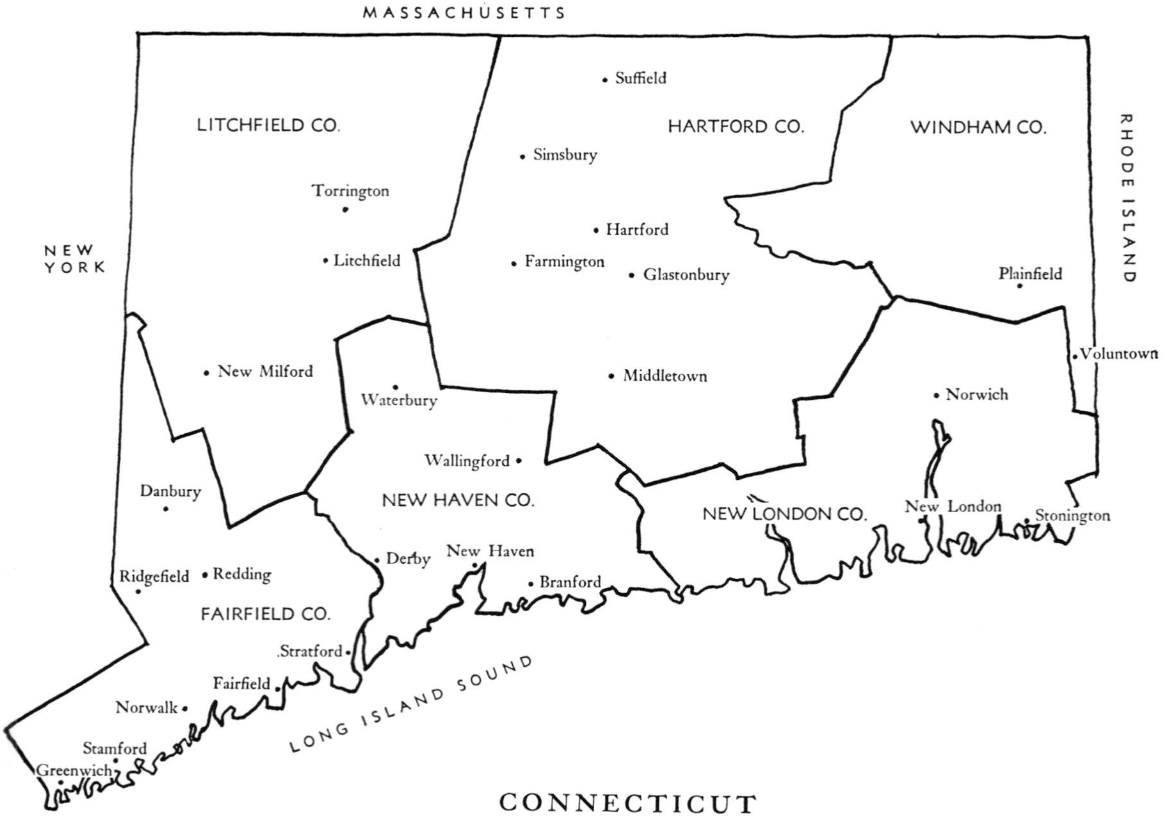

RHODE ISLAND

MASSACHUSETTS

NEW YORK

WINDHAM CO.

HARTFORD CO.

LITCHFIELD CO.

NEW HAVEN CO.

NEW LONDON CO.

FAIRFIELD CO.

LONG ISLAND SOUND

CONNECTICUT

Voluntown
Plainfield
Norwich
Stonington
New London
Suffield
Simsbury
Hartford
Farmington
Glastonbury
Middletown
Branford
Wallingford
New Haven
Torrington
Litchfield
Waterbury
Derby
New Milford
Stratford
Danbury
Redding
Fairfield
Ridgefield
Norwalk
Stamford
Greenwich

ONE HUNDRED and fifty claims are analyzed in the Connecticut tables,[1] and the number is increased to 153 by the addition of three persons about whom there is no information. This is approximately 0.08 per cent (a fairly low proportion) of the white population of 191,763 in 1776.[2] If Connecticut Loyalism was numerically quite feeble, it was overwhelmingly a native movement, over 84 per cent of the claimants whose birthplaces are known being American born. (There was, of course, comparatively little immigration to the colony). The fifteen claimants who were not natives were all from Great Britain; the loyalty of six of them is easily accounted for; four were royal officials and two retired soldiers who had arrived during the Seven Years War.

Although the claimants are quite widely scattered throughout all the counties (but with the concentration toward the coast—Windham, an inland county, has only two), the outstanding fact is the preponderance, eighty out of a known 146 (55 per cent), in Fairfield County, the westernmost seacoast county which borders on New York and is less than thirty miles from New York City. Within Fairfield County the claimants are strung out among the coast towns: Greenwich, Stamford, Norwalk, Fairfield, and Stratford. There is no equivalent to the overwhelming concentration of Loyalism in Newport, Rhode Island, or Boston, Massachusetts, but Norwalk and Stamford with forty-three claimants between them account for 30 per cent of the total. Add New Haven's sixteen and the total is about 40 per cent. There was no really dominant town in Connecticut, but New Haven far outstripped its rivals in commerce and in population, with 8,295 inhabitants in 1774. The record of a mere sixteen claimants suggests the weakness of Loyalism there. Stamford with eighteen claimants out of a population of 3,563 in 1774 stands out as the strongest center of Loyalism in Connecticut. (A witness maintained that Filer Diblee, a native-born Stamford lawyer and representative in the General Assembly, had kept the town loyal until 1776 when he "was overpowered by mobs from neighbouring Towns.")[3] It is followed closely by Norwalk with twenty-five out of a population of 4,388 in 1774. Eastern Connecticut Loyalism was clearly the weaker. Two Scottish brothers, Alexander and James Robertson, who printed a newspaper at Norwich, soon found they could not carry on "without making it subservient to the Cause of Rebellion," and that was probably typical.[4]

By occupation, the Connecticut Loyalists are divided rather evenly, but the commercial element is the largest with over 43 per cent, about 14 per cent being artisans and 25 per cent merchants and shopkeepers. Farmers and landowners with over 42 per cent are almost as large a group. Most of them were yeoman farmers because thirty-seven out of a known fifty-four claimed for £500 or less. The loyal gentleman farmer is a rarity. The occupation analysis is completed by 8 per cent professional men and nearly 6 per cent royal officials. As the bulk of Connecticut's population was on the land, Loyalist claimants there had a distinct but not overwhelming commercial tendency.

The table giving the value of the claims suggests that most Connecticut Loyalists had only moderate means. Almost half (a rather startling figure) were for no more than £500, while nearly 70 per cent claimed £1,000 or less and 84 per cent, £2,000 or less. The bulk of the claims under

£500 came from yeoman farmers, almost all the rest from artisans and traders. The general absence of wealth among most Connecticut claimants partly reflects the economically homogeneous nature of society there. Although there were twelve claims for more than £5,000 (particularly wealthy were Elihu Hall and the Reverend Samuel Peters, who claimed losses of £20,000 and £40,000 respectively),[5] Connecticut lacked the merchant aristocracy of Massachusetts or Rhode Island. Henry Hulton, an English customs official in Boston, gave a valuable insight into Connecticut society when he wrote in October, 1772: "Nobody in These parts has the idea of a Superior, or of a Gentleman, other than themselves. They seem to be good substantial kind of farmers, but there is no break in their Society, their Government, Religeon, and Manners all tend to support an equality. Whoever brings in your Victuals sets down and chats to you."[6]

Forty-six per cent of the claimants served in the armed forces or militia and, including those who served the British in some other official way, the figure is raised to a very high 62 per cent (the highest in New England), which indicates that Connecticut Loyalists were very active. Connecticut men served in several regiments, in particular the Prince of Wales Volunteers, the Queen's Rangers, and Fanning's King's American Regiment.[7] There is some reason to agree with one claimant's assertion that "in their Supplying men for his Majesties Service they [Connecticut men] can claim Precedence with any Colony in America."[8] A few Loyalists mention serving in the American militia under duress, but apart from this there is little evidence of equivocation. Only three claimants refer to their families as split. Zephaniah Beardslee was disinherited by his Whig father, Ralph

Earl's father was a rebel colonel, and Azariah Pritchard noted that he was leniently treated because his father and brother were "both violent friends to the Rebel Cause." Joel Stone, a Woodbury shopkeeper, had a partner who remained in Connecticut and was therefore at least neutral.[9] Stephen Jarvis, later a public figure in Canada (but not a claimant), was the nephew of the Whig Major Starr.[10]

The structure of Connecticut Loyalism which emerges from the statistical tables is of a native-born, numerically weak, but physically active movement, urban in the sense of being concentrated in numerous small towns, quite widely scattered geographically and economically, but with a concentration (as is also the case with radicalism) in Fairfield County in the southwest (in particular at Norwalk and Stamford). There was a slight tendency to commerce, and a notable tendency to very modest wealth. Connecticut Loyalism did not command a mass following, but it did command considerable support from the masses.

All evidence, the claims commission testimony and the history of Connecticut during the revolutionary period, points toward the general weakness of Loyalism. The basic reason for the strength of the Whigs is probably, as G. A. Gilbert put it, that for nearly 150 years Connecticut "had been an independent republic *de facto*," and it was difficult to advance antirepublican sentiments in a successful republic.[11] Similarly the contemporary Loyalist, the Reverend Samuel Peters, observed that republicanism had been established in Connecticut and some other colonies.[12] This is perhaps what Joshua Chandler was hinting at in a petition for relief when he wrote, "I have Sometimes thought it a misfortune to have been Born in Connecticutt, that Colony has been but Little known or noticed until these unhappy

Times." [13] Connecticut's charter was satisfactory enough to serve as the state constitution until 1818, and alone of all the colonial governors, Connecticut's Jonathan Trumbull (whose cousin, John Trumbull, wrote the celebrated anti-Tory satire *M'Fingal*), was a firm Whig. He came to power at the election following the Stamp Act and remained governor until 1784. The renunciation of British rule was accomplished with hardly any opposition. In June, 1776, the Assembly vote in favor of independence was unanimous. [14] Central and local political leadership was solidly Whig. Only one local official, a justice of the peace, put in a claim, and only two members of the Assembly (one of whom was also a local magistrate).

The one reference in the Connecticut claims record to the Stamp Act controversy further suggests Tory weakness. Jeremiah Miller, Sr., lost his seat in the Assembly never to return because his loyal stand "gave umbrage to my constituents." It is worth noting that although Miller was a customs official at the beginning of the Revolution he "took no active" part and, as his son testified, was allowed to remain in Connecticut. [15]

A few Tories, such as the Reverend Samuel Peters, had Yale degrees, but of the 1,000 Yale graduates surviving at the beginning of the Revolution fewer than twenty-five or one-fortieth were genuine Loyalists. [16]

Official policy towards the Loyalists was generally quite mild, a sign of Tory weakness. [17] However, there are several examples of the persecution of Loyalists. [18] It might be simply economic boycott as, when James Sayre told the commissioners, the local committee forbade "all Persons whatever viz. Merchants Mechanicks Millers and Butchers and Co. from supplying the said John Sayre or Family with any manner of Thing whatever." ¹⁹ David Pickett, a Stamford weaver, was advertised as an enemy in the newspaper and thus lost his business.²⁰ Zephaniah Beardslee, who evidently took his Loyalism extremely seriously, was "very much abused" for drinking the king's health and naming his daughter Charlotte after the queen.²¹ But the Patriots could get more violent. William Davies was tarred and feathered and beaten with muskets, mistreatment which, he claimed, had affected his memory; the Reverend Samuel Peters was awaiting a similar fate upon the gallows in 1774 when some neighbors rescued him. Samuel Jarvis related that the following treatment made his whole family very ill: "That your Memorialist for his Attachment to constitutional Government was taken with his Wife and Famely, consisting of three Daughters and one little Son by a Mob of daring and unfeeling Rebels from his Dwelling House in the dead of Night Striped [*sic*] of everything, put on board Whale Boats and Landed on Long Island in the Month of August last about 2 oClock in the Morning Oblieging them to wade almost to their Middles in the Water." ²²

In 1775 Dr. Nehemiah Clarke claimed that he nearly died at the hands of a mob at Hartford; Peter Guire was branded on the forehead with the letters "G.R."; Seth Seely, a Stamford farmer, was brought before the local committee in 1776, and for signing a declaration to support the king's laws was "put on a Rail carried on mens Shoulders thro the Streets, then put into the Stocks and besmeared with Eggs and was robbed of money for the Entertainment of the Company." ²³

Nathan Barman (or Barnum), a native-born farmer, imprisoned (falsely, he said) in 1779 for passing counterfeit money, recounted the following romantic tale. "Knowing the Apprehensions and Prejudices of the Country against the Small-Pox," he inoculated himself just before his trial and was "sent to the Hospital, where he was chained to the Floor to prevent his Escape," but "he found Means to bribe one of the Nurses, who not only brought him a File to cut off his Irons, but amused the Centinal [*sic*], placed over him while he effected it . . ."[24]

Connecticut claimants provide two more examples of colorful escapes. Samuel Jarvis and his brother got out of prison "by the assistance of Friends who had privately procured some Women's apparel which they Dressed themselves in, and by that means made their escape through the Rebel Army." James Robertson asserted that while he was in jail at Albany, the British attacked and set the building on fire, whereupon, unable to walk, he managed to crawl into a cabbage patch "and chewing them to prevent being suffocated" was found three days later badly burnt.[25]

At least four Loyalists suffered death. During the war one was shot for being out of bounds in Simsbury; another was hanged at Hartford; Joshua Stone reported the execution of his father, William, for raising troops for the British at Hartford; Moses Dunbar, significantly a convert to Anglicanism from Congregationalism, was hanged for accepting a British commission and recruiting troops.[26]

Claims were made for two Loyalists whose deaths were attributed to the harsh treatment they had suffered. Filer Diblee, whose family was plundered four times (the first time the rebels "took even the Children's Hats from their Heads and shoes from their feet," Diblee's brother-in-law claimed), collapsed under the strain, "took a Razor from the Closet, threw himself on the bed, drew the Curtains, and cut his own throat." Millington Lockwood, after receiving a head wound, lost his reason and drowned himself.[27]

Connecticut was considered a good place for the im-

prisonment of Tories from other states. This reasoning was
not entirely due to the strength of Whig feeling there, but
rather because of the famous Tory jail, or "Catacomb of
Loyalty" as Thomas Anburey called it, the Simsbury Mines.
These old converted copper mines contained cells forty
yards below the surface of the ground into which "the
prisoners are let down by a windlass into the dismal cavern,
through a hole, which answers the purpose of conveying
their food and air, as to light, it scarcely reaches them."[28]
Justus Sherwood regarded being sent there as a "shocking
Sentence (worse than Death)."[29] The mines received such
celebrated Loyalists as William Franklin, governor of New
Jersey, and Mayor Mathews of New York.[30]

Further suggestion of the weakness of the Tories in
Connecticut is that they were rapidly readmitted at the end
of the war, although there was sometimes an initial burst of
animosity.[31] Thus just after the signing of the peace treaty
Prosper Brown, a Saybrook Loyalist, returned to New London on his way home, whereupon a mob hung him up by
the neck on a ship at the wharfside, took him down, stripped
him and gave him the cat-o'-nine-tails, tarred and feathered
him, hoisted him naked from the yard-arm for a quarter of
an hour's exhibition, and then put him on a boat for New
York without his belongings and with a warning not to return on pain of death.[32]

But his seems to have been a rare case. At any rate persecution was temporary.[33] The quick rehabilitation of Loyalists (which had also been going on *during* the war—a proclamation of May, 1777, offering pardon to Loyalists who
would take an oath of allegiance before August 1 was
followed by a similar one in May, 1779, and "hundreds had
recanted before 1783")[34] had certain economic causes, at

least in New Haven where business favored the return of wealthy Loyalists to bolster the city's economy.[35] A Norwich Loyalist admitted in 1785 that his lands had been restored to him.[36]

The tables which show nearly half the Loyalists claiming for sums of £500 or less are at variance with the often-held opinion that Connecticut Loyalists were generally the well-to-do.[37] The reason may well be that most of the wealthy Loyalists either returned to the state after the war (which, as we have seen, they were encouraged to do) or, like the Reverend Calvin White, never left it in the first place.

White, a descendant of John White who came to Massachusetts in 1632, was born at Middletown, Connecticut, in 1762, and died at the age of ninety-one within a few years of the Civil War. It is significant that this Yale graduate was at first a Congregationalist, but was converted to the Anglican faith, and finally in 1822 embraced Roman Catholicism, a logical end, perhaps, to his spiritual journey. In the years following independence White remained an unrepentant aristocratic Tory. He never voted or recognized the republic in any way except to pay taxes. It is related that as late as 1850 while out driving near Orange, New Jersey, he was shown a spot known as "Tory Corners" because it had been a Loyalist stronghold, whereupon "the old man uncovered his head and bowed in reverence."[38]

Isaac Wells Shelton, who helped guide Governor Tryon's expedition against Danbury in April, 1777, continued to reside at his home in Bristol where he was known as "Tory Shelton," and maintained his predilection for swimming against the tide by keeping slaves as long as it was legal to do so.[39]

If Connecticut had been dominated by a large town which

the British had held for a length of time, or if a British garrison had been present, there would undoubtedly have been many more Loyalist claimants. Military occupation was the great precipitator of Loyalism. But Connecticut lay outside the main fields of combat (although the occupation of New York City and Long Island was a stimulus to some Connecticut Loyalists), and apart from some harassment of the coast by the British fleet, forays by Governor Tryon against Danbury in 1777 and New Haven in 1779, and an attack on New London by Benedict Arnold in 1781, the province escaped serious fighting. It is significant that in 1779 several Loyalists joined Tryon and withdrew with him.

Why were the Connecticut claimants loyal? The assertion by James Ketchum, a Norwalk merchant, that he "was led by the dictates of Reason to oppose the Factious multitude at the first dawning of the Rebellion" somewhat begs the question, but the reasons for the loyalty of some Connecticut claimants are self-evident. Isaac Hubbard, a royal official, informed the commissioners that "being a Servant of the Crown therefore he was in Duty bound to be loyal." [40] It was as simple as that. Similarly a Kirk of Scotland minister, the Reverend George Gilmore, wrote, ". . . of course as I could not from principle and according to my Ordination Oath deny my Allegiance to my gracious Sovereign not chusing to adopt the Country Mood of Cursing the King and blessing their Congress. Refusing to pipe the popular Tune of Tumult Faction Sedition and Rebellion, I was Judged unworthy to share in the priviledges of another lives [sic] of Community." [41]

As for the mercantile class, the history of the decade following 1763 does not reveal that Connecticut merchants were backward in their patriotic obligations, although, as one would expect, there were some difficulties (but only temporary) over the acceptance of the Continental Association in Fairfield County.[42] Most of the merchants must have remained true to the Association, but not all, as the tables show. Economic and political conservatism inclined many merchants throughout the colonies to Loyalism, and it is clear that trading with the British forces was a constant temptation. Nathaniel Hubbard, a Stamford merchant, sold supplies to the British troops.[43] One Connecticut claimant, Isaac Moseley, even mentions trading with the British from rebel-held territory. Goods were put on ships ostensibly bound for the West Indies; meanwhile the British were informed and cruisers would lie in wait and "capture" them as if they were American vessels. Moseley noted with apparent pride that "he contrived the Plan himself." His ships were finally taken to New York and handed over to his agents. "It was a Risk but if they succeeded they were paid very well." Other merchants, such as Jacob Loder, simply shifted their business to British-held New York.[44] But trading was not always confined to merchants. John Winthrop, a rich New London farmer, sold cattle "for the preservation of the Lives of his Majesty's Troops" and was accordingly the object of Whig attention, his widow testified.[45]

The partial concentration of Connecticut Loyalists in the west, in Fairfield County, demands an explanation. One obvious factor is the distance from the Boston stronghold and the proximity of New York City, significant as the entrepôt of Connecticut and as a long-held, powerful British base. It was to New York that most of the claimants fled, and it was from there that most of them finally sailed into exile.

Another factor is the Church of England. It was widely

The King's Friends

held by contemporaries such as Ezra Stiles that Anglicanism was the key to Connecticut Loyalism, an opinion shared by modern scholars[46] and echoed by Ralph Isaacs, a Branford merchant, who recalled that his parents were Anglicans and thus "in his early education he received impressions in favour of the British, which were never eradicated." The zealous missionary work of the Society for the Propagation of the Gospel which controlled the church in New England had aroused strong antagonisms. It is clear that Anglicanism was strongest in southwestern Connecticut, precisely the area of Loyalism's strength. One-third of the population of Fairfield County was reportedly Anglican compared with one-thirteenth for the colony as a whole. These western Connecticut Anglicans had close ties with New York. It may be that most of the claimants were Anglicans (the commissioners' evidence does not usually reveal religious affiliations), but it is notable that of the twenty Church of England ministers in Connecticut only two, the Reverend Samuel Peters, the rector of Hebron and Hartford, and the Reverend John Sayre, the rector of Fairfield, are found among the claimants. They were in an unenviable position. They could not be expected to desert their flocks, and all but two being natives of Connecticut, exile would be a far different matter for them than for immigrant English clergy. Gilbert calls Newtown, strongly Anglican, a center of Toryism, yet not a single claimant is found there; indeed a contemporary wrote in 1781 that "Newtown and the Church-of-England part of Redding were, he believed, the only parts of New England that had refused to comply with the doings of Congress," yet only three claimants from Redding are identified. On the other hand these three claimants asserted that their town was strongly Tory, mentioning

Connecticut

in particular the "Reading Resolves against Congress and Committees."[47]

Connecticut had developed deep religious, political, and economic sectionalism following the Great Awakening. After 1760 British policy, together with certain other issues, produced two definite parties, the conservatives (strongest in Fairfield County and composed mostly of Old Light and Anglican freemen) and the radicals (strongest in New London and Windham Counties, and composed largely of Congregationalists, especially New Lights).[48] The Congregational church, of course, was the established church. Thus the Anglicans favored an increase in royal power as a means of alleviating their own position. Conversely the Congregationalists feared any royal encroachments, especially the possibility of an American bishop. Following the Stamp Act crisis the conservatives' Governor Fitch was ousted permanently by the radicals' Jonathan Trumbull, a setback from which the conservatives never recovered. It is striking that as early as 1768 Connecticut's conservatives were labeled "Grumbletonians" and "Tories." However, the subsequent history of the conservatives makes it clear that the Loyalists were only a wing of that party, to the left of whom stood neutralists and then moderates who finally went over to the Whig side. Thus the moderate Benjamin Gale joined the radicals, while Jared Ingersoll, the one-time stamp collector, George Wyllys, the secretary of Connecticut, and the ministers Benjamin Woodbridge and Nehemiah Strong finally accepted the new regime.[49]

Even the much-hated Reverend Samuel Peters told the commissioners that he hoped to return to Connecticut, although he did not actually reach the United States until 1805.[50] William Samuel Johnson, a Connecticut-born Anglican council member, supporter of the episcopacy plan, and moderate Whig at the time of the Stamp Act and Townshend duties, remained neutral at first during the war, but finally accepted the drift of events and went on to serve in the Confederation Congress and Federal Convention before becoming the first president of Columbia College and a United States senator.

The evidence is strong that most Anglicans were simply neutralists (like a claimant, Samuel Miles, who "kept out of the way as much as possible")[51] who strongly disliked the Revolution but were eventually reconciled to it (partly because of the state's mild treatment of them).[52] When the Connecticut Anglican clergy met in convention at New Haven in July, 1776, apparently only the indomitable John Beach, rector of Newtown and Redding (significantly a converted Congregational minister), protested the resolve to suspend public execution of churchly duties.[53] Outspoken as Beach was, and often threatened, even shot at, he succeeded in dying peacefully in his own home in 1782.

Most Anglicans and most Loyalists (to use the term loosely) remained in Connecticut. There are many examples of Loyalists, or alleged Loyalists, in positions of responsibility during the war. For example, the Newtown regiments tried to elect Tory officers in May, 1778.[54] One meets the epithet "Tory" in elections *after* 1783. Ezra Stiles wrote in February, 1784, of New Haven that "the Episcopalians are all Tories but two, and all qualified on this Occasion, tho' dispising Congress government before—they may perhaps be 40 Voters," adding, "Perhaps one Third of the Citizens may be hearty Tories."[55] Further, it was in Connecticut that locally-born Samuel Seabury after the war became the first Episcopal bishop in America. Bishop Jarvis, a member of a well-known Connecticut Loyalist family, became the second Episcopal bishop of Connecticut and the first prelate consecrated in the United States.

In summary it must be said that there is a world of difference between genuine, active Loyalism and mental Loyalism or neutralism. Most Loyalists in Connecticut seem to have been Anglicans, but most Anglicans were not really Loyalists.

In Benedict Arnold (not a claimant), Connecticut, of course, furnished one of the best-known Tories of all. He is the most notorious example of a whole class of Loyalists who joined the British for reasons (sometimes justified, sometimes not) of personal pique.[56] The famed turncoat is mentioned once in the claims testimony by Samuel Ketchum, who recalled that being forced into the rebel militia "but not doing his Duty General Arnold who then Commanded the Rebels ordered that he and a few more Tories should be shut up in a House and burnt."[57]

But apart from Arnold, the Reverend Samuel Peters, and perhaps a few others, the bulk of Connecticut's talent—such as General Israel Putnam, Jonathan Trumbull, the Reverend Benjamin Trumbull, Ezra Stiles, Eliphalet Dyer, Roger Sherman and even, in the long run, William Samuel Johnson—were on the Patriot side.

In the last analysis, why a considerable number of merchants and small farmers should have taken the opposite course to the majority of their brethren remains something of a mystery, probably not susceptible to any generalized answer. The preamble to the pardon act of May, 1779, called Toryism a heinous crime, but went on: ". . . it is apprehended that very different motives and principles have influenced the conduct of the deluded few . . . Some through ignorance of the nature and grounds of the dispute between Great Britain and America; some through particular prejudice, prospects of reward and gain, or through timidity; others, deceived by the treacherous arts of subtle and secret enemies, have without deliberation given way to the force of various temptations . . ." [58] This is another way of saying that, as in all the colonies, each man had his reasons.

V. NEW YORK

CHARLOTTE CO.

Lake Champlain

GLOUCESTER CO.

Crown Point

Ticonderoga

TRYON CO.

Lake George

CUMBERLAND CO.

Saratoga

Stillwater • Cambridge

BallsTown

MANOR OF RENSSELAER

Albany

Schoharie

Rensselaerwick

MASSACHUSETTS

ALBANY CO.

MANOR OF LIVINGSTON

Hudson River

DUTCHESS CO.

PENNSYLVANIA

ULSTER CO.

Poughkeepsie

MANOR OF CORTLANDT

CONNECTICUT

ORANGE CO.

WESTCHESTER

NEW YORK (City & Co.)

SUFFOLK CO.

NEW JERSEY

QUEENS CO.

KINGS CO.

RICHMOND CO. & STATEN ISLAND

NEW YORK

IN THE second half of the eighteenth century, New York (which includes Vermont for the purposes of this study) was dominated by rich merchants and the great semifeudal families who lived on landed estates (often called "manors") lying along the Hudson and Mohawk Rivers. During the pre-Revolutionary years politics was the preserve of this ruling class, which divided into two factions: the ruling, Anglican, DeLancey party and the opposition, Presbyterian, Livingston party. When the poor farmers rose in an antirent riot in 1766, both factions combined to suppress them fiercely. Resistance to British policy after 1763, if not quite on the same plane as in Massachusetts or Virginia, also came from both political sides; it was vocal and vehement, but, uniquely among the colonies, remained in the hands of moderates and future Loyalists. In fact, as the agitation shifted to outright war and independence, many "Whigs" became "Tories," and the latter party stood forth with a strength rarely equaled in any other part of America. But, although the Loyalists kept control of all three branches of government, the news of Lexington put real power into the hands of the Whigs. However, New York City, a British military stronghold during the entire war, became the mecca of the Loyalists from the area and eventually from most of the other colonies.

Eleven hundred and six New York claimants are analyzed and the number is increased to 1,107 by the addition of one claimant about whom there is no information. This is approximately 0.54 per cent of the population of 203,747 in 1776,[1] the highest percentage for any colony except Georgia. New Yorkers make up nearly half the total of claimants analyzed in all the colonies, and contemporaries[2] and modern scholars are agreed that New York was the great Loyalist stronghold.

It has been estimated that New York provided 23,500 men for the British armed forces (including the militia), a figure perhaps equal to the total supplied by all the other colonies combined, although New York ranks only seventh out of thirteen in population size. About 67 per cent of the claimants mention serving in the armed forces. Apart from the militia, units frequently joined included DeLancey's Brigade, the Westchester Refugees, Sir John Johnson's Regiment (the New York Volunteers), the Orange Rangers, the Guides and Pioneers, the Loyal American Regiment, the King's Rangers, the Queen's Rangers, the King's American Regiment, and Jessup's Corps. No colony contributed more to British military power.[3]

No province passed harsher laws against the Loyalists than New York.[4] Numerous examples of unofficial and illegal persecution are found in the claims commission testimony—burnings, mobbings, and, in New York City, "grand Toory [*sic*] Rides," as a contemporary called the grisly riding on a rail.[5] Only one tarring and feathering is mentioned but there certainly were others.[6] Margaret Francis Hill, Colonel Guy Johnson's housekeeper, related suffering singularly cruel treatment; she was "stripped naked of all her Cloaths confined to a cold Room in Bedford New England" for three months in winter. She believed that the reason (which perhaps lends credence to her story) was the American hatred of the Johnsons for using Indians in the war. Also, she had refused a bribe to poison her master.[7]

The statement of George Folliott, a rich New York

merchant, that the rebels "made a practice of hanging people up on a slight pretence" doubtless is an exaggeration,[8] but the claims commission testimony reveals fifteen executions of Loyalists (whether after a legal trial is rarely mentioned) and the attempted execution of Benjamin Whitecuff, a Negro, who maintained that having been caught as a spy he actually hung by his neck for three minutes before being cut down just in time by a detachment of British troops.[9] Throughout the colonies there are examples of the execution of military prisoners. A contemporary French account of the Loyalist defeat at the battle of Bennington related that "les royalistes Américains se comportèrent bravement, le Col. Peters fut tué et presque tout son monde. Les rebelles les assassinèrent après qu'ils étoient prisonniers." [10]

But perhaps more touching across the years than accounts of atrocities are the more pedestrian misfortunes of civil war. In 1780 Mary Donnelly petitioned the British authorities in New York for relief. Her husband had been serving on board a privateer when "about seven months ago as my youngest Child lay expireing in my Arms an account came of the Vessil being lost in a Storm." Mrs. Donnelly was now destitute, "frequently being affraid to open my Eyes on the Daylight least I should hear my infant cry for Bread and not have it in my power to relieve him. the first meal I had eat for three days at one time was a morsel of dry bread and a lump of ice." [11]

On June 6, 1783, Phebe Ward of East Chester wrote to her husband Edmund at New York,

Kind Husband

I am sorry to aquant you that our farme is sold. . . .

thay said If I did not quitt posesion that thay had aright to take any thing on the farme or in the house to pay the Cost of

a law sute and imprisen me I have sufered most Every thing
but death it self in your long absens pray Grant me spedy
Releaf or God only knows what will be com of me and my
frendsles Children

thay said my posesion was nothing youre husband has forfeted his estate by Joining the British Enemy with a free and
vollentery will and thereby was forfeted to the Stat and sold

All at present from your cind and Loveing Wife

phebe Ward

pray send me spedeay anser.[12]

At the time of the peace treaty (at least in the upstate
areas) there was a good deal of rough expulsion of unpopular Tories who tried to remain,[13] and David Colden noted
that the treaty had not affected the "spirit of persecution and
violence." [14] Similarly a hot reception awaited anyone who
attempted to return.[15] But most Loyalists were not exiled,[16]
although great numbers were disenfranchised, and such incidents as the case of *Rutgers* v. *Waddington* exacerbated bad
feelings.[17] John Jay and Alexander Hamilton, among others,
opposed harsh treatment of the Loyalists, arguing that it
was bad for business, and by 1788 all anti-Tory legislation
had been repealed.[18] As early as November, 1785, an inhabitant of Albany assured a friend that most exiles from
that area had returned and "live Quiet and unmolested." [19]
Eleven (seven of whom supported ratification of the federal
Constitution) out of sixty outstanding New York leaders
during the "critical period" had been Loyalists.[20]

If the Loyalists were powerful, however, they were probably not a majority. This is indicated by the fact that they
were unable to prevent the province from falling to the
Whigs and were able to hold power only because of the
British occupation. Also, the manpower (41,633) supplied
to the rebel forces was nearly double that supplied to the

British.[21] Alexander Flick, the most thorough chronicler of the New York Tories, guessed that the Loyalists numbered 90,000, 35,000 of whom emigrated.[22] This accords with Alexander Hamilton's statement that at the outbreak of the war nearly half of New York's population was Tory,[23] a view echoed by John Adams.[24]

The table showing the residences of the Loyalists reveals that the great concentrations of Tories were (in numerical order) in Tryon County, Albany County, Charlotte County, New York City, Dutchess County, and Westchester County; this area included the heart of New York running north from Manhattan up the east bank of the Hudson as far as the southern boundary of Albany County, and then on both sides of the river up to Lake Champlain (with notable concentrations around Albany and Saratoga), and along the Mohawk into Tryon County. Staten Island (Richmond County), Long Island (Kings, Queens, and Suffolk Counties), the western frontier areas of Orange and Ulster Counties, and the Vermont area of Cumberland and Gloucester Counties were weak in claimants although these areas also had comparatively small populations.

Tryon and Albany Counties, with almost equal numbers, account for about 50 per cent of the claimants. Charlotte County (14 per cent), New York City (13 per cent), Westchester County (11 per cent), and Dutchess County (7 per cent) make up most of the remainder.

Counties with the most claimants were not necessarily the areas of the greatest Loyalist strength. Most of the numerous Tryon County claimants, mainly Highland Catholic tenants and followers of Sir John Johnson, were part of a body of Loyalists forced to flee to Canada in 1776, outnumbered ten to one by the Whigs, according to the Catholic priest, John McKenna.[25] In other areas prompt Whig action may have squashed Tory resistance before it had any real chance to get organized. For example, Governor Tryon wrote to the Earl of Dartmouth on February 7, 1776, that in the previous month 1,200 men from New Jersey had entered Long Island and disarmed 600 Queens County Loyalists.[26]

Based on the percentage of claimants of the white population of 1771, the list of counties in descending order is as follows:[27]

County	Percentage
Charlotte	5.45
Tryon	2.9
Albany	0.96
New York	0.74
Westchester	0.65
Gloucester	0.56
Dutchess	0.305
Cumberland	0.23
Ulster	0.22
Queens	0.182
Orange	0.18
Richmond	0.178
Kings	0.12
Suffolk	0.0425

This analysis of the claimants is not fully in accord with the usual estimates of the distribution of Loyalists, in particular with their much-noted strength on Long Island and Staten Island. The explanation probably is that in many parts of southern New York the Tories were so numerous and powerful that it was impossible for the Whigs to force them into exile. Flick estimated that the disfranchising act of May 12, 1784, took the vote from "two-thirds of the inhabitants of New York City, Richmond and Kings Counties, one-fifth of those of Suffolk County, nine-tenths of Queens County, and all of the borough of Westchester."[28] It is probable that a much smaller proportion of active Loyalists in New York was forced into exile than in other states. If this is true the great strength of New York Loyalism compared with other areas is increased.

There may be no contradiction between Moses Knapp's assertion to the commissioners that "the Inhabitants of Dutchess County were in general Loyal" and the low proportion of claimants for that county noted above.[29] In November, 1781, John McGinniss argued that New York Loyalists were in a majority of five to one "if properly supported," and a petition of the previous month to Sir Henry Clinton signed by sixty-three persons declared that two-thirds of the men able to bear arms would do so "when ever they can be properly supported and Furnished by his Majesty's Troops."[30] But of course by this time the British cause was virtually lost, and most Loyalists' future interests lay in accepting the republican regime.

New York City, the center of the colony's political, economic, and social activity and a key city in the colonies as a whole, has a special interest. One hundred and thirty-eight persons (nearly 13 per cent of the total claimants) from the city submitted claims; this is 0.55 per cent of the city's population of 25,000 in 1775,[31] a proportion a little more than half that for Boston, and a little less than twice that for Philadelphia or Newport. This does not support the view of Flick that the Loyalists were a majority in the city,[32] although it does indicate that they were strong. The population dropped from 25,000 in 1775 to 5,000 in 1776 at the prospect of the British invasion (a drop of four-fifths compared with drops of about one-half in Philadelphia and Newport, and three-quarters in Boston), a figure which does not suggest a widespread enthusiasm for the advancing army.[33] Thus it seems that William Cunningham was closer to the truth than Flick when he told the commissioners concerning New York City that "the Rebellious party were rather more in Number" than the Loyalists.[34] The Tories were unable to retain control of the city before the arrival of British troops. Many claimants recounted hiding in the woods and swamps of Long Island or retiring to the Jersies until the British came.

A majority of the city's population was Whig, or, at least, as James Devereux recounted, the departure of the British troops at the beginning of the troubles "so intimidated and alarmed the people that almost every Person in the City of New York joined the Association and Signed their Articles."[35] There was also fear of the Whigs in other colonies. James DeLancey, Jr., the son of the lieutenant-governor, said that in 1775 he and several of the "principal Citizens . . . were of Opinion they could have mastered the disaffected in New York, but were apprehensive of being overpowered by those from New Jersey and Connecticut."[36]

The area which became Vermont (Cumberland, Gloucester, and Charlotte Counties, and part of Albany County) is a special case. It gained a reputation for Toryism because of the celebrated intrigues and negotiations with the British, but few claimants were found in this area. Those who were generally joined General Burgoyne in 1777 during his campaign in those parts. The Vermonters sought independence from whichever side would grant it. Abijah Hawley said as much when he told the commissioners, "Vermont did not join Congress but were [*sic*] violent against Great Britain." [37]

Patriot strength lay in New York City, the town of Albany, and Orange County (few Loyalist claimants are recorded from this latter area). New York City, of course, was also a center of great Tory strength and is considered more fully below. Albany was the only other place in the province where the economic boycotts which preceded the Revolution were received with any enthusiasm; however, as in New York, the Albany Loyalists were, as Colonel William Edmeston put it, "a very considerable and respectable body," [38] but again not considerable enough to hold their own. Abraham Cuyler held a party there on June 4, 1776, which featured carousing and the singing of "God Save the King," whereupon the enraged citizens broke in and carried the merrymakers off to jail. [39]

The claimants are almost equally divided between native- and foreign-born. American-born is easily the largest single category, but the combined total of foreign-born is slightly greater. The great majority of this latter category came from the British Isles: over half from Scotland, roughly equal numbers from Ireland and England, and a handful from Wales. The only other important country of origin is Germany, with slightly over 7 per cent of the Loyalists. As in most other colonies, considerably more of the immigrants had arrived after 1763 than before.

Two German-born ministers of religion submitted claims: John Michael Kern of the German Reformed (Lutheran) Church at Wallkill, Ulster County, and Bernard Michael Houseal of New York City, who seems to have been Anglican (he was later a minister of the Society for the Propagation of the Gospel at Halifax, Nova Scotia). Neither gave any indication of the general attitude of their fellow countrymen toward the Revolution. It is generally held that most New York Germans were Whig.

The vast majority, nearly 75 per cent, of the New York claimants were farmers, followed by the commercial, generally urban, element with about 18 per cent; then royal office-holders with almost 4 per cent, and professional men with well over 3.5 per cent.

The preponderance of farmers is reflected by the fact that the largest claim category (64 per cent of the whole) is for amounts of £500 or less, and over 77 per cent of the claims were for £1,000 or less. But the seventy-two who claimed £5,000 or more, and the thirty-nine persons who claimed £10,000 or more, show that the very wealthy, if a small minority of the claimants, were nevertheless substantially represented in the Loyalist ranks.

However, the picture of the typical New York Loyalist which emerges from the tables is of a farmer of moderate means, living in the Hudson or Mohawk Valley, equally likely to be native or foreign born (if the latter, probably from the British Isles, but possibly from Germany).

This description obviously applies to the rural Loyalists only; the great urban center of New York City requires separate analysis. The differences are those to be expected. The port claimants were composed of a little over 60 per cent immigrants as compared with about 50 per cent for the colony as a whole. Also hardly any Germans are found (they were mainly farmers), and the English are the largest immigrant group as opposed to the Scots (mainly tenant farmers in Tryon and Charlotte Counties). The city immigrants were a much longer-established group, forty-four arriving before 1763 and eighteen after.

New York

Not surprisingly, most of the wealthy claimants came from New York City; for example, about three-quarters of the thirty-nine who claimed £10,000 or more. About 19 per cent of the city claimants (the same percentage as claimed £10,000 or more) claimed £500 or less compared with 64 per cent for the colony in general. In New York City almost equal numbers claimed over £2,000 or less; in the colony as a whole only about 14 per cent claimed £2,000 or more. On September 5, 1776, General Greene wrote to Washington: "Two-thirds of the property of the city of *New York* and the suburbs belongs to the Tories. We have no very great reason to run any considerable risk for its defence." [40]

Among the claimants, the majority (five-eighths) of the merchants and shopkeepers lived in the city, as did a little over half of the professional men and somewhat less than half the office-holders (seventeen out of forty-two).

In short, the active Loyalist of New York City was a member of a substantial minority, was more probably wealthy than his fellow Loyalists in other parts of the state, was usually a long-standing immigrant from the British Isles, and was more likely to be a merchant or shopkeeper than anything else.

These conclusions lend weight to William Cunningham's statement to the commissioners that in the city "the Loyalists were the better sort of Inhabitants—the Rebellious party were . . . of the lowest order." [41]

Perhaps one-third of the military engagements of the Revolutionary War took place in New York. This reflects the colony's strategic and commercial importance, a result of the great port of New York City which also provided a central harbor for troop concentrations. Accordingly, the British occupied the city from late 1776 until the end of

The King's Friends

the war. The Hudson Valley-Lake Champlain route was a means of access to and from Canada, the control of which could split New England off from the rest of the colonies. This, indeed, was the object of an abortive three-pronged British campaign in 1777 under Burgoyne, St. Leger, and Howe. Years of stalemate followed in the southern part of the colony, the British holding New York City, the Americans entrenched at West Point. At the same time, the Loyalists and the Indians under Sir John Johnson, John Butler, and the Mohawk chief Joseph Brant campaigned at the frontier, the last major engagement being the Loyalist defeat at the battle of Johnstown, October, 1781. This was the end of fighting, but Washington did not march into New York City until November 25, 1783.

Several explanations for Loyalist strength in New York can be given, but the occupation of New York City for the whole period of the war as the prime military stronghold of the British forces was a major stimulant. "We are at present all Whigs until the arrival of the King's troops," wrote one Tory in June, 1775.[42] It is significant that New York province, with the most Loyalists, was occupied longer than any other colony. The city was the colony's only port; thus its capture put a stranglehold on all who depended on commerce of any kind for a livelihood. The city was also the haven for Loyalists from throughout the thirteen colonies, and gradually, as one city after another fell to the Americans, it became the last resort, the final refuge, until in the end the sad convoys of exiles reluctantly sailed down the Hudson bound for Nova Scotia, New Brunswick, or Great Britain.

Allied to the occupation was the belief, increasingly difficult to sustain, in British invincibility. Neil McLean was even capable of recalling this state of mind when he maintained to the claims commissioners that in 1776 he had induced 400 to 500 American soldiers to desert General Wooster: "Amongst other Motives I represented the Consumate Knowledge of the British Commander in the Art of War. The fine Discipline and determin'd Resolution of the British Troops. The cruel outrageous and ungovernable Fury of the Canadians and Indians when set Loose on a defeated Enemy and the total Incapacity of Mr. Wooster as an Officer." [43] John Weatherhead had supposed "as every body else did, that the Rebellion would be easily extinguished in a short time after the Army should take the Field." [44]

But wherever British armed forces were present in America they restrained as well as encouraged Toryism. This restraint was the result of harassment and neglect. In New York City, December 5, 1781, Frederick Smyth, the moderate former chief justice of New Jersey, wrote of Loyalist disillusionment: "I have seen our affairs year after year growing from bad to worse and little prospect of any amendment. I think it high time to terminate the war in this Country—for in truth the war in this Country it['s] now little more than a war upon the Treasury and we have a list of Generals in this place under the denomination of Quartermaster—Barrackmaster etc. etc. etc. who have shown vast intrepidity, good generalship and by no means like some other Generals any sign of fainting in the chase." [45]

In the testimony to the claims commissioners there are numerous references to British, and more often Hessian, depredations. Judge Thomas Jones, a leading New York Loyalist, devoted a whole chapter in his partisan history of the state to the "Illegal and Cruel Treatment of Loyalists

by the British Military during the War." [46] The Reverend
Leonard Cutting lamented from Hempstead, Long Island,
in 1781, "We have nothing to call our own, and the door
to redress is inaccessible. The army has done more essential
injury to the King's cause than the utmost efforts of his
enemies." [47] In 1782 Jacobus Cropsey, also of Long Island,
complained to the authorities about "the wanton Destruction" to his property and the "great abuse of his Family"
by the British soldiers. [48]

In 1783 the inhabitants of Westchester County petitioned
Sir Guy Carleton that they were experiencing great evils
from "a lawless Banditti" which was "within reach of your
Excellencys Command." Isaac Heron, a Brooklyn watchmaker, said that the rebels first plundered his property but
the Hessians "complet'd his Ruin." [49]

In a memorial to Sir Henry Clinton of May, 1782, 220
New York City Loyalists, fearing the impending peace,
expressed their feelings with a delicate sarcasm, writing that
the king's "Paternal regard for all his Subjects cannot be
more fully evinced than by the gentle Means he has hitherto
exercised towards the Rebellious part of them. . . ." [50]

Another underlying factor in New York Loyalism, as in
other colonies, is the large number of immigrants whose
loyalty to the home country comes as no surprise, especially
those sixty claimants who mention having arrived as soldiers
during the Seven Years War, and therefore evinced a
natural loyalty.

Although they made up less than 4 per cent of the
claimants, Flick considers the royal officials as the most
active and powerful class of Loyalists, [51] as, indeed, they
were. Many of the great landlords like Sir John Johnson
belonged to this group. Rich New York City officials allied

with certain wealthy merchants and upcountry aristocrats provided the dynamic leadership for the Loyalist party. Lieutenant-Governor Cadwallader Colden, a versatile Scot who had resided in America since 1710, ruled the colony most of the time from 1760 until in 1775 he was forced by popular uprisings to return to Long Island, where he died a year later. Colden, as governor, was the leader of the official class and a particularly intransigent and unpopular upholder of royal authority after the Stamp Act troubles.[52]

Important royal officials who were claimants include: Governor William Tryon, who was resident in New York from 1771 until April, 1774, when he went to England, not returning until fourteen months later when the Revolution was already under way; Chief Justice William Smith; Thomas Jones and George Duncan Ludlow, both judges of the supreme court; John Tabor Kempe, the attorney-general; Robert Bayard, judge of admiralty; Beverley Robinson, judge of Common Pleas and a great landowner; John Peters, a judge in Gloucester County; James DeLancey, high sheriff of Westchester County; John Roberts, sheriff of the city and county of New York; Alexander White, high sheriff of Tryon County; David Mathews, mayor of New York and holder of various legal offices; Samuel Bayard, Jr., deputy secretary of New York; Samuel Kemble, naval officer of the province; David and Nicholas Colden, office-holding son and grandson of the governor; Sir John Johnson, Guy Johnson, and Daniel Claus, Indian agents; Philip Skene, lieutenant-governor of Crown Point and Ticonderoga; Ebenezer Jessup, a deputy in the land office and a large landholder in Albany County; and finally Abraham Cuyler, mayor and an official at Albany.

The motives of the royal officials are not hard to discover; of all classes of Tories their loyalty was the most ingrained. Robert Bayard was doubtless telling no more than the simple truth when he asserted that on being offered command of the rebel army in Canada, "his answer was that he had been a Crown Officer all his life and should never think of changing his Sentiments." [53] William Friend, who had commanded a British sloop on Lake Champlain, recalled that when he was a prisoner at Albany, one Franks, an aide-de-camp of the rebel Benedict Arnold, "told him if he had acted as their friend, he would by that time have been Commodore of all the Lake. He told Franks he had rather serve as a Swabber on board any of His Majesty's Ships than be their Admiral." [54]

Another recurring group which usually included many royal officials might be termed the intellectual Loyalists. Chief Justice William Smith is a good example. He has been aptly designated "an eighteenth-century Whig"; he opposed the Stamp Act, and indeed all Parliamentary taxation, as unconstitutional, but independence he could never concede. In 1788 he wrote, "You know my enthusiasm respecting the Constitution of England. Every encomium I ever read in its favour is short of my idea of its perfections; . . . of all modes of government I pronounce it to be the best . . ." [55]

Henry Van Schaack was a crown officer whose loyalty was *not* ingrained. In fact this American-born official and merchant consistently opposed British policy after 1763, and only the question of independence drove him into Tory neutralism. Henry Cruger Van Schaack (a nephew) argued that his uncle's "great difficulty, and it was that which mainly deterred him from participating in the revolution (as declared by him to a friend in after life), was the oaths he had taken as a public officer." [56]

A leading royal official in New York was the native American Sir John Johnson, Indian superintendent, and owner of a vast estate in frontier Tryon County. His father, Sir William Johnson, an Irish immigrant who had made good, was his son's predecessor in the Indian Department. As an early writer on Sir John put it, "birth and training, family honors and vast possessions due to the generosity of the British government" account for his loyalty. [57] Almost every intellectual Tory in America had a good deal in common with the Whigs. Dr. Myles Cooper, a leader of the Anglicans in New York, opposed the Stamp Act, the Townshend Acts, and the tea duty. Flick concludes that the Loyalists "if anything, in the days before the revolution . . . were more active than the Whigs" in working for reform. [58]

Peter Van Schaack, the lawyer brother of the above-mentioned Henry, argued in an extremely subtle and learned fashion against the Declaration of Independence and armed rebellion and attempted to remain neutral. Drawing largely on Locke, he wrote that his principles were "founded on the immutable laws of nature, and the sacred rights of mankind," but he sympathized with much of the Whig cause and supported non-importation, non-consumption, and the Continental Association. His neutralism separated him from what his son termed his "particular friends, John Jay, Egbert Benson, Theodore Sedgwick, and Gouverneur Morris," all of whom took the Whig side. [59] Carl Becker [60] has examined the subtle process which put the two friends John Jay and Peter Van Schaack, with similar backgrounds and views, into opposite camps. Jay submitted to a *fait accompli*, Van

Schaack followed his conscience. James Duane is another example of a very conservative Whig. His conservatism dated from 1765 when he tried to disperse a Stamp Act mob and continued with his support for Galloway's Plan and later for the federal Constitution.

The kind of personal and social rift observable between Jay and Van Schaack was general in New York. In 1780 Thomas Anburey remarked upon it,[61] and the claims commission testimony, as usual, reveals many examples of divided families and business relationships. Flick has noted that the following families were divided: DeLanceys, Livingstons, Van Schaacks, Crugers, Morrises, Youngs, Boyntons, Van Cortlandts, Floyds, Lows, Herkimers, Jays, and Subers.[62] But it was not just the great families which were so affected. At the opposite end of the social scale, Benjamin Whitecuff, a Negro Loyalist claimant, declared that his father took the rebel side.[63]

Local politics were involved in the Tory-Whig division. As Van Tyne has put it, as the imperial quarrel deepened polarization took place; the Loyalists "merged into the old Episcopal or DeLancey party, and all the opposition became identified with the Presbyterians or the Livingston party." The Tory party was partly a clan: the DeLanceys, DePuysters, Waltons, and Crugers were related "by blood or marriage to more than half of the aristocracy of the Hudson Valley."[64] Among the Loyalist claimants who were members of the DeLancey faction are Brigadier General Oliver DeLancey, James DeLancey, John Harris Cruger, Jacob Walton, David Colden, William Bayard, Abraham Cuyler, John Watts, Roger Morris, Sir John Johnson, and Thomas Jones.

The DeLanceys and Livingstons had been in constant

opposition in the decades preceding the Revolution, and Van Tyne even maintains that the former were "forced" into the Loyalist side because their enemies were Whig.[65] The mixture of principle and expediency in politics is always difficult to measure, but one faction tends automatically to oppose what its rival favors. Flick notes that by 1770 the two parties were quite well defined, and that after that date every question became a party issue. However, apart from the ultra-Tories led by Governor Colden, the quarrel was over the *mode*, not the question, of opposition. Both groups opposed the Stamp Act, only Cadwallader Colden, typically, attempting to enforce it. He and the Reverend John Milner, who was "obliged" to give up his Westchester parish for taking a "warm part . . . in the Support of it," were very exceptional cases.[66] The moderates continued to support most anti-British measures up to and including the First Continental Congress,[67] but at the Second Continental Congress only one of the five New York delegates supported independence.

The claims commission testimony supports the view that the Loyalists had great political strength. On the eve of the Revolution, the twelve-man New York council was unanimously loyal, and all members submitted claims except the two who had died—Sir William Johnson (in 1774) and Daniel Horsmanden (in 1778). In addition, nine members of the Assembly and twelve justices of the peace submitted claims.[68] Only in New York did the Loyalists succeed in keeping control of the legislature, and indeed of the whole early revolutionary machinery, in particular the well-known Committee of Fifty-one and the election of delegates to the First Continental Congress (the Assembly refused to elect any to the second). This control was the result of the

DeLancey party's machinations, as James DeLancey was quick to point out to the claims commissioners,[69] but in the long run it proved of no avail. After Lexington the Whigs simply superseded the Assembly with an extra-legal convention, a provincial congress, although at first even it did not favor the Declaration of Independence.

Although the New York merchants took the lead in the opposition to imperial policies after 1763,[70] the majority were what Virginia D. Harrington has called "eventual conservatives," ending up as neutralists or Loyalists as they gradually lost control of the pre-Revolutionary movement.[71] Such was Isaac Low, head of many merchant committees, who retained the confidence of both radicals and conservatives as late as 1775, but could not accept independence and became a Loyalist and a claimant.[72] Of the 104 members of the New York Chamber of Commerce living in 1775, fifty-seven became Loyalists, twenty-one were neutral, and twenty-six became Whigs.[73] Most merchants were Loyalists, but most were not exiled, and the majority even escaped confiscation. As Robert East has shown, real persecution would have "decimated" the merchant class.[74]

Motives of trade, fear of the lower classes, and general social outlook are responsible for the loyalty of the merchants. But, of course, some merchants were Whigs. For example, of the Committee of Fifty-one, twenty-six were loyal, seven neutral, and eighteen (including twelve merchants) Whig. Miss Harrington offers only tentative reasons for the split: the factors leading towards Toryism were official connections, recent immigration, Anglicanism, and relationship with the DeLancey party, whereas Whig merchants were all engaged in illicit trade and were usually in the distilling and sugar-refining business, or at least the West Indies trade.[75]

The proximity of the British armed forces presented a temptation to trade. The temptation existed not just for a wealthy merchant like John Dawson who secretly supplied the British fleet with £4,000 worth of provisions,[76] but also for modest traders like Mary Airey, an enterprising widow of New York City, who recalled "that upon the expectation of his Majesty's Forces becoming Masters of N. York your Memorialist laid in a considerable quantity of such kind of Provisions as it was in her power to procure and she judged would be most necessary for their refreshment." [77]

It is difficult to judge the mixture of profit and principles in the merchants' actions. Dawson's partner, Patrick Dennis, was a rebel, yet the pair presumably had similar economic interests.[78] The brothers Alexander and Hugh Wallace, rich Irish immigrant merchants, lent Clinton £4,000 toward his southern expedition in 1776. Was this action a business venture, an act of patriotism, or both? Hugh Wallace told the commissioners that no one else would lend the money and that, although he took 10 per cent interest, he could have got more elsewhere. At the same time he refused to lend to Congress and turned down Washington's offer of "any Situation he desired." [79]

Many of the Loyalists who were professional men were connected with the aristocratic governing clique and royal officials.[80] One professional group, however, the Anglican clergy, requires further discussion.

Nine Anglican clerics (five Americans, three British, and one German) submitted claims: Harry Munro of St. Peter's, Albany; Samuel Seabury of Westchester County; Charles

Inglis of Trinity Church, New York; Myles Cooper, second president of King's College; John Vardill, professor of divinity; John Doty of St. George's, Schenectady; Samuel Auchmuty (posthumously) of Trinity Church, New York; John Milner (Milner had no parish when the Revolution began); and Bernard Michael Houseal, a German who seems to have been an Anglican because he was later a missionary of the Society for the Propagation of the Gospel in Halifax, Nova Scotia.[81]

Like that of the royal officials, the loyalty of the Anglican ministers and much of their congregations was almost automatic. As Henry Cruger Van Schaack put it, "The sentiment of allegiance and loyalty was with many an absolute religious sentiment."[82] Timothy Buell, an American-born tenant of the DeLanceys, remarked dryly to the claims commissioners that having been educated an Anglican "the Consequence has been detrimental to his Worldly Interest, but not to his Conscience."[83] Religion and politics were closely linked; Governor Colden connected the two when he wrote in 1770, "From the different political and religious Principles of the Inhabitants, opposite Parties have at all Times, and will exist in this Province . . ."[84] The DeLancey party was generally Anglican, of course, while the Whigs tended to be Presbyterians.[85] The Reverend Charles Inglis declared that the Anglicans in New York City comprised three congregations of at least 2,000 each, almost all of whom stayed loyal and "among whom were the principal Gentlemen of the province for rank and fortune."[86] The entire congregation of Trinity Church, New York, went to Nova Scotia with their minister.[87] On August 26, 1783, Sir Guy Carleton informed Lord North that the "greater part" of the settlers going to Nova Scotia were Anglicans.[88] The bulk of the New York Loyalists (certainly most of the leaders) were probably Anglicans, but there were claims from Irish and Scottish Catholics, a Quaker merchant, and a Lutheran minister; Flick identified Presbyterian, Methodist, Lutheran, and Quaker Tories.[89]

The Anglican position was partly an intellectual one. The Reverend Charles Inglis (born in Ireland), perhaps the most articulate Anglican cleric in New York and a leading promoter of the American bishopric, in his memorial to the claims commissioners listed the reasons for his loyalty as attachment to the king, attachment to the British constitution, "the best political fabric that ever existed," and a desire to defend the Church of England, "which naturally results from a full conviction that her doctrines and plan of Government are conformable to Holy Scripture and that her Spirit are more libral [sic] and mild than that of any other Christian Church whatever." Before the Revolution "the Americans were . . . in possession of as large a portion of freedom as could well consist with a state of Civil Society—that if they were not happy the want of Liberty was not cause, that they could not change but for the worse—and that a separation of the colonies from the parent State must be highly injurious perhaps ruinous to both Countries." Inglis sometimes slid over into king-worship. In a sermon he argued that the key precept must be *"Honour the King"* which is the "Cause of truth, of real Liberty." [90]

The Anglicans in New York, backed by the Society for the Propagation of the Gospel, had been an aggressive force for many years. In 1754 they had succeeded in establishing King's College. The entire faculty was loyal when the Revolution came and all submitted claims: the Reverend Myles Cooper, the president; the Reverend John Vardill, regius professor of divinity; and Dr. Samuel Clossy, professor of anatomy and natural philosophy. The alumni were divided. At least one in eight was a Loyalist claimant, and many more were probably loyal but not claimants. Among the claimants are found Richard Bayard, James DeLancey, Peter Van Schaack, John Watts, Frederick Phillipse, Beverley Robinson, and Isaac Wilkins. Distinguished Whig alumni include John Jay, Robert Troup, Henry Rutgers, Leonard Lispenard, Alexander Hamilton, Gouverneur Morris, and Chancellor Robert R. Livingston.[91]

Allied with their colleague, Thomas Bradbury Chandler, across the water in New Jersey, the New York clergy presented the most formidable Anglican clerical group in the colonies. Seabury, Inglis, Cooper, and his protégé (and finally successful British spy) Vardill were leading advocates of intercolonial Anglican unity and the establishment of an American episcopate, the hoped-for political effects of which they were well aware. Cooper and Vardill joined in the newspaper controversy in 1768 over William Livingston's "The American Whig," which had opposed the bishopric. In 1772 they were engaged in a pamphlet battle with President Witherspoon of Princeton, and also wrote a series of papers signed "Poplicola." Inglis, a close associate of Chandler, told the claims commissioners that he observed "a restless and seditious spirit to prevail in some parts of America long before the proceedings there occasioned any public Alarm," and he accordingly joined with Chandler, Cooper, and Seabury to refute them. After the Revolution began, Inglis wrote as "Papinian" and produced a reply to *Common Sense*, "a most inflammatory pernicious pamphlet."[92]

Seabury, later first Episcopal bishop of the United States, in his memorial to the commissioners, echoed Inglis' assertion of a very early opposition to future rebels. He noted that in 1753 the contribution of William Livingston (the future governor of New Jersey) to the "Watch Tower" column in the *New York Mercury* tended "to corrupt the principles of the People with regard to Government." [93] The "Watch Tower" had opposed the episcopacy and the DeLancey faction. Some years later, he continued, it became evident from publications "and from the uniting of all the Jarring Interests of the Independents and Presbyterians from Massachusets [*sic*] Bay to Georgia under Grand Committees and Synods that some mischevious [*sic*] Scheme was meditated against the Church of England and the British Government in America."

Thus he joined with Chandler and Inglis "to watch all publications either in Newspapers or Pamphlets and to obviate the evil influence of such as appeared to have a bad tendancy by the speediest answers." They "bore the whole weight of the controversy with the American Whig" (mentioned above), and "this Paper was the immediate forerunner of the late rebellion . . ." [94] The culmination of Seabury's writing was, of course, the letters signed "A Westchester Farmer," answered by the precocious undergraduate from King's College named Alexander Hamilton.

One layman, Isaac Wilkins, should be added to the list of Anglican writers. Wilkins was associated with the foregoing clerics, wrote several pamphlets, and was at the time reputed to be the "Westchester Farmer." [95]

Unlike data for most other colonies, the New York tables show a mass of poor farmers (a majority of the claimants) who were Loyalists. This seems to stem partly from the antirent riots of 1766, which were harshly suppressed by the landlords, aided by such New York City magistrates as John

Morin Scott who later became a Revolutionary leader. The farmers noted that whereas the Stamp Act rioters were mildly treated, their own leaders were condemned to death. Thus the pardon given to Prendergast revealed the king to the tenants as "a shield against rapacious landlords." Many farmers, as a recent historian has put it, "when the Revolution came, turned against it wherever the landlords were for it."[96]

This attitude was implied by Abraham Yates, Jr., in a 1787 Independence Day oration, when he said, "It is admitted that there are poor as well as rich Tories . . . yet we know by experience that there would not have been a Tory in fifty in our late struggles if they had not been disaffected by the rich."[97]

Some Tory tenants hoped for land reform if the king defeated their landlords, and William Smith claimed that the Quaker Hill area, where the tenants made their last stand in 1766, was forty to one against independence.[98] Irving Mark has noted that many small farmers in Albany, Westchester, and Dutchess Counties, the scene of agrarian disturbances in the 1760's and earlier, were Loyalists, and certainly many yeoman claimants are found there. Mark discovered about twenty Loyalists who seemed to have a connection with the agrarian riots but concluded that in general the evidence was "insufficient."[99]

The table of residence of Loyalist claimants does not prove widespread Toryism among the tenants of Whig landlords. Only a tiny handful of claimants gave their residence as Livingston Manor, the Manor of Rensselaer, or Rensselaerwick. However, a petition from the inhabitants of Livingston Manor of September 20, 1781, addressed to Sir Henry Clinton upon his arrival, claimed that over 800 men would bear arms "whenever they can be properly supported and furnish'd," and that Loyalists on the manor "compose a larger majority than other Districts of the Province."[100] But the Livingston Manor Loyalists were not "properly supported." A revealing letter from Samuel Hake to Clinton, dated February 15, 1782, recounts that John Cook and Abraham Freleigh, two leading Loyalists from the manor, were refused an interview with Clinton and were instead received "with . . . cool indifference" by Colonel Robinson. Hake noted the possibly fatal effects on the Loyalists whom the two men represented and added that if this was the way friends were treated, "permit me to remark, how can your Excellency reasonably suppose any Man of Honour will risque his All, as those have done to support the royal Cause."[101] Neither Cook nor Freleigh appears among the claimants.

Most of the great landlords were in fact Loyalists, including the following claimants: Sir John Johnson, Guy Johnson, Oliver DeLancey, Frederick Phillipse, Philip Skene, Roger Morris, John Watts, Beverley Robinson, John Harris Cruger. There were also claimants from the following large landholding families: the Floyds, the Jessups, the Purdys, the Rapaljes, the Waltons, the Joneses, the Bayards, and the Cuylers. Some other important loyal landed families from which there are no claims are the Baches, the Van Cortlandts, and the DePuysters.[102]

These great proprietors were some of the richest men in the colonies. Sir John Johnson claimed £103,162, Oliver DeLancey £108,957, Beverley Robinson £79,980, and Roger Morris £68,384. Most, but not all, were natives of America. Many like Guy Johnson, Indian superintendent, or Judge Thomas Jones, were royal officials; several served on the council, all were part of the aristocratic governing clique which was tied together by marriage and kinship. Both Beverley Robinson and Roger Morris, for example, married daughters of Frederick Phillipse. Much of their land came from royal grants. Phillipse mentioned to the claims commissioners that his manor had been granted in 1693 by William and Mary.[103] The Johnson family fortune had been built up by royal favor. Politics, religion (the proprietors were normally Anglican), social position, and self-interest all conspired to keep most of the great landlords loyal.

It is not surprising, therefore, that most farmer-claimants were not tenants of Whig landlords involved in the antirent riots. The majority were following their landlords rather than opposing them. Twenty-two claimants were from Cortlandt Manor, sixteen from Philipsburg, and thirteen from Skenesborough. Beverley Robinson told the commissioners that the regiment he raised and commanded was mainly made up of his own tenants.[104] But the most imposing examples are the claimants who resided on land belonging to the Johnson family. At least one hundred and forty-nine, nearly 15 per cent of the total individuals whose residences are known, definitely lived on the Johnson domain. The bulk of these specifically say that they were tenant farmers of the Johnsons. Many of the remaining Tryon County claimants may well have been tenants of the Johnsons (the claims records are often not specific); certainly many of them served in the army under Sir John.

Sir William Johnson died on the eve of the Revolution, but his son Sir John and his nephew Guy ably maintained the family's interests and took most of their tenants with them to the British side. As early as May, 1776, Sir John fled to Canada with 175 followers.[105] A substantial segment of these tenants were Scottish Highland Catholics who had arrived as recently as 1773 and who were naturally dependent on, and owed gratitude to, their landlords.[106] Such contemporaries as General Philip Schuyler testified to the Toryism of the New York Highlanders.[107] Of the 149 claimants who seem to have been Johnson tenants twenty were American born, three English, seven Irish, ninety-two Scottish, twenty-three German, and four unknown. Seventy-two of the Scots had arrived in America in 1773 or later. One other notable fact is that one-third of the total German claimants is represented here. The claims records do not say so, but presumably most of the seventy-two newly-arrived Scots were Highland Catholics. There is a claim from their Irish priest, the Reverend John McKenna, who told the claims commissioners that he went to New York in 1773 with 300 Highlanders from Fort William, not one of whom joined the rebels; all instead followed him to Canada where they formed the Royal Highland Emigrants and the Royal Yorkers with McKenna as chaplain.[108] In their decision regarding his claim the commissioners made a characteristic comment, ". . . appears to be (as they generally are) a Man of low Extraction," and awarded him a mere £20 per annum.[109]

It must be noted that not all tenants of Loyalist landlords followed their leaders. William Houghton, who had four tenant families settled on his land at the head of Lake George, Albany County, told the claims commissioners that all chose the rebel side.[110]

Farmers are usually conservative people, and the mass of New York farmers were no exception. Most were probably content with their lot and had little interest in the political issues of the Revolution and no taste for rebellion. Further, the New York countryside was never alerted in the way the Massachusetts hinterland was. Rural New York had an almost feudal air; there was no vigorous local government, no town meeting, no Samuel Adams in New York City to bestir and organize the country dwellers.[111]

New York is one of the few colonies where the Indians make up an important segment of the Loyalists.[112] An engraved copy of a lost painting by Benjamin West depicting the "Reception of the American Loyalists by Great Britain" includes an Indian chief.[113] The artist may well have had in mind Joseph Brant, chief of the Mohawks, who led the Six Nations against the Americans. The reasons for the loyalty of these Indians are basically the same as those of loyal tenant farmers. They considered the British in general, and the Johnson family in particular, as their protectors and leaders, an attitude which dated from the acquisition of Fort Niagara from the French during the Seven Years War, and the friendly activities of Sir William Johnson.[114] The military operations of Brant and his followers in association with Sir John Johnson and Connecticut-born Colonel John Butler added an extra bitterness to the civil war in New York. Butler, probably unfairly, became a sort of folk villain (D. W. Griffith cast him for this role in his last great spectacle, *America*), but General Haldimand told the claims commissioners that Butler was largely responsible for the support given by the Six Nations.[115]

In conclusion, the outstanding fact about the Loyalist movement in New York is not just its great numerical strength, but also its wealth of political, military, and literary talent, and its representatives of leading families, which could only be matched by Massachusetts among the twelve other colonies.

Only Massachusetts can compare with New York for outstanding or powerful Loyalists—such politicians or soldiers (or both) as Governor William Tryon, Sir John Johnson, Joseph Brant, John Butler, Daniel Claus, John Harris Cruger, Abraham Cuyler, Oliver DeLancey, James DeLancey, and Lieutenant-Governor Cadwallader Colden (also a pioneer scientist); such jurists and historians as Chief Justice William Smith and his rival, Judge Thomas Jones, such distinguished Anglican clergymen and polemicists as Seabury, Inglis, and Cooper.

VI. NEW JERSEY

NEW JERSEY

HISTORIANS are agreed that the political pressure in New Jersey was low during the Revolutionary period preceding the war. There were no sectional or other conflicts; the great issues of the day were remote from the daily lives of the yeoman farmers who constituted the bulk of the population. There were no important class divisions. Nicholas Collin, the Swedish cleric, wrote in July, 1771, "Here everyone is of the same Stamp. . . . All are called gentlemen and ladies." [1]

Yet there are 239 New Jersey claimants,[2] about 0.19 per cent of the white population of 121,185 in 1776.[3] This is higher than any New England percentage, and the fourth highest of all the colonies. Five thousand is the accepted number of active male Loyalists during the Revolutionary period in New Jersey,[4] and all historians agree on the comparative strength of Toryism in the colony. It is significant that Cortlandt Skinner's New Jersey Volunteers was the largest American Loyalist regiment produced by the war. In December, 1776, Washington wrote to his brother complaining of "the defection of New York, Jerseys and Pennsylvannia," and singled out the conduct of New Jersey as the "most Infamous. Instead of turning out to defend their Country and affording aid to our Army, they are making their submissions as fast as they can." [5]

The Loyalists would have appeared even stronger in New Jersey if it had not been for many outrages committed by the British army (usually Hessian regiments). In his history of the war Charles Stedman noted that when the people of New Jersey found "that their property was seized, and most wantonly destroyed . . . they determined to try the other side . . ." [6] In 1778 a New Jersey Loyalist told Thomas Anburey that the "desolation of the Jersies, which included friends, and moderate persons, as well as enemies, had done great injury to our cause, as it had united the latter more firmly, and detached numbers of the former." The result was that there remained "few, or scarce any friends to Britain in the province." [7]

Daniel Coxe related the following incident to the claims commissioners:

But the British Army in the meantime very unexpectantly advancing from Brunswick to Trenton in pursuit of Washingtons Army over the Delaware, and taking post there, his Houses Offices and Estate were seized up as Quarters for Hessian Troops under the Command of Col. Rhode, and not withstanding his well known public and loyal character and every remonstrance of his ffriends and Servants to the Contrary, his Rooms, Closets Stores and Cellars were all broke open ransacked and pillaged and every species of Furniture, China, Glass, Liquors etc. plundered destroyed or taken away, his Servants compelled to fly for safety and Shelter elsewhere, and most wanton Desolation committed on his Property and Estate . . .[8]

Examples could easily be multiplied from the claims testimony and from other sources. How many instances of British maltreatment were never told to the commissioners because the victims ceased to be loyal, we will never know. There are indications that the majority of New Jersey inhabitants were favorably disposed towards the British, at least in the beginning. Stedman implies as much;[9] Daniel Isaac Browne stated that Bergen County "contained a Majority of Loyalists";[10] William Taylor related that in June, 1776, in Monmouth County he and his family got "a very great Majority of the Inhabitants" to sign a petition opposing the Declaration of Independence.[11] Isaac Ogden, an equivocal Newark lawyer, wrote to Joseph Galloway in November, 1778, that "the men of property in general (excepting only such as have held posts under Congress, and the Assembly) wish for reconciliation" with England, and "among the common ranks of life a great majority" wanted peace, but Ogden also noted British depredations "making many persons rebels" and he advocated the execution of hostages, if Loyalist prisoners were not spared, because it would evince "a certain *spirit* that has long been wanting" and show the Loyalists that "some attention is paid to them." [12] Claims that a majority of New Jersey people were loyal are probably exaggerated. More likely, as Jonathan Odell put it for the town of Burlington, "people were in general peaceably disposed," [13] from which standpoint they would drift into the Whig or Loyalist ranks according to economic, military, and psychological pressures. The very large number of claimants who admitted either signing the Association, or serving in the rebel militia, or both, stands out. Usually they explained that their action came as the result of fear or persecution, but it was probably a reflection of the apathy of the population.

At first the British military presence, in spite of depredations, encouraged the Loyalists, but finally the "unfortunate" (as it was usually called by the claimants) British defeat by Washington at Trenton and Princeton during the Christmas–New Year period, 1776–1777, put an end to serious Loyalist military chances, although guerrilla fighting was to persist throughout the war.[14]

The New Jersey Loyalists were quite strong, but their strength did not lie in the political leadership of the colony. There was no public opposition to the formation of committees of observation in 1774 and 1775, and in January,

1775, the proceedings of Congress were approved by the Assembly with only the Quakers showing misgivings—concerning the possibility of the use of force.[15] Governor William Franklin pluckily braved it out until his arrest in June, 1776, but could be no more than a helpless spectator. Only one member of the Assembly, Joseph Barton, voted against his impeachment. (Barton's Loyalism was no surprise, for he was the agent for the East Jersey Proprietors.)[16]

In Franklin, of course, the Loyalists had an able and famous governor, but only two members of the lower house and only six local officials submitted claims. Even the council, often a predominantly Loyalist body, gave only weak support to the governor. Franklin, testifying in the case of Daniel Coxe, said that Coxe was one of the "two or three" loyal members of the council, but that even they were "not active to embark in Matters of risque, they declined to do somethings proposed by the Governor as too hazardous alleging they were unsupported."[17] In January, 1776, Franklin had written of the "trimming conduct" of the loyal councilors.[18] Four members of the council were Whigs, one was retired; the remaining seven, Frederick Smyth, David Ogden, Stephen Skinner, Daniel Coxe (all claimants), Peter Kemble, James Parker, and John Lawrence, were Loyalists, although two of these (Parker and Kemble) are probably more accurately described as neutralists.[19]

The College of New Jersey at Princeton was solidly Whig from 1763 onward. Only five graduates took the Loyalist side, a fact partly attributable to the influence of President Witherspoon.[20] Of these five, one was David Mathews, mayor of New York, another was David Zubly of Georgia; the remaining three were from New Jersey and all claimants—Daniel Isaac Browne, the Reverend Jonathan Odell, and the Reverend Garrett Lydecker.[21]

Turning to the persecution of Tories, the evidence in general suggests their strength. In 1777 a Loyalist wrote: "No country has ever been more harrassed than Jersey; those who are called Tories, tho' they have been passive, having been plundered and imprisoned without mercy."[22] Official action and legislation were undoubtedly very thorough (a sign of Loyalist strength), culminating in 1778 with the extensive confiscation of Tory estates, 1,200 in all.[23]

But the claims commission testimony reveals comparatively little mob action before or during the war. Prior to the fighting there was an absence of strong partisan feelings, but with the advent of civil war it is surprising that more instances of persecution are not recorded. However, three executions are mentioned to the commissioners. Jonathan Clawson related that his eldest son was taken prisoner in 1780 and executed without trial by General Maxwell; Francis Hutchinson said that his brother, a member of Skinner's Brigade, was similarly put to death while visiting his parents in Morris County; George Mount's father was apparently "murdered" by a scouting party within half a mile of his own home.[24] These were not the only executions. For example, Sabine records that Stephen Edwards of New Jersey, while on a spying mission to Monmouth County, was arrested in his father's house, court-martialed, and executed.[25] The Swedish pastor Nicholas Collin wrote in his journal for 1779 about accompanying to the scaffold a young man convicted a second time for serving with the British troops.[26] These last two were legal executions, if the Revolutionary regime is considered legal.

Some mob action which inflicted something less than death is recorded. Two claimants got coats of tar and feathers (than which there was "no better proof of Loyalty," as the commissioners noted in one of the cases), and Edward Bowlby received 500 lashes at Bergen in 1778 for an unmentioned offense.[27]

New Jersey furnishes two examples of the mental effects of the times. John Hinchman's wife lost her mind when her husband was persecuted, and William Franklin's wife died of a "broken heart" while he was in prison.[28]

There is no doubt that New Jersey was the scene of some of the bitterest civil war in all the provinces. The Reverend Nicholas Collin commented accurately, ". . . it is apparent how terrible this Civil war raged . . . because both parties fought not like real men with sword and gun, but like robbers and incendiaries."[29] British and Loyalist parties ranged in from New York and Philadelphia, and it was to New Jersey that most of the activities of the Board of Associated Loyalists at New York were directed. The culminating act which resulted in the dissolution of the board was the hanging of Captain Joshua Huddy from a tree on the Jersey shore of the Hudson by Captain Richard Lippincott (a New Jersey claimant) in reprisal for the murder of the Loyalist Philip White.

Several New Jersey claimants returned to the province (or never left it), but no one who could really be called an active Loyalist (except perhaps Thomas Bradbury Chandler) returned. Political disabilities remained with the Tories until 1788,[30] and several would-be returners got an unpleasant unofficial reception. In early 1783 Cavalier Jouet was ejected—"A number of fellows came about me with sticks and whips"—and two discharged privates of the New Jersey

Volunteers were beaten when they ventured into Sussex County the same year. When John Hinchman returned home after the peace treaty, he was mobbed, which gave him a palsy stroke.[31] All this indicates the strength of Loyalism in New Jersey. But rough treatment was reserved for active Loyalists; those who had not actually aided the British were leniently treated (former Chief Justice Frederick Smyth, an inactive Loyalist, had no difficulty in returning), and there was even a campaign, following the peace, to encourage the return of Loyalist merchants to aid the state's economy.[32]

The Loyalist claimants were not distributed evenly throughout the colony. The tables show that Middlesex County with sixty-three, or 27 per cent of the claimants, heads the list. It is followed by three counties with roughly equal representation: Monmouth (thirty-six), Essex (thirty-one), and Bergen (twenty-nine). The four total 159, or a little over 68 per cent of the whole. Perth Amboy (a site of the royal administration) with twenty claimants (nearly all merchants or officials) is the leading Loyalist town, although it by no means dominates the scene any more than it dominated the colony. Washington wrote more than once of the "known Dissafection of the People of Amboy." [33] The town is followed closely by Woodbridge (fifteen), Newark (fifteen), and Hackensack (thirteen). If the whole Raritan Bay and estuary is considered, with Perth Amboy as the center, the region becomes much more dominant, for the total claimants from Perth Amboy, Woodbridge, Raritan Landing, New Brunswick, Piscataway, Spotswood, and Blazing Star in Middlesex County; Bound Brook, Hillsborough, and Middlebrook in Somerset County; and Middletown, Shrewsbury, and Sandy Hook in Monmouth County amount to one-third of the whole.

In short, Loyalism was centered mainly in the three northern, or East Jersey, counties, although claimants are found in every county except desolate Cape May. Whereas the Raritan Bay, Hudson River, Long Island Sound periphery was strongly Loyalist, the counties bordering Delaware Bay (Cape May, Cumberland, and Salem), produced a mere six claimants. West Jersey was much more sparsely populated than East Jersey, but not, however, enough to explain the disparity. Middlesex County remains easily the leading Loyalist area even on a proportional basis of Loyalists to population. In the north, as in so many colonies, the concentration is on the seaboard; the three inland counties, Sussex (twelve), Morris (eleven) and Hunterdon (fifteen), account for only thirty-eight, or 16.4 per cent of the claimants. This conclusion is partly supported by a contemporary witness, Cortlandt Skinner, who commented to the claims commissioners that the area of Hanover Township in Morris County was inhabited by descendants of New England immigrants "bred in Republican principles." [34]

The modest economic status of the claimants is unmistakable. Less than 10 per cent claimed over £5,000 while 26 per cent claimed £500 or less, and forty-six per cent £1,000 or less. Unlike in many other colonies the claimants asking £500 or less were not generally immigrants: of those whose nationalities are known, fourteen were foreign and thirty-two American born.

Loyalism in New Jersey, as revealed by the claimants, was a native movement. Seventy-seven per cent of the claimants were American born. The remainder, mainly quite recent British immigrants (the largest group being the English with 12 per cent), show a similar distribution to the claimants as a whole except in one particular; the farmers are a minority while the commercial element preponderates. The British compose over half the commercial group listed in the tables.

Analysis and statistics are not enough to indicate fully the quality of Loyalism in a colony, although the high percentage who served the British shows how active the New Jersey Tories were.

The outstanding native-born Loyalists, Thomas Bradbury Chandler and Jonathan Odell, were produced by the Anglican clergy. Chandler, the rector of St. John's, Elizabeth, a graduate of Yale and a convert from Congregationalism, was the author of several pro-British pamphlets, including *A Friendly Address to all Reasonable Americans* in 1774, and the next year *What Think Ye of Congress Now?* which attacked that unlawful body. He had advocated the repeal of the Stamp Act, but "finding that the evil spirit in the Colonies . . . had not subsided on the repeal of it," he had undertaken to defend the government.[35] He was also a long-standing and leading advocate of the American bishopric, in the middle colonies, about which he wrote several pamphlets. Chandler was American enough to return to his parish after the war where he lived out his days, ill health preventing him from accepting the bishopric of Nova Scotia.

Odell, a descendant of one of the early settlers of Massachusetts, minister at Burlington and Mount Holly and part-time doctor, was very active on the British side, playing a major part in the negotiations with Benedict Arnold. He wrote newspaper articles, but his reputation then as now rests on his ability as a satirical poet, unequaled in the Tory ranks, according to that wise authority, Moses C. Tyler, and paralleled only by the Whig, Philip Freneau, also a New

Jersey man.[36] After the war Odell had a distinguished career in New Brunswick.

William Franklin and Brigadier General Cortlandt Skinner have already been mentioned.[37] Franklin was an able governor, and his name added luster to the British cause. Although he was a tenacious Loyalist, his views had always been moderate and well advised. He was not in favor of the Stamp Act, and in May, 1775, he wrote to Lord Dartmouth advising the government to call a congress of the colonies to discuss grievances because he was "convinced . . . that the Americans in general are disposed to run the Risk of a total Ruin rather than suffer a Taxation by any but their own immediate Representatives . . ."[38] Later in New York he became president of the Board of Associated Loyalists.

Skinner, former attorney-general of New Jersey and one of the colony's largest landowners, organized the New Jersey Volunteers, who ravaged the Jerseys extensively. Daniel Coxe, member of the council and successful lawyer, helped organize the West Jersey Volunteers at Philadelphia while the British were in control there and later was on the Board of the Associated Loyalists.

Other leading lawyers who were Loyalist claimants were David Ogden, Edward Vaughan Dongan, Isaac Allen, Bernardus La Grange, Daniel Isaac Browne, John Taylor, and his son William.[39] But lawyers, in general, were apparently Whigs.[40]

Three more distinguished claimants can be added: Dr. Abraham Van Buskirk (an eminent physician), Robert Drummond (a prominent merchant), and Richard William Stockton (of the well-known Princeton family).

In summary, the New Jersey Loyalists were quite numerous and quite active, and comprised a creditable share of the province's talent. From the tables it can be adduced that the most likely New Jersey Loyalist (especially if he was native born) was a farmer, usually of moderate means. But this description applies equally well to any typical inhabitant of New Jersey. The question is why a strong minority chose a different path from that of the majority whom they so strongly resembled.

Some standard groups such as royal officials, British immigrants, and the mercantile class are obviously explained.

Anglicanism was probably important also. Nineteen claimants specifically reveal themselves as Anglicans, including five missionaries of the Society for the Propagation of the Gospel: Jonathan Odell, Isaac Browne, George Panton, Samuel Cooke, and Thomas Bradbury Chandler.[41] The clergy seems to have been loyal almost to a man; only one, Robert Blackwell, missionary at Gloucester for the Society for the Propagation of the Gospel, became a Whig.[42] All but one of the Anglican claimants whose birthplaces are known were American born, as were three of the five missionary claimants. The Reverend Mr. Chandler certainly believed in the connection between Anglicanism and Loyalism. He wrote to the Society in 1776 that if "the interest of the Church of England in America had been a national concern from the beginning, by this time a general submission in the Colonies to the Mother Country, in everything not sinful, might have been expected . . ." And he added, with the splendid egotism of his calling, "Who can be certain that the present rebellious disposition of the Colonies is not intended by Providence as a Punishment for that neglect?"[43] Conversely, in 1778 Isaac Ogden singled out "the dissenting Parsons" as instrumental in preventing the supersession of Governor William Livingston.[44]

Many names indicative of Dutch descent occur in the lists

of claimants, and a recent study of Bergen County shows that the majority of Loyalists there were so descended.[45] Whether, in general, the proportion of Loyalist Dutch names is above that to be expected in the population as a whole is difficult to say.[46] But there is some indication to the contrary. The proportion of the New Jersey population of Dutch descent in 1790 was 16.6 per cent, whereas the proportion of claimants with Dutch-sounding names is about 11 per cent.[47] Some were doubtless members of the Dutch Reformed church. One minister of this church, Garrett Lydecker, who apparently commuted from his farm in Bergen County to a congregation in New York, submitted a claim.[48] So did Elias Cooper, the son of the Dutch Reformed minister at Hackensack, who was advised by his father to join the British. The son recalled that his father remained with his congregation "and by his precepts and example has in great Measure confirmed Several of His Congregation in their loyalty to the King"—a statement suggesting that they were a minority.[49]

For the Hackensack Valley Adrian C. Leiby has demonstrated that the Whig-Tory split was preceded and prefigured by a violent division of the Dutch Reformed church between the conferentie group (largely future Whigs) who, swept along by the Great Awakening, wanted an independent American church, and the coetus group (a minority and largely future Tories) who opposed the Great Awakening and for tactical reasons supported the authority of the mother church in Amsterdam, but whose "real objective" was power. Thus, before the Revolution the majority already had a commitment to independence, the minority a commitment to overseas protection.[50]

Lawrence Van Buskirk, a claimant and prominent Lutheran and political figure in Bergen County, became a Loyalist and carried with him a good many members of the two small Lutheran congregations there. Apart from Van Buskirk's prestige, the fact that many of his coreligionists were recent immigrants may explain their Loyalism,[51] and this may be another example of a minority's fear of Whig subjection.

Only two Quakers submitted claims. One of them, Robert Fitzrandolph, told the commissioners that at Woodbridge, Middlesex County, "none of his profession took part with the Americans." [52] But neither did the Quakers take active part with the British. The Quakers were, of course, opposed to violence of any kind, and their Hobbesian attitude towards constituted authority was in favor of the state government once the British had been ejected. The Quakers in New Jersey, as elsewhere, came under strong suspicion, but their stand was really neutral rather than loyal.

For New Jersey in general, as Miss Keesey has suggested for Bergen County, the status quo was satisfactory[53] either under the new Republican government or where the British were still in power. Hence the correlation between occupied areas and Loyalism. Beyond this it was a matter of individual choice, of individual conscience, of individual circumstances.[54]

This point is illustrated by the case of native-born James Moody, who has left a partial explanation of his choice of Loyalism in his pamphlet, *Narrative of the Exertions and Sufferings of Lieut. James Moody ... since 1776.* When the troubles began Moody was a "happy farmer" in Sussex County who "seldom thought much of political or state questions; but he felt and knew he had every possible reason to be grateful for, and attached to, that glorious Constitution to which he owed his security." Resisting the temptation to follow the "multitude," and in spite of the dangers to his family, he realized that "however real or great the grievances of the Americans *might* be, rebellion was not the way to redress them." Nevertheless he tried to remain "silent" on his farm and "not to give offence," but was "harrassed" by committees, and even shot at. Finally, in April, 1777, he set out for the British lines with seventy-three neighbors. Moody went on to become one of the most glamorous Loyalists, a leading spy, a daring soldier, the Scarlet Pimpernel of New Jersey. When he was captured by the Whigs, only escape prevented his execution.[55]

This view of Loyalism as an individual matter is always reinforced by examples of family and other splits. As the Reverend Nicholas Collin put it, "Everywhere distrust, fear, hatred, and abominable selfishness were met with. Parents and children, brothers and sisters, wife and husband, were enemies to one another." [56]

The most famous split family of all was that of the Franklins. William told the commissioners that his father made him pay a debt of £1,500, "which would not have been demanded had he not been on the British side." [57] The following claimants were members of divided families: Thomas Skinner, whose two sons were rebels; David Ogden, Sr., with two sons rebels but three Loyalists, and a rebel brother who became a United States senator; Dr. Absalom Bainbridge, whose two sons served in the United States Navy; John Vandyke, whose father was a Whig; and Arthur Neilson, whose brother was similarly inclined.[58] One Whig, Captain William Howard, blessed with a Loyalist wife, was obliged to have the injunction, "No Tory talk here," painted above the mantelpiece at his home, Castle Howard, as a constant reminder for his errant spouse.[59] The two partners of Anthony Mosengeil, a copper mine expert, were Whig; Benjamin Thompson related that the rebel Dr. John Cochran under whom he was studying failed to persuade his pupil to follow the same course.[60]

But the key to New Jersey Loyalism lies in the explanation for the geographical distribution of the claimants. The recurring story of the northern New Jersey claimants is the arrival of the British army, support for it, sometimes enlistment in it, often trade with it, then military withdrawal accompanied willy-nilly by Loyalist withdrawal, the exiles being obnoxious to their patriotic fellow citizens. Northern New Jersey, like western Connecticut, had natural economic and geographical ties with the New York City area. These were reinforced by the long British occupation of the city and environs, especially of Paulus Hook and Staten Island. And, of course, northern New Jersey itself was partly occupied by the British for long periods. For example, parts of Bergen County supported a British army for seven and one-half years. It was often difficult to pick the winner. Abraham Vanderbeck, of Hackensack, Bergen County, admitted that his father, aware of his son's Tory activity and "thinking the British would get the better," made over his land to him. Finally, the British paid for supplies with gold, which was much preferred, even by many Patriots, to continental currency. Hard cash may well have influenced Ellis Barron, of Woodbridge, who provisioned the navy, or Philip Summer, who baked bread for General Meadows.[61]

In southern or West New Jersey the British occupation of Philadelphia similarly stimulated Loyalism, as the Reverend Nicholas Collin recorded at the time in his journal for 1778,

"It looked as though America would soon be conquered. The people around here began as early as last autumn, to trade with the English in order to obtain specie coin. . . . The severest laws were passed against such trading and caused many people to suffer. These in order to take revenge and others to avoid punishment, went over to the English side." [62]

New Jersey laws were of no avail in stopping illicit trade with Philadelphia or New York, and Collin noted that a man was flogged to death for the crime. The tables show the weakness of Loyalism in the south as compared with the north; this reflects the fact that Philadelphia was occupied for a much shorter time than New York (September, 1777, to June, 1778, as opposed to seven years).

VII. PENNSYLVANIA

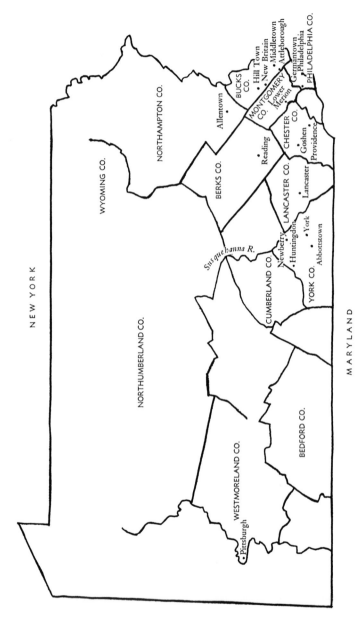

NEW YORK

WYOMING CO.

NORTHAMPTON CO.

Allentown

BUCKS CO.

Hill Town

New Britain

Middletown

Attleborough

MONTGOMERY CO.

Lower Merion

Germantown

Philadelphia

PHILADELPHIA CO.

Reading

BERKS CO.

CHESTER CO.

Goshen

Providence

LANCASTER CO.

Lancaster

York

Abbottstown

Susquehanna R.

Newberry

Huntingdon

CUMBERLAND CO.

YORK CO.

NORTHUMBERLAND CO.

BEDFORD CO.

WESTMORELAND CO.

Pittsburgh

MARYLAND

PENNSYLVANIA

AMONG the thirteen colonies Pennsylvania was one of the richest and most diversified, a diversification seen in many aspects, from the economy, notably iron smelting and mixed farming, to the abundant religious sects, notably Quakers and Mennonites (the Quakers controlled the colony after its foundation but formally withdrew from politics in 1756). Philadelphia, the metropolis, was probably the second city of the British Empire, certainly the major port of the colonies, and the main disembarkation point for immigrants. For this reason and because of the colony's early history, the population was very cosmopolitan, containing people of English, Scottish, Scotch-Irish, Irish, Welsh, German, Swiss, Dutch, French, and Swedish birth or ancestry. In particular Pennsylvania was the center of the German-American population, and an important area of Scotch-Irish settlement. In 1790 persons of German origin made up 33.3 per cent of the population and the Scotch-Irish 11 per cent.[1]

Pennsylvania was a proprietary province in the hands of the descendants of the great Quaker, William Penn. This form of government, added to a strong tradition of religious freedom, augured ill for the future strength of Loyalism. Penn's Charter of Privileges, the constitution from 1701 until 1776, established an unusually powerful unicameral legislature which was independent of the governor and made the colony a semiautonomous republic. Government appointments from the governorship down were in the hands of the proprietor. Thus, largely outside the royal orbit, Pennsylvania politics revolved around the question of the proprietorship and such local issues as those represented by the march of the Paxton Boys in 1763. There was no embryonic Tory party associated with a royal governor.

Even the proprietors themselves were by no means adamant Loyalists,[2] and support for the Penns was no evidence of Loyalism. For example, John Dickinson, who led the proprietary party, is known as the "Penman of the Revolution." Conversely the future Loyalist, Joseph Galloway, and the future Patriot, Benjamin Franklin, were united, during the Seven Years War and afterwards, in seeking the substitution of royal for proprietary government, and the party which they represented dominated the colony's politics until the eve of the war. During the imperial quarrels of the period 1763–1775, almost all shades of opinion opposed British policy and any unrequested British interference and supported the freedom of Pennsylvania. It was only when the question was independence that agonizing decisions as to Loyalism or Whiggism were forced on anybody.

Finally, in 1776, after the meeting of the First and Second Continental Congresses, Philadelphia adopted a radical state constitution which extended the suffrage to all freemen over twenty-one years of age. But the colony's strategic position made it unlikely that it would be left in peace to enjoy its consummated independence. In the summer of 1777 General Howe invaded by sea from New York and on September 11 defeated the rebels at Brandywine. Fifteen days later he entered Philadelphia and on October 4 repulsed Washington's counterattack at the battle of Germantown, meanwhile generally securing Delaware Bay. Washington retired to the ill-famed winter quarters at Valley Forge while, in bitter contrast, Howe, aided by Tories and collaborators, inaugurated a brilliant season in the city. There was little more formal warfare, and the British evacuated Philadelphia at last, for strategic reasons, in June, 1778. The only further military action was some sporadic guerrilla fighting inland, in particular the notorious raid on the Wyoming Valley (mainly by Butler's Tories and Indians out of New York) also in June, 1778.

One of the prime features of Pennsylvania Loyalism (and chief reason for its feebleness) is its equivocal, neutral, and, it must be argued, sometimes subtle nature. A striking number of Pennsylvanians did not know which way to turn. Writing about those banished by the Whigs from Philadelphia at the end of 1777 before the British arrived, Robert Proud, the Quaker schoolmaster from Yorkshire, observed "that they with many others, not withstanding the general Revolt, had remained entirely inactive either for or against it . . ." [3]

This was a course of action which Proud himself (not a claimant) followed. He informed his brother that since the Revolution he had escaped "abuse" by living "in a very private and retired Way, even like a Person dead amidst the Confusions, and conversing more with my Books than with Persons . . . and scarcely ever departing above two miles from my Place of Abode for several years." [4] Proud never left Pennsylvania; he reopened his school and went on to write a well-known history of his adopted state.

Among those who were claimants and undoubtedly genuine Loyalists a great amount of halting, trimming, or erratic behavior is found. At least twenty-three persons admitted to some action which compromised their loyalty—usually service in the American militia or trade with the rebel forces, although normally such behavior was attributed to threats or the use of force. Apparently even the loyalty of the customs officials at Philadelphia was not complete. Zacharias Hood, the comptroller there, said at the outbreak of the Revolution that John Wormington was the only tidesman who could be trusted.[5] Significantly, untrustworthy conduct is true of the leading Loyalists.

Like so many intelligent Loyalists, Samuel Shoemaker, the most notable of all Quaker claimants, opposed early British policy, having signed the non-importation agreement in 1765, but he drew the line at independence. His brother, Joseph, was a definite Whig until after the Declaration of Independence, and Samuel himself returned to Philadelphia in 1789 and died there in 1800.[6]

William Rankin, a leading figure in York County, freely admitted that he considered the Declaratory Act "oppressive."[7] He was a colonel in the rebel militia until the Declaration of Independence caused him to change sides. Even the stern claims commissioners noted in their decision that "it is very possible that he might have done it upon Real Principle as many other good Men stopped at that period."[8]

There was no more distinguished Philadelphia family than the Allens, headed by Chief Justice William Allen, one of the richest and ablest men in the colony, with decades of service to his credit. He had been associated with Franklin in various ways. The chief justice was a Loyalist (although not a claimant—he died in 1780), but a moderate; he opposed the Stamp Act and worked for compromise to the extent of outlining a program in *The American Crisis* in 1774. A witness even told the commissioners that he was "a great Enemy to this country [England]."[9] His son Andrew was a claimant but, like his father, had considerable sympathy for the American cause, and was chosen a member of the Continental Congress by the Pennsylvania Assembly in 1775. As the commissioners remarked, "He makes no scruple to avow that his Sentiment was ever opposed to the Idea of unlimited Taxation . . ." [10] Another son, William Allen, Jr. (not a claimant), originally served as a lieutenant colonel under St. Clair, but in 1776 went over to General Howe and raised the Pennsylvania Loyalists. [11]

The lawyer Phineas Bond, a member of an old Pennsylvania family, the son and nephew of two leading Philadelphia doctors, and one-time protégé of Mrs. Franklin, was less spectacularly, but nevertheless somewhat, equivocal. He recognized Parliament's right to tax the colonies, but thought it inexpedient, and had, like many others, mustered with the rebel militia because he believed it "improper for the Gentlemen of America to suffer the power to get into the hands of the lowest people." [12] The commissioners considered him a Loyalist although he had signed the Association and mustered with the militia. [13] Bond later had a very successful career as British consul to the middle states.

Perhaps the ablest Loyalist in the whole of America was the Philadelphian Joseph Galloway, yet he epitomized the characteristics of the Allens and others. Elected as speaker of the Assembly from 1766 to 1775, he championed the American cause, but was a moderate and a compromiser. The result of his efforts was the narrow rejection of his famous plan by the First Continental Congress. When Howe took Philadelphia, Galloway served as the extremely zealous civil administrator of the city and later went to England where he became the leading Loyalist spokesman, pamphleteer, and critic of Howe.

John Dickinson, the celebrated "Penman of the Revolution," although not a claimant or even a Loyalist, fits well into the Pennsylvania syndrome of moderation and concilia- tion. He was a leader of the opposition to Great Britain in the years before the Revolution, yet could not sanction violence and opposed independence. But unlike his rival Galloway he did not go over to the Tories; after a quietist period he returned to politics and was finally a Delaware delegate to the Federal Convention and, appropriately enough, a strong advocate of the Constitution. A considera- tion of Galloway and Dickinson gives a good idea of the fine line which could separate Loyalism and Whiggism.[14]

The roots of Loyalism in Pennsylvania do not go back in any obvious way to the period following 1760. This is not surprising when the Whiggish role of such Loyalists as Galloway, Duché, and Shoemaker is recalled. Many Loyal- ists supported the Whigs in everything short of actual independence, and James Allen wrote ruefully in July, 1777, that within the term Tory "is included every one disinclined to Independence tho' ever so warm a friend to constitutional liberty and the old cause."[15]

Legislation against the Loyalists in Pennsylvania was harsh,[16] notably the test act of June 13, 1777, which de- nied citizenship to those refusing the oath of allegiance. Four legal executions (those of James Molesworth, George Spangler, John Roberts, and Abraham Carlisle) are men- tioned in the claims commission testimony. Molesworth was executed before a great crowd in Philadelphia in 1777 for spying for Galloway.[17] Mary Spangler recalled that her husband George, who had been a guide to Sir William Howe, remained in Philadelphia after the evacuation to look after his family, but was tried, hanged, and buried under the gallows.[18] Roberts and Carlisle were both apparently scapegoats executed on the excuse that they (among so many) had accepted office from Howe during the occupation.[19]

Elias and Peter Snyder recounted that being captured on their way to the British lines, they were condemned to death and only escaped the sentence by joining the rebel army.[20] William Caldwell and George Harding said that they were also sentenced to death, but escaped the penalty.[21]

There were several examples of mob action. James Sheppard, a recalcitrant blacksmith who refused the American oath, was tarred and feathered. The Reverend Daniel Batwell was tossed into a river; Isaac Hunt (the father of the famous Leigh Hunt) was paraded through Philadelphia in a cart; John Wormington, the tidewaiter at Philadelphia, suffered four broken ribs for seizing a vessel in 1776; and Zacharias Hood, comptroller of customs at Philadelphia, said he "was beat and obliged to fly" by Franklin's son-in-law, Beach, for mentioning the doctor's trial before the Privy Council.[22]

Probably the best-known mobbing in Philadelphia was that of the brave Quaker, Dr. John Kearsley, whose widow later submitted a claim to the commissioners. Kearsley, a leading physician, pill manufacturer, and horse dealer, was a pugnacious English immigrant with strong Loyalist views. He was seized by a mob in September, 1775, and had his hand bayonetted; then he was carried through the streets to the tune of "Rogue's March." Sabine reports that he took off his wig with his injured hand "and swinging it around his head, huzzaed louder and longer than his persecutors." His widow said that he nearly died following this treatment. His house was later ransacked, and he was arrested and finally died in jail.[23]

These incidents seem to have been rather exceptional. More usual was some form of ostracism. Chief Justice Allen's son James wrote in his diary for February 17, 1777, "I never knew, how painful it is to be secluded from the free conversation of one's friends, the loss of which cannot be made up by any other expedients." Later, in July, "The Tories seldom venture from home, as they run a risk of being stopt. I have not been to Philadelphia these six weeks . . ."[24]

Any Loyalist depending on the public for a living ran grave risks. John Webster was in business for himself as a whitesmith and employed several journeymen, but his political views led to the closing of his shop, and he himself had to work as a journeyman, as he was still doing when he presented his claim. The weekly wage, he noted, was "too little to maintain his Family in the same manner as when he did Business for himself . . ."[25]

Not many claimants have anything to say about returning to Pennsylvania, but it is clear that many Loyalists did return after the war, including the claimants Jacob Duché, John Penn, and James Humphreys. By 1787 the last of the punitive laws had been repealed, but as late as 1793 Joseph Galloway was refused permission to return. Several notable Loyalists (not claimants) never left Pennsylvania in the first place: for example, Edward Shippen, who became chief justice in 1799; the historian Robert Proud; and Benjamin Chew, whose legal career continued successfully.[26] These facts suggest the weakness of Loyalism in Pennsylvania. On the other hand, the harsh legislation and the comparatively severe persecution reported to the claims commissioners show that the Tories were feared in Pennsylvania, a fear partly stimulated by the British occupation and by the significant body of pacifists in the population.

Although the figures in this chapter do not bear it out, Pennsylvania has a reputation as a Loyalist stronghold. Long ago, Van Tyne pointed out that the colony delayed independence longer than any other save New York.[27] The truth is that Pennsylvania was a stronghold of moderates, pacifists, and neutralists. It also probably contained many *potential* Loyalists. Joseph Galloway, for one, was always insisting that with British encouragement mass Loyalist support would reveal itself. It will never be known how many more Loyalists could have been created by a different British policy in Pennsylvania, or in any other colony. What is certain is that Pennsylvania claimants were preeminent in complaining of British neglect, which must have affected popular attitudes. Most notable are Galloway's celebrated strictures on Sir William Howe, strictures echoed by his wife Grace Galloway, who agreed with her husband in little else. She wrote in her diary in 1778, "I abused how [Sir William Howe] as the Author of all our ruin . . ."[28]

The *coup de grâce* for the Tories was, of course, the evacuation of Philadelphia. John Potts, an American-born judge, informed Galloway on December 17, 1778, that with the evacuation most people had lost "their confidence in government" and had "abandoned themselves to a lethargy very nearly bordering on despair."[29] Thomas Anburey wrote at about the same time:

The Loyalists in Pennsylvania generally accuse General Howe with ungrateful conduct, in abandoning Philadelphia, after all the assistance they had given him, and not having during the Winter, endeavored to dislodge General Washington at Valley Forge, suffering the enemy to harrass and distress the loyal inhabitants on every side of the British lines. . . .

Indeed, the Loyalists of Pennsylvania are greatly to be pitied, for they have been much persecuted since our troops evacuated

Philadelphia, their loyalty is greatly abated, as they conceive themselves made sacrifice of by the conduct of General Howe; and are so exceedingly incensed [that they say] . . . that his whole conduct was founded on private interest and ambition . . .[30]

Even while Howe and his army were still present the situation was anything but roses. There were complaints of Loyalist advice and intelligence going unheeded,[31] and claims against the *British* army were not unknown to the commissioners. Thomas Coombe claimed over £500 for the "depredations" of the troops on Chestnut Hill.[32] Galloway complained that the British "burnt and destroyed his Estate on Hogg Island," and that it "appeared to be done wantonly and not for the Public Service." [33] Nor was it only the British troops who alienated the people. William Moore told a typical story: ". . . unfortunately the Royal and American Army by Turns encamped upon the said Estate threw down burnt and destroyed the inclosures wasted the Stock and cut down the Timber thereon." [34] Nevertheless there was much truth in Mrs. Galloway's comment of July 20, 1779, that "the King's greates[t] enemies ar[e] his own Armies." [35]

Active Loyalists were a minority in Pennsylvania. Two hundred and six are analyzed in the tables, and the number of claimants is raised to 208 by the addition of two more for whom there is no information. This is approximately 0.07 per cent of the population, not a very high proportion, less than in Rhode Island and Massachusetts.[36]

The Loyalists were concentrated in Philadelphia; 104, or more than 54 per cent, of the claimants whose residences are known lived there. One hundred and thirty-one, or more than 68 per cent, of the claimants were from the three original eastern counties, Chester, Philadelphia, and Bucks. Other eastern counties, Lancaster (6), York (7), Berks (2), Montgomery (1), Northampton (4), and Wyoming (1), bring the total to 152 or precisely 80 per cent. This leaves thirty-eight, or 20 per cent, scattered around central and western Pennsylvania in the four counties of Northumberland, Cumberland, Bedford, and Westmoreland. Loyalism in Pennsylvania, as reflected by the claims, was largely an eastern and in particular a southeastern phenomenon. The far west (Bedford and Westmoreland Counties) had only nine, or less than 5 per cent, of the claimants. However, in central Pennsylvania, notably along the Susquehanna River in Northumberland County, a strong pocket of Loyalists is found with twenty-six, or more than 13.5 per cent of the claimants.[37]

A similar distribution of Loyalists is shown by an analysis of the 453 persons declared traitors by the state between 1778 and 1781 for having joined the British.[38]

Philadelphia	109
Philadelphia County	76
Bucks County	77
Chester County	87
York County	9
Northampton County	35
Bedford County	4
Trenton, N.J.	3
Maryland	1
New York	1

Although Nicholas Cresswell found the landlady of the best inn at Fort Pitt a Tory,[39] there is no evidence of Loyalist strength there except that as usual the British and the Tories secured the support of the Indians. Like most royal officials, the Indian agents were nearly always loyal, as were the Indian traders. The Indian agent at Fort Pitt was Alexander McKee, assisted by Simon Girty (both were native born). The two of them finally fled with Mathew Elliott, an Indian trader, to Detroit, where they helped rally the aborigines to the British cause.[40]

Part of the reason for the distribution of the Loyalists in Pennsylvania is that the population was much denser in the east, but the basic cause is that Philadelphia was the center of Loyalism in the colony. For the apparent concentration in Northumberland County there is no obvious explanation, although it is possible that the water transportation which linked the area with Philadelphia played a part. The twenty-six claimants from that county were all farmers but one, twenty-one claimed for £500 or less, and nineteen served in the British armed forces or militia, almost always in the ranks. The only unusual fact is that, contrary to the general Pennsylvania trend, fifteen, the great majority of the twenty-five whose nationalities are known, were American born, and of the remaining ten, seven were German (over half the total number of German claimants), two Dutch, and one Irish.

A look at the claimants from Bedford, Westmoreland, and Cumberland Counties, areas where they were very few, reveals little. Half of these odd men out served in the British armed forces, four-fifths were farmers, all were of modest wealth, and all but one migrated to Nova Scotia. Of those whose nationalities are known, four were Irish, two German, and five American.

As for the Patriots, they were strong in Philadelphia, but they also commanded great support from the Scotch-Irish of the west, support which finally produced a much more radical revolution than the eastern leaders wished for. The famous Pennsylvania constitution of 1776 was the consummation of this radical western movement.

The claims tables show that all economic levels are represented, and that wealth was rather evenly spread. Eighty-eight claimed £1,000 or less, eighty claimed more. Nearly three times as many Loyalists claimed for £2,000 or less as for over £2,000. The fifty-eight claims for £500 or less are easily the largest category; thus, compared with most colonies, persons of modest wealth are strong in the ranks of Pennsylvania Loyalists.

In some colonies the humble Loyalists are usually immigrants. This is not so in Pennsylvania. Of those who claimed £500 or less and whose origins are known, 57 per cent were immigrants, an only slightly higher figure than the percentage of immigrant Loyalists for the province as a whole. The group claiming £500 or less does have one distinct characteristic, however; more than 66 per cent were farmers.

The largest single occupation category is the combined commercial element with 42 per cent, followed by the farmers with 33.5 per cent. The rest is comprised of 13 per cent officials and 11 per cent professional men. As the great majority of Pennsylvanians got their living from the land, the commercial and urban bias of Loyalism there stands out in bolder relief.

As Philadelphia was the leading port of entry for immigrants to America, it is not surprising that a majority (55 per cent) of the Pennsylvania claimants came from across the Atlantic: in order of importance, from England, Ireland, Scotland, Germany, Holland, and Switzerland. Twice as many immigrants arrived after 1763 as before. As usual, recent arrivals were less likely to have become Americanized, although it must be remembered too that they were also less likely to be dead.

Perhaps the Germans in Pennsylvania were overwhelmingly Whig, or at least indifferent. There are only twelve German-born claimants, yet in 1755 William Smith had estimated the German population as nearly 100,000 out of a total of 220,000.[41] Only three Germans from Philadelphia, one from Cumberland County, and seven from Northumberland County submitted claims. From Northampton County, a largely German area, no German-born persons are found among the four claimants. The twelve German-born claimants were mostly farmers, mostly poor (eight claimed £500 or less), and two-thirds of them served in the armed forces or militia, usually in Butler's Rangers. They were an active group but apparently highly untypical of their nation in general. Christopher Sower, Jr., a first-generation American and an ex-Dunker, or Seventh Day Baptist, minister turned successful printer, was a claimant, but again untypical, although he said that his pacifist sect excommunicated anyone who opposed the government, and that he kept his *Germantowner Zeitung* pro-British.[42] He and Abraham Pastorious (also native born) were the only claimants from Germantown, the center of the Dunkers. In November, 1775, the German Baptists and the Mennonites issued a statement that although pacifists they would support the Whigs without actually fighting, in order to escape being branded Tories like the Quakers.[43] However, it is necessary to be extremely cautious in drawing any definite conclusions about the Germans. The language barrier, national suspicions, and ignorance may have prevented many Germans from filing claims.

Twelve claimants, about one in sixteen of the total, reveal

themselves as Quakers. They do not show any markedly different characteristics from the other claimants, except perhaps a tendency towards considerable wealth; more than half claimed over £1,000 and four claimed more than £2,000. Also a greater percentage of the Quaker claimants were native born; seven were Americans, four British, and one German. Six lived in Philadelphia, the others being scattered around York, Bucks, and Chester Counties. One was an official, four were farmers, and the rest were in commerce.

As in other colonies where they were a significant part of the population, the small number of Quaker claimants suggests that they were usually genuine neutralists and unfairly branded as Tories because of their pacifism. Robert Proud wrote in 1777 that many Quakers banished to Virginia from Philadelphia before the British arrived had been neutral except for "occasionally using their Persuasions to Peace." [44]

In Samuel Shoemaker the Quakers had an outstanding Loyalist, a leading citizen of Philadelphia (he had held the office of mayor among other posts and was a representative in the provincial Assembly), a prominent merchant, and one in whom the claims commissioners decided to put their trust because of his distinguishedly loyal behavior.[45]

The weakness of Loyalism in Pennsylvania is underlined by consideration of the apathetic Anglican clergy, from whom strong support might have been expected. Only seven Church of England clerics submitted claims, but two of these, Isaac Hunt and John Lott Phillips, did not follow the calling until after the Revolution began. The five claimants who can really be counted are William Stringer, rector of St. Paul's, Philadelphia; Jacob Duché, rector of Christ

Church and St. Peter's, Philadelphia; Bernard Page of Wyoming; Alexander Murray, Society for the Propagation of the Gospel missionary at Reading, Berks County; and Daniel Batwell, missionary for the same society to York and Cumberland Counties. Of these five, only Duché was a native of America.

The Anglican clergy were waverers. This was not necessarily the result of timidity or weak thinking any more than Galloway's behavior was. The eloquent Reverend Jacob Duché is the leading example of equivocation. He has been called "the Benedict Arnold of the American Clergy"[46] because he was chaplain to the First Continental Congress, but cooled after the Declaration of Independence and finally, after Howe's capture of Philadelphia, became an adamant Loyalist. As a witness for Duché, Samuel Shoemaker pointed out that Duché's father and all his wife's relations were "Violent" Whigs, and "this induced him to be Chaplain of Congress."[47]

William Stringer, the other Philadelphia claimant, was not apparently of dubious loyalty in his conduct, although he did attempt to remain after the British evacuation;[48] but, like Duché, the rest of the Philadelphia Anglican clergy were suspect; among them were William White, William Smith, the first provost of the College of Philadelphia, and Thomas Coombe, although only White remained unerringly Whig.[49] He served Congress as a chaplain and then became rector of Christ Church.[50]

Thus the Reverend Thomas Bradbury Chandler's remark to the claims commissioners that "all the Clergy in Philadelphia were promoters of the rebellion" was barely an exaggeration.[51] Two of the remaining claimants, Daniel Batwell and Alexander Murray, seem to have been steadfast Loyalists, but it was rumored that the third, Bernard Page, had been a rebel chaplain, and the Reverend Charles Inglis certainly believed him to be an "indifferent Character."[52] Batwell fled to the British lines rather than take the oath to the rebels, and Murray explained his own loyal conduct by the fact that he had married a rich wife and took no money from his parishioners; he "was better able to preach to them for nothing than they to pay him."[53] Murray's remark hints that his parishioners were not particularly loyal. This is just what one would expect, for if the pastors were equivocal the flocks would be more so. The weak loyalty of the clergy was probably often the result of a fear of alienating the congregations and the ultimate loss of position and salary (apart from what the Society for the Propagation of the Gospel paid). Murray also noted that he had tried to preach against rebellion, "but his Voice was drowned in the General Cry of Liberty."[54] Batwell recounted being tossed into the river by the townspeople and being imprisoned in Huntingdon where his church was.[55] William Stringer clearly indicated the outlook of his parishioners in Philadelphia by telling the commissioners that early in the troubles many of them had refused to pay pew money because of his loyal conduct.[56]

The conclusion must be that as a whole neither the Anglican clergy nor the laity was a particularly strong element in Pennsylvania Loyalism.

Loyalism was weak in Pennsylvania, but strongest in Philadelphia. Even there it was quite feeble. The proportion of claimants to the whole population of 40,000 in 1775 is 0.26 per cent. This is slightly less than the proportion in Newport, Rhode Island, considerably less than at Portsmouth, New Hampshire, or Norfolk, Virginia, and only a little over one-quarter the proportion at Boston in the same year.

This fact may come as something of a surprise, as it did to Samuel Curwen. After the battle of Lexington, he fled to Philadelphia because of its reputation for moderation but discovered that his Toryism was not acceptable. As he put it, "At this period the political phrenzy there had risen to an equal height with New England." [57] When the British evacuated Philadelphia in 1778, 3,000 Loyalists went with them,[58] while about 1,100[59] left Boston two years earlier in similar circumstances. Proportionately many more Tories left Boston than left Philadelphia, 1,100 out of a population of 3,500 (almost one in three) compared to 3,000 out of a population of 21,767 (about one in seven).[60]

Yet, writing to Lord George Germain on June 15, 1778, just before the evacuation of Philadelphia, the Carlisle peace commissioners noted the "Consternation" of "those who had put themselves under His Majesty's Protection." But, the commissioners went on, all were not fleeing; "many of the principal Inhabitants" were endeavoring to save their property by taking oaths of allegiance to the rebel states.[61] Thus it is clear that not all the Philadelphia Loyalists (including those who had come from outlying parts) were represented by the 3,000 who were evacuated. The change in allegiance is not necessarily evidence of opportunism. The British in fact were abandoning the Loyalists in Pennsylvania and, indeed, in the whole Chesapeake Bay area. This was clear to Ambrose Serle, the perceptive secretary to Lord Howe. On May 22, 1778, the day after the announcement of the decision to evacuate Philadelphia, Serle noted in his journal, "I now look upon the Contest as at an End. No man can be expected to declare for us, when he cannot be assured of a Fortnight's Protection. Everyman, on the contrary, whatever might have been his primary Inclinations, will find it his Interest to oppose and drive us out of the Country." At the same time he advised his very despondent friend, Joseph Galloway, to reconcile himself to the rebel authorities.[62]

More than 54 per cent of the claimants lived in Philadelphia. An analysis of them does not reveal trends strikingly different from the analysis of the whole, except for the necessary absence of farmers. All economic levels are found; claims of £500 or less are still the biggest category, but there is a higher incidence of greater wealth, fifteen of the twenty-two claims for more than £5,000 coming from the city. Finally the ratio of immigrants to native-born Americans is higher (about two to one as compared with about nine to seven for the colony in general), not surprising considering that Philadelphia was a port of entry.

The commercial element is the nucleus of Philadelphia Loyalism, but even the loyal merchants were a small minority of their class. In 1765 there were about 400 merchants and traders in Philadelphia; yet only twenty-seven claimants are found,[63] and by 1775 the number of merchants and traders must have been considerably more than 400 because of the growth of the city.

The figures support Robert East's assertion that, unlike Boston and New York, Philadelphia lost few leading merchants.[64] Isaac Wharton, banished as a Loyalist, and John Parroch, a claimant, are the exceptions among such great merchant families as the Morrises, Willings, Pembertons, and Whartons; and Thomas Wharton, Jr., even became president of Pennsylvania.

Joseph Galloway remarked to the commissioners that

most of the magistrates under the proprietary government were Whig and therefore the loyal conduct of Samuel Shoemaker was "striking." [65] Only two members of the assembly submitted claims, speaker Galloway and James Rankin. Only five local officials are found: Abel Evans, the clerk of the assembly; William Rankin, a colonel in the militia; Samuel Shoemaker, mayor and magistrate of Philadelphia; and John Potts and Hugh Ferguson, justices of the peace. This is indicative of the weakness of Loyalism in the province.

Pennsylvania was a proprietary province and proprietors were naturally inclined to Loyalism. But the two members of the Penn family, John and Richard, who were resident in the province at the time of the Revolution, although claimants, were anything but Tory firebrands. Lieutenant-Governor John Penn, a grandson of the great William and himself finally a proprietor, was the family's leading representative in the colony and chief executive from 1763 to 1771 and from 1773 until the Revolution ended his tenure of office in 1776. John Penn was not a popular governor and in 1764 the Assembly petitioned for the establishment of royal government. But this was not a premature Whig-Tory split; Galloway as well as Franklin was on the antiproprietary side, and John Dickinson, more Whiggish than Galloway in the Revolution, favored the proprietors. Although briefly under arrest, Governor Penn was a quietist as the Revolution got under way and returned to live in the province until his death in 1795. His brother Richard, naval officer in the port of Philadelphia and briefly lieutenant-governor (1771–1773), left Pennsylvania permanently in 1775, but he had been popular (Caesar Rodney, in 1774, called him "a great friend to liberty").[66] He was commissioned by the Continental Congress to deliver the Olive Branch Petition to the king. The new regime in Pennsylvania showed no animosity toward the proprietors; they were allowed to keep their personal estates and also received a large cash compensation.[67]

In summary, a Pennsylvania claimant, a member of a small minority which rarely included anyone from the ruling class, probably lived in Philadelphia, or at least Philadelphia, Bucks, or Chester County; was somewhat more likely to be an immigrant than native born; was unlikely to be a German or Quaker; was likely to be engaged in some commercial activity or might quite possibly be a professional man or office-holder; but if he lived outside Philadelphia, he was probably a farmer, in which case he could be expected to be a man of modest wealth.

So much for the structure of Pennsylvania Loyalism as revealed by the claimants. Now to consider the question of motives. The loyalty of British immigrants, officials, professional men, and merchants in Philadelphia is fairly easily comprehended. The military occupation of the city was the opportunity for sincere Loyalists to stand up and be counted (many worked for Galloway's administration) and for others to trade or work for British gold. George Napper, a Quaker, baked for the troops; a witness remarked of James Henderson, a wagoner who joined the British after service in the American militia, that it "might be his motive to get good Employment as much from principle of Attachment to Britain"; John Granger, the keeper of a livery stable, bluntly admitted that he "was in the way of making a Fortune when the British Army arrived"; James Humphreys, whose Tory *Pennsylvania Gazette* had failed in November, 1776, after less than two years in print, resurrected his newspaper under official patronage during the occupation.[68]

For others the occupation was a time to pick what they fancied was the winning side. Samuel Shoemaker, when asked what people thought of the war in 1776, replied that "all the Loyalists and most of the rebels thought that Great Britain would prevail," which, if true, is a comment on the boldness of the Whigs and the timidity of the Tories.[69] Thomas Badge, a Philadelphia grocer, announced baldly that "his motive for joining the British was because he thought the British army would conquer . . ."[70] The Reverend Mr. Duché, somewhat in anticipation of the recent "better Red than dead" controversy, wrote to Washington in October, 1777, forecasting American defeat: "Perhaps it may be said, that it is 'better to die than be Slaves.' This indeed is a splendid maxim in theory. . . . But where there is the least Probability of an happy Accomodation, surely Wisdom and Humanity call for some Sacrifices to be made, to prevent inevitable Destruction."[71]

As already mentioned, the Loyalist merchants were a minority of the whole. Some must have acted from principle; others were compromised by trade with the occupation forces; others, such as Charles Startin, who "was in good Business there [Philadelphia] as a factor for Birmingham Ware," may well have seen no future for themselves outside imperial trade circles.[72]

No one who watches the current scene could lightly dismiss the allure of the British monarchy. Admittedly George III was belatedly, unfairly, and rather successfully cast in the devil's role by the Patriots, but Loyalists sometimes gave glimpses of king-worship. During the war the exiled Samuel Shoemaker came away from an interview (conducted partly in German) at Windsor Castle, enthralled by George III. Perhaps the meeting merely served to confirm long-held views. "I cannot say, but I wished some of my violent Countrymen could have such an opportunity as I have had. I think they would be convinced that George the third has not one grain of Tyrany in his Composition, and that he *is* not, he *cannot* be that bloody minded man they have so repeatedly and so illiberally called him. It is impossible; a man of his fine feelings, so good a husband, so kind a Father *cannot be a Tyrant.*" [73]

Pennsylvania is one of the colonies which show most signs of social conflict during the Revolution. Fear of this influenced some of the conservative, well-to-do Loyalists. James Allen's diary shows this fear at work, apparently as the decisive factor in edging him from the Whig into the Tory camp. In May, 1772, he wrote, "I am at present much engaged in prosecutions for breaches of the laws of Trade and have libelled four or five Vessels and Cargoes for Captain Talbot of the Lively Man of War. I am doing as a Lawyer what I would not do as a politician; being fully persuaded of oppressive nature of those laws."

Three years later in July, 1775: "The Eyes of Europe are upon us; if we fall, Liberty no longer continues an inhabitant of this Globe: for England is running fast to slavery. The King is as despotic as any prince in Europe; the only difference is the mode; and a venal parliament are as bad as a standing army."

By October, 1775, he was cautiously drilling with the American militia. "My Inducement principally to join them is; that a man is suspected who does not; and I chuse to have a Musket on my shoulders, to be on a par with them, and I believe discreet people mixing with them, may Keep them in Order." The same day he complained that "the most insignificant now lord it with impunity and without discretion over the most respectable characters."

Five months later, in March, 1776: "The plot thickens; peace is scarcely thought of—Independency predominant. Thinking people uneasy, irresolute and inactive. The Mobility triumphant. . . . I love the Cause of liberty; but cannot heartily join in the prosecution of measures totally foreign to the original plan of Resistance. The madness of the multitude is but one degree better than submission to the Tea-Act." Next month: "A Convention chosen by the people, will consist of the most fiery Independants; they will have the whole Executive and legislative authority in their hands. . . . I am determined to oppose them vehemently in Assembly, for if they prevail there; all may bid adieu to our old happy constitution and peace." [74]

In 1777 a contemporary wit put the point nicely, writing of William Allen, Jr., who had been a lieutenant colonel in the American army, "which station he resigned—not because he was totally unfit for it, but because the Continental Congress presumed to declare the American States Free and Independent without first asking the consent, and obtaining the approbation of himself and wise family." [75]

Somewhat on the same lines and also illustrating another point, an anonymous witness told the claims commissioners, "The great proprietors of Lands thought if they could be Independent of this Country they should be petty princes but when they saw that the Rebels confiscated their Estates they turn'd about and became very loyal." [76]

Thus some light can be thrown on the motives of certain classes of Loyalists and certain articulate individuals. It may be the rather sophisticated reasoning of James Allen, or the blunt assertion by the Marquis de Chastellux that Simon Girty, the Indian agent, went over to the British after being discovered in "some malversations of the public money." [77]

The Pennsylvania Loyalists were comparatively rich in talent and members of leading families. They do not measure up to such outstanding Whigs as Benjamin Franklin, John Dickinson, Joseph Reed, Charles Thomson, Thomas Miflin, and Robert Morris, but such Tories as Joseph Galloway, the Allen family, Samuel Shoemaker, Phineas Bond, James Humphreys, Christopher Sower, Jacob Duché, Charles Stedman (author of a well-known history of the Revolutionary War), and Joseph Stansbury (not a claimant, but a leading Tory poet), make an impressive showing.

VIII. DELAWARE

PENNSYLVANIA

Wilmington •

New Castle •

NEW CASTLE CO.

NEW JERSEY

Delaware R.

Dover •

MARYLAND

KENT CO.

SUSSEX CO.

DELAWARE

TEN DELAWARE Loyalists, a mere handful, submitted claims. This is about 0.02 per cent of the population of 40,695 in 1776,[1] the lowest percentage of any colony. This figure would seem to support the opinion that Delaware was almost unanimously Whig. But against this there is Joseph Galloway's statement to the claims commissioners that "they were very moderate People in the Delaware Government. There was throughout the War a Majority of the Assembly in favour of retaining their Allegiance, but it was a small Government surrounded by larger ones and incapable of acting of itself." [2]

This view that the Loyalists were a majority, or at least very strong, is supported by such contemporaries as John Adams, Thomas McKean, Caesar Rodney, and British officers.[3] Harold B. Hancock, the leading student of Delaware Loyalism, guessed that 50 per cent of the inhabitants were Loyalists, 30 per cent Patriots, and 20 per cent "pacifist and hesitant"; and it cannot be denied that the great majority either opposed or were indifferent to independence.[4]

Thomas Robinson told the claims commissioners that in June, 1776, he collected 5,000 signatures (a figure confirmed by Galloway) on a petition opposing the Declaration of Independence, while supporters of the Declaration could only get 300. John Clark was mobbed while carrying the petition to Congress, whereupon Robinson with 1,500 followers tried to restore law and order, but was refused arms by Sir Andrew Hammond, commander of the "Roebuck," and finally was completely subdued by 1,500 riflemen dispatched into Sussex County by the council of safety at Philadelphia.[5] Further, there were some small Tory uprisings against the state, the most serious occurring in April, 1778, in Kent County where Cheney Clow (later captured and executed) led 100 Tories in a brief engagement.[6]

Some early Delaware historians such as Henry C. Conrad and the Reverend Joseph B. Turner have taken the opposite view, the latter urging that the state contained fewer Loyalists than any other south of New England except Virginia.[7] This conclusion is supported in varying degrees by the very small number of claimants; the ease with which Clow's "rebellion" was put down; the fact that the Tories never came anywhere near controlling the state; the sterling service rendered the American army by the Delaware regiment;[8] some contemporary statements—Thomas McKean wrote to his wife in the middle of the war that "the inhabitants of Delaware are said to be on the verge of total Revolution to Whiggism";[9] the patriotic course followed by the state during the economic troubles during the period 1763–1776;[10] and the lenient treatment of the Tories by the republican government. This last point requires elaboration: very little persecution was reported to the claims commissioners beyond the mobbing of two claimants, Dr. John Watson and Joshua Hill, a rich farmer.[11]

It may be that Professor Hancock has exaggerated the numbers of Delaware Loyalists, and it is probable that contemporaries did; for example, Ambrose Serle wrote to Lord Dartmouth in 1777 that the people of Delaware were "well-affected" and implied that the evidence for this was that they "have brought us large Supplies of everything we wanted,"[12] but, of course, British gold often obliterated principles. Revolutionaries have a tendency to exaggerate the strength of the enemy to justify their extreme measures, and even a Loyalist such as Joseph Galloway had a vested interest in stressing alleged Loyalist strength which, he claimed, the British neglected to encourage. Nevertheless, the weight of evidence seems to support Hancock and his impressive array of contemporary witnesses.[13]

How then can the paradox of the dearth of Loyalist claimants be explained? Galloway has already been quoted to the effect that Delaware "was a small Government surrounded by larger ones and incapable of acting of itself." As already noted, troops were dispatched from Philadelphia in 1776 against Thomas Robinson, and there are many other such examples.[14] There was no dominant town like Philadelphia, the occupation of which by the British could focus and encourage the Loyalists, nor any major evacuation to take the Loyalists into exile.

Philadelphia, of course, was close enough for its occupation to stimulate Delaware Loyalism, as did the presence of a British fleet in Delaware Bay. But the British undoubtedly neglected to support the Tories in the lower counties. Galloway's strictures were echoed by Thomas Robinson, a leading citizen and the outstanding Loyalist of Delaware, who complained that Sir Andrew Hammond denied arms to Robinson and his followers, and that Sir William Howe turned down his offer to raise Delaware men for the expedition to the head of the Elk River.[15]

Finally, a great many Delaware citizens were apathetic, neutralist, or conservative, or all three, rather than actively Loyalist, and were never turned into true Loyalists because of British neglect and failure allied with Whig success. Hancock argues that because the majority of the inhabitants of Delaware were contented small farmers living in an isolated environment with few schools or roads and no newspaper, the result was an automatic conservatism.[16] (But conservatism is not synonymous with Loyalism.) Because of this situation, avowed, secret, or potential Loyalists were rarely forced into exile. Theodore Maurice, the comptroller of customs at New Castle, did finally leave "in despair" in June, 1778, but asked by the commissioners how he had managed to remain so long, he replied that leaders in Delaware "were his Friends and very moderate People," and in this he was backed up by Joseph Galloway who confirmed that Maurice was able to stay without "trimming." [17]

After the war Thomas Robinson, Delaware's leading Loyalist, returned to the house of his brother Peter (later chief justice of Sussex County) and died there in 1789. [18] The next richest claimant, Joshua Hill, had a rebel wife and eldest son who remained in Delaware. [19]

The strongest religious sect in Delaware was the Presbyterian, mainly Scotch-Irish, and as usual mainly Patriot. [20] The next strongest denomination was the Anglican, and Hancock states that they were usually Loyalists. [21] The Reverend John Patterson, of Maryland, testified before the claims commissioners that Thomas Robinson was "head of the Church Party who were generally Loyal." [22] However, like Delaware Loyalists in general, the Anglican Loyalists were inarticulate. The American-born Reverend Daniel Curry, who kept a school, submitted a claim, but none of the other five (four being native born) Anglican priests in Delaware did, although they were all missionaries of the Society for the Propagation of the Gospel. The Reverend Philip Reading was a firm Loyalist; his church was closed down, but he is not a claimant because he died in 1778. The other three clerics were Patriots, including the Reverend Aeneus Ross (his brother signed the Declaration of Independence, and his sister-in-law supposedly stitched the first American flag). [23] The congregations were probably

even more divided than the ministers; such outstanding
Patriots as George Read, Caesar Rodney, and John Clowes
were Anglicans.[24]

The next strongest sect seems to have been the Methodists, at that time still theoretically Anglicans.[25] Few, however, seem to have been loyal (although John Wesley's Tory
position put them under grave suspicion) as is suggested by
the sojourn of Francis Asbury in Kent County, which began
in 1778 and from which the great growth of Methodism
in Delaware stems.[26]

The attitudes of the powerful Anglican (and Methodist)
church illustrate that Delaware Loyalism was largely a
product of surmise and accusation, a potential rather than
an achieved reality. The evidence is somewhat conflicting
and puzzling, and there are so few Delaware claimants that
generalizations can be made only with extreme caution.
Slightly over half of the claimants were natives of America
(all but one wealthy), the rest from the British Isles, twice
as many of whom emigrated after 1763 as before. There was
a slight tendency towards wealth, five claiming for more
than £1,000 as compared with four for less. Thomas Robinson and Joshua Hill were rich claimants, but the two richest
men in Delaware, George Read and John Dickinson, were
moderate Whigs.[27] The majority of the inhabitants of
Delaware were modest farmers; yet only three farmers
submitted claims, the commercial element (four) being the
largest category, followed by three professional men. Only
one office-holder appears, but of course there were very
few in the colony, partly because of the proprietary form
of government. (Delaware had the same governor as
Pennsylvania, but had its own unicameral legislature.) There
is little sign of the political leadership among the claimants:
just Thomas Robinson and Joshua Hill, who were members

of the Assembly and also local magistrates. No claimant came from Wilmington, the leading town; three came from Kent County, two from Sussex County, and five from New Castle County (three from the town of New Castle). The assumption would be that New Castle County was somewhat more strongly loyal than the other two, although Hancock comes to exactly the opposite conclusion, considering it the most strongly Patriot and least Loyalist county.[28] Yet in 1778 John Potts considered the area between New Castle and Chesapeake Bay "better disposed towards Government than any other country in the middle colonies."[29]

A supplementary source of simple statistics, which on the whole confirm the claims tables on distribution by geography and occupation, is the list of "Loyalists Excepted from Pardon by the Act of June 26, 1778,"[30] which contains twenty names from New Castle County, and thirteen each from Kent and Sussex Counties. The breakdown by occupation is as follows:

Farmers	11[a]
Artisans and craftsmen	12[b]
Merchants and shopkeepers	1
Seamen and pilots	9[c]
Innkeepers	2
Captain of militia	2
Lieutenant	1
Physicians	2[d]
Lawyers	1
Members of Assembly	3[e]
Sheriff of Sussex County	1
Unknown	1

[a] Nine husbandmen and two yeomen.
[b] Three coopers, two laborers, and one each: saddler, bricklayer, hatter, weaver, cordwainer, coppersmith, and tailor.
[c] Four pilots, three shallopmen, and two mariners.
[d] One also a combmaker.   [e] One also a physician.

IX. MARYLAND

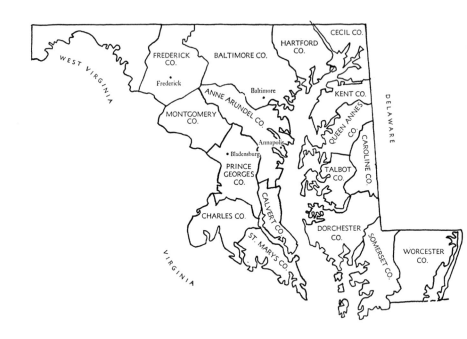

MARYLAND

LOYALIST claimants in Maryland were overwhelmingly immigrant British.[1] Less than 27 per cent were white Americans, the rest British (apart from four Germans) with almost equal contingents from England, Scotland, and Ireland. About two-fifths of the immigrants had arrived before 1763, the rest afterwards.

The general commercial element of merchants, shopkeepers, artisans, innkeepers, and seamen constitutes the largest occupation category with thirty-three claimants, or 42 per cent of the whole. Professional men with over 24 per cent, office-holders with about 19 per cent, and farmers with about 14 per cent complete the total. Nine (nearly half) of the professional men were Anglican clerics, followed by five doctors, four lawyers, and one schoolmaster.

The table of the amount of the claims reveals a distinct tendency toward wealth. The largest single category is for claims between £2,000 and £5,000, and the third largest is for amounts over £10,000. Only eight claims were for £500 or less; only fourteen, or 22 per cent, were for £1,000 or less; more than 54 per cent claimed for £2,000 or more.

Baltimore, the largest town in Maryland, had the most claimants: twenty-five, or more than 35 per cent of those whose residences are known. Annapolis, the capital and only other real urban center, follows quite closely with over 24 per cent. On a proportionate basis both towns are about the same: Annapolis has 0.55 per cent of its population of 3,700 in 1775 as claimants, while Baltimore has 0.52 per cent of a population of 5,934, also in 1775.[2] The proportion for each is much less (by one-half) than that for Boston, greater than Philadelphia's or Newport's, and slightly less than Norfolk's.[3] If the Negro population of the two Maryland towns is discounted, the proportion rises considerably, perhaps by a third. The two towns combined account for about 60 per cent of the claimants. The only other concentration is in Maryland's west, in Frederick County, with twelve claimants (half residents of Frederick), or 17 per cent of the whole. Outside these three areas, Loyalists were almost non-existent. Major Swiney, a merchant and planter, told the commissioners that he knew of no other Loyalist besides himself in Charles or St. Marys County.[4] The few remaining Loyalists, about 12 per cent, were scattered about St. Marys, Charles, and Prince Georges Counties on the western shore of the Chesapeake and on the eastern shore in Worcester, Somerset, and Kent Counties.

The concentration of the Loyalists in Annapolis and Baltimore comes as no surprise when the predominantly commercial, professional, office-holding nature of Maryland Loyalism is considered. As the clergy were appointed by the proprietor in Maryland, they were in effect office-holders, so the relative weight of this category is greatly enhanced. William Eddis noted, "In England there are few, even in great departments of state, who possess so extensive a patronage as the governor of Maryland." For example, Eddis estimated that All Saints Parish in Frederick County was well on the way to being as lucrative as many English bishoprics.[5]

The reason for the slight concentration in Frederick County is less obvious. However, none of the twelve claimants were American born (four were German and the rest British), and three were Church of England ministers (although one was ordained after the Revolution began).

The Patriots were overwhelmingly strong in all parts of

Maryland

Maryland, but were strongest in Baltimore and especially Annapolis. More than one Loyalist asserted that Annapolis took the lead in the rebellion.[6]

Briefly, a Maryland Loyalist was likely to be a British immigrant, well-to-do, in commerce or a profession, or holding an office, and resident in Annapolis or Baltimore. Also he was a member of a small minority because the proportion of claimants to white population is approximately 0.05 per cent, one of the lowest figures.[7]

Most of the other evidence points to this weakness. A. M. Schlesinger has shown that Maryland's record in the opposition to imperial policy after 1763 was firmly Whig, more so than Virginia's, partly because there were more native merchants there than in the Old Dominion.[8] Only six merchants in overseas trade can be definitely identified among the claimants and only one of these was American born.

Serious Loyalist opposition to the Revolution never really materialized in either Annapolis or Baltimore where it had the most chance of success. In Baltimore, on May 31, 1774, George Chalmers, a British lawyer and later a historian of the colonies, made his first and last attempt to influence a public meeting. He was not even allowed to speak, and his friend, Henry Thompson, was threatened with defenestration for making the attempt. As Chalmers put it, from then on "neither himself nor any of the friends of Government attended any Meeting, as they had tried at one what could be done and found great danger from it, but no Service had arisen."[9] Chalmers made it clear that he was a member of a tiny minority, noting that through his loyalty he lost "his friendships and his station in life."[10]

During the Revolution Maryland was, of all the colonies, the conservative one par excellence. James Brooks, an English immigrant and holder of several proprietary offices, told the commissioners that he believed that "Maryland was the most moderate of all the Provinces, Annapolis excepted." [11] Even as late as March, 1776, William Eddis, an English office-holder, was able to write, "In Maryland, a spirit of moderation is yet predominant." [12] Power was kept firmly in the hands of a rich, conservative aristocracy. Apart from the ending of the proprietorship and a somewhat tardy confiscation of Tory property all radical measures were eschewed, as the moderate state constitution well illustrates.[13] The result was that few conservatives were likely to be repelled by the Revolutionary party or driven into the Loyalist ranks. George Chalmers told the commissioners that many Loyalists stayed "without making any real Sacrifice of their Principles but that of remaining quiet." [14]

Claude H. Van Tyne rightly estimated that the laws against the Tories in Maryland were among the lightest in America.[15] At least seven claimants were actually resident in Maryland, or about to return, when they submitted their claims, and former Governor Eden died in Annapolis in 1784 while trying to recover his property. Philip Barton Key was a zealous Tory who fought as a captain in the Maryland Loyalists, receiving half-pay, yet managed to return to his native state after the war, practice law, get elected to the legislature and finally, in 1806, to the United States Congress.[16]

Only a few instances of Loyalist persecution appear in the Maryland claims. Samuel Skingle, a stuccoworker in Annapolis, had his business boycotted in 1775 and was subsequently tarred, feathered, and carted for his Loyalism.[17] Two German brothers, Adam and George Graves, and an Irishman, Hugh Kelly, recounted that having been captured while recruiting troops, they and four other officers were tried and sentenced to hanging, drawing, and quartering, but only three of them (all German) were actually executed at Frederick (by simple hanging). William Garrett, an overseer of a plantation, claimed he was under sentence of death when rescued by some Hessians.[18]

Joseph Galloway claimed that many potential Loyalists in Maryland merely awaited a British military presence to rally them. He may have been mistaken. But Hugh Kelly told the commissioners that by 1781 nearly 1,300 had joined his "Maryland Royal Retaliators" before his capture ended the enterprise.[19] However, the British army was only very briefly in one small part of Maryland, and Annapolis and Baltimore were never occupied. Had they been captured, the strength of Maryland Loyalism would probably have appeared very differently, as Galloway suggested.

In the years preceding the Revolution, Maryland politics had been dominated by a constant struggle between the court party, consisting of the governor, the council, and officials (including the Anglican clergy) appointed by the proprietor, and the country party, consisting mainly of the rich planters who controlled local affairs and the lower house of the legislature.[20] When the Revolution came the court party undoubtedly contributed substantially to the Loyalist ranks. This is shown by the fifteen office-holders, nine Anglican clergy, and no member of the lower house found among the claimants. Similarly only four local officials (justices of the peace in this case) filed claims; local officials, although appointed by the proprietor, were normally members of the country party. George Chalmers wrote despairingly of the justices of the peace that they "were themselves the promoters of Sedition."[21] Significantly, two of the four justices of the peace who were claimants had been appointed in 1775 following a purge of the Whigs by the governor. Even in the ten-man council only two members, Philip Lee and George Steuart, submitted claims, and two others, Daniel of St. Thomas Jenifer and John Beale Bodley, became Patriots although the latter was inactive. At least two others, Benedict Calvert and Colonel William Fitzhugh, remained in Maryland, and Doctor Upton Scott, clerk of the council, returned to a peaceful retirement near Annapolis in 1780.[22]

Seven more claimants—the Reverend John Montgomery, a close friend of the governor; Richard Lee, the son of the councilor of the same name; three Dulanys, including Daniel Dulany III; the Reverend Henry Addison, a representative of one of the first families of Maryland; and the Reverend Jonathan Boucher, the leading Anglican in Maryland—illustrate further that part of the court party which became Loyalist, but clearly not all did; at least a couple became Patriots and others remained neutral or passive.

The career of Governor Robert Eden, a claimant and undoubtedly a Loyalist, illustrates further the general weakness of the movement. This able governor and *bon vivant* who held office from 1769 to 1776 became very popular in Maryland and was sympathetic to the American cause. Hence, as the Revolution approached, his own disposition and the neutralism or desertion of some of the court party, plus the ardent Whiggism of the great majority of the ruling aristocracy entrenched in the House of Delegates, led inexorably to a draining away of his authority which he was powerless to halt. He was not even prepared to act provocatively. Early in 1775 George Chalmers, a very active Loyalist,[23] promoted a "private Association" of Loyalists to defend themselves from mobs and asked the governor for arms. The arms were not supplied nor did the governor lend any support to the Association.[24] All the while Eden was treated with great respect and moderation, and he finally left in comparatively friendly circumstances. William Eddis noted as late as June, 1776, on the eve of Eden's departure, that "he is treated with every exterior mark of attention." [25] In 1784 he was back in Annapolis seeking his property and was well received.[26]

If the governor himself was not a violent Tory, it is not surprising that others close to him were also moderate. For example, his secretary William Eddis, who wrote the well-known *Letters from America* . . . , called the repeal of the Stamp Act "a wise and necessary measure," wanted the repeal of the Townshend duties, and acknowledged the justice of most of the American grievances, though he could not support the mode of opposition. Robert Christie, sheriff of Baltimore County and a claimant, was critical of the Stamp Act and the Townshend Acts.[27]

Robert Alexander, a native-born Baltimore lawyer, was at first a leading Patriot and went as a delegate to the Continental Congress in December, 1775. He told the claims commissioners that he believed the British Parliament could not legally tax Maryland, but he withdrew when independence became the issue.[28] But by June, 1778, he was writing in vain to his ex-colleague at the Congress, Thomas Johnson, now governor of Maryland, about the conditions under which he might return; if they were honorable "I shall most readily embrace them, and return immediately to my Country my Family and Friends." [29]

The outstanding Maryland example of a moderate Loyalist is Daniel Dulany, American born, but educated in England and one of the ablest of all colonial lawyers, who wrote the celebrated pamphlet following the Stamp Act which refuted the argument that the colonies were virtually represented in the British Parliament. He has been called the "most active defender of the proprietary interest." [30] He was not a claimant and remained in Maryland in neutral retirement until his death in 1797. His son of the same name fled to England in 1778 from New York and did submit a claim.[31]

In sum, the story of Maryland during the Revolution is that of an aristocratic body politic which simply sloughed off the excrescence of the proprietorship without causing any major splits and continued along the path it was already traveling with a minimum of disruption, not even experiencing military occupation. This is why the Loyalist movement barely counted there. Like the Virginia ruling classes, the Maryland aristocracy had power and defended it from both British and local interference. Maryland Loyalism boasted a few outstanding men such as Daniel Dulany, Jonathan Boucher, George Chalmers, William Eddis, and James Chalmers, commander of the Maryland Loyalists and author of *Plain Truth*, a rebuttal to *Common Sense*, but they were an impotent handful and significantly all British except for Dulany.[32]

Anglicans in Maryland were merely one religious group among many, including Catholics, Presbyterians, Quakers, German Reformed, and Lutherans.[33] But the Anglican church was established, and the more than forty livings (including some of the richest in America) provided the proprietor with a fine source of patronage which sometimes led to very unsavory appointments. Not surprisingly, most of the Episcopal clergy seem to have remained loyal,[34] and ten (two of whom were ordained after the Revolution began) submitted claims. Six of those claimants were British and four were American.

The Reverend Jonathan Boucher, the leading Anglican cleric in Maryland, a lexicographer and at one time a teacher of Washington's stepson, nevertheless wrote in October, 1771, that the American-born Anglican clergy were inclined to Whiggism, at least in the case of his own curate "who being a Native gave them such a Sermon as they wish'd for" on a patriotic fast day. Later, to Boucher's mortification, the curate succeeded to the living in 1777.[35] Most Maryland Loyalists were perhaps Anglicans, but they were probably a minority of the church. This was certainly the case if William Eddis' assertion that Anglicans outnumbered "the aggregate body of the dissenters of every denomination" is true.[36] Boucher's letters make it clear that his congregation was solidly Whig, and even his initial attempts at remaining neutral were not acceptable.[37] It is significant that Boucher, although undoubtedly a Loyalist, was no firebrand. He wrote in May, 1775, "for my part I equally dread a Victory on either side."[38]

Office-holders, Anglican clergymen, immigrants—these groups who make up a good proportion of the Maryland Loyalists are not difficult to understand. In July, 1775, William Eddis wrote, "I wish well to America—It is my duty—my inclination so to do—but I cannot—I will not—consent to act in direct opposition to my oath of allegiance, and my deliberate opinion."[39]

The remainder, especially if native born—farmers, lawyers, doctors, merchants, shopkeepers, and artisans—are harder to explain. They were a tiny minority of their classes. Some merchants were tied to British houses. (Only six claimants can be positively identified as overseas merchants, and two, James Christie and Robert Buchanan, certainly were closely connected with British houses.)[40]

The commissioners' reports reveal little about motives for Loyalism in Maryland. Lawrence Kellar, one of the four Germans who claimed, reported that he refused the rank of major offered by the rebels "unless they could prove to his satisfaction that it was lawful to take an Oath one day and to forswear it the next." (He had also served in the British army during the Seven Years War.)[41] It may well be that, to some of those few colonists who had taken them, oaths of allegiance were treated as binding. The Reverend John Patterson said his brother favored the rebels until he (John) was ill-treated, whereupon blood proved thicker than water.[42] This suggests the personal nature of Loyalism. Similarly, Robert Buchanan, a Scottish merchant claimant from Annapolis, had a partner, John Briscoe, who was a rebel. Presumably their economic outlook was the same, yet they split.[43]

The most enigmatic Maryland Loyalists (and a tiny minority) were the native born. A look at the twenty such claimants reveals no striking characteristics except that they were generally wealthy. But this does not mean much; the leading native-born Maryland Patriots, men like Charles Carroll and William Paca, were also wealthy.

Some of the few leading Maryland families which produced Loyalists were characteristically divided. The Dulanys are a prime example: Daniel of pamphlet fame was neutral; his sons were all Loyalists except Benjamin, who was a Patriot. David Steuart, an American-born claimant and former member of the council, had two brothers who were rebels; and Philip Barton, a member of an old Maryland family, had a brother who was a lieutenant colonel in the American army.[44]

Daniel Dulany III stated categorically that he "inherited" his Loyalism from his father and grandfather,[45] while a relative, also called Daniel Dulany, noted his English education and the fact that he was "bred from his infancy in an affectionate regard for Great Britain, in veneration for her constitution and Laws." [46]

On March 29, 1783, Major Walter Dulany (not a claimant) of the Maryland Loyalists wrote to the commander-in-chief in New York, Sir Guy Carleton, about the prospect of being given a permanent commission, explaining his position thus:

My duty as a subject; the happiness which America enjoyed under the British government; and the miseries to which she would be reduced by an independance [*sic*]; were the motives that induced me to join the British Army; nor are there any dangers, or difficulties that I would not cheerfully undergo, to effect a happy restoration.

But, at the same time, that I acted, with the greatest zeal, against my *rebellious* countrymen I never forgot that I was an American—If therefore, Sir, Independance should be granted, and the war still continued, I should deem it extremely improper to remain in a situation, obliging me to act either directly or indirectly against America.[47]

X. VIRGINIA

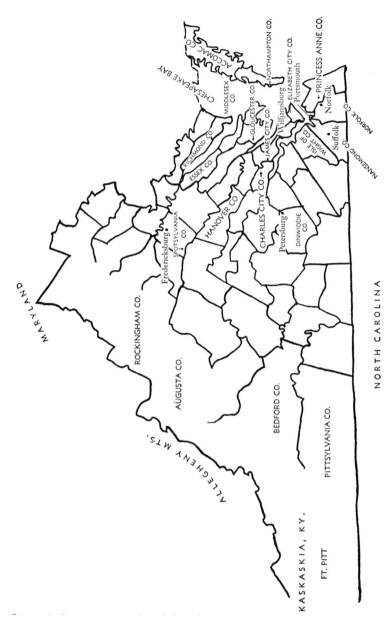

VIRGINIA

ACCOMAC CO.

NORTHAMPTON CO.

CHESAPEAKE BAY

MIDDLESEX CO.

ELIZABETH CITY CO.
Portsmouth

PRINCESS ANNE CO.

GLOUCESTER CO.

Williamsburg

Norfolk

RICHMOND CO.

JAMES CITY CO.

NORFOLK CO.

ESSEX CO.

ISLE OF WIGHT CO.

Suffolk

Fredericksburg
SPOTSYLVANIA
CO.

HANOVER CO.

CHARLES CITY CO.

NANSEMOND CO.

Petersburg

DINWIDDIE
CO.

MARYLAND

ROCKINGHAM CO.

AUGUSTA CO.

BEDFORD CO.

NORTH CAROLINA

PITTSYLVANIA CO.

ALLEGHENY MTS.

KASKASKIA, KY.

FT. PITT

DURING the eighteenth century Virginia had developed what Carl Bridenbaugh has called a "unique bourgeois aristocracy,"[1] a ruling class retaining the confidence of the rest of society, which it led in remarkably unified opposition to British encroachments during the fifteen years preceding the Revolution. The Old Dominion shared with Massachusetts the leading colonial role in the imperial quarrel, from the Stamp Act until the outbreak of war.

When Lord Dunmore succeeded the popular Lord Botetourt as governor in 1771, he found himself powerless seriously to influence events, and in the summer of 1775 had to retire to Norfolk, the only place in Virginia congenial to Tories. In November, as a war measure, he proclaimed Virginian slaves to be free; in December, after an earlier success at Kemp's Landing, he suffered military defeat at Great Bridge and fled to the safety of his ships in Chesapeake Bay, whence he was not permanently driven until July, 1776. Meanwhile, in the spring of 1776, an expedition planned by Dunmore and led by John Connolly to rally the Loyalists in the west had failed. For the next three years while the war raged to the north and south, Virginia, unmolested except on the western frontier, but contributing greatly to the Revolutionary armies, established its state government under the reforming leadership of Thomas Jefferson.

In 1779 and 1780 British armies based at Portsmouth carried out a series of raids; finally, in 1781, General Cornwallis lost the initiative and, surrounded on the Yorktown peninsula, was forced to capitulate on October 19, an event which marked the end of fighting not only in Virginia but throughout America.

The King's Friends

The tables reveal that Loyalism in Virginia was mainly a British, and more specifically a Scottish, affair. More than 40 per cent of the claimants were Scottish, and more than 73 per cent came from the British Isles. Date of arrival was not important; only a slight majority emigrated after 1763. A mere 21.5 per cent were Americans. In Virginia Loyalism represented wealth more than in most colonies; over 54 per cent claimed for over £2,000, 28 per cent for over £5,000, and 16 per cent for over £10,000. At the other extreme only eleven claimants wanted less than £500 compensation. Clearly, Toryism in Virginia attracted few people in humble situations. Only one man signed his memorial with a cross.[2]

The bulk of the Loyalists, 64 per cent, were involved in commerce, and many of the large merchants were connected with, or part of, British houses. James Miller, Michael Wallace, Neil Jamieson, Anthony Warwick, and George Logan are the five claimants who specifically mention their Scottish (in four cases Glasgow) partners; but frequent references by other claimants to their dealings in English goods and their re-establishment in trade on returning to Great Britain suggest that they too had intimate transatlantic connections. Further, the antagonism between the planter aristocracy who ruled Virginia and the "foreign" traders, an antagonism heightened by these traders' increasingly suspect behavior as the Anglo-American quarrel advanced, is a commonplace of Virginia history.[3] In December, 1776, the Virginia House of Delegates ordered that all the "natives of Great Britain who were partners with agents, storekeepers, assistant storekeepers, or clerks for any merchant in Great Britain—except only such as heretofore uniformally manifested a friendly disposition to the American cause, or are attached to this country by having wives or children here" be given forty days in which to leave the country.[4]

The merchants seem to have been almost unanimously loyal. Of the seventy-two listed in 1774 as members of the Virginia Merchants Association, four at the most became Patriots.[5] Only one merchant, Jonathan Eilbeck, reported having a partner, David Ross, who was a rebel.[6]

Not surprisingly, Norfolk, the commercial hub of Virginia, was the geographical center of the claimants. Nearly one-third lived there; more than 43 per cent lived in Norfolk and nearby Portsmouth and Gosport combined; if Williamsburg and Petersburg are added about 56 per cent are accounted for. Virginia was a rural colony but Loyalism there was urban. It was also a tidewater phenomenon; all but four claimants lived in tidewater counties.[7] Perhaps if John Connolly's expedition to link up with the west in 1775 had succeeded, many claimants from the back country would have appeared. As it was, potential Loyalism in that area received scant encouragement and did not manifest itself.

All the evidence confirms that the Scots made up the backbone of Virginia Loyalism. An analysis of the forty-seven Scottish claims shows that they usually reflect, as would be expected, the general characteristics of Loyalism in the colony. Half lived at Norfolk or Portsmouth, thirty-six, the great majority, were connected with commerce and trade, and twenty-seven, well over half, had emigrated before 1763. In short, the Scottish Loyalists were a long-established commercial element centered on the Norfolk area.

Virginia Loyalism may have been weak in numbers,

but the evidence suggests that those who were loyal were active participants. Fifty-six, or 43 per cent of the 130 claimants, served in the armed forces, particularly in the Queen's Own Loyal Virginians, which later amalgamated with the Queen's Rangers. Sixty-nine, more than half, served the British in some official capacity. This is a higher proportion than in some colonies.

A high percentage were captured or imprisoned (this partly reflects British military setbacks at Yorktown and earlier). However, Virginia produced no outstanding Loyalist soldier, and military activity was extremely limited because of the failures of Dunmore, Connolly, and Cornwallis.

As with Massachusetts, the other storm center of the Revolution, Virginia has a special interest because of its dominant position. Virginia poses the question, like that which faced Sherlock Holmes, of the dog which did *not* bark at night. There were hardly any Loyalists in the Old Dominion although it was so Anglicized and aristocratic. This study analyzes 130 claimants, but if missing claims are included the number of whites is increased to 157. If the white population was 294,218 in 1776,[8] this is a proportion of 0.053 per cent, one of the smallest. Thus Virginia, with the largest population, had proportionally the third fewest Loyalists. Even in Norfolk, that "infamous nest of Tories," the Loyalists were probably a minority. Mary Rothery, who lived there, suggested as much when she recalled, "Few people would permit Tea to be drank in their Houses."[9] These conclusions agree with the judgment of modern scholars and contemporaries alike who concur that Virginia Loyalism was feeble.[10] In a memorial to William Pitt, the wife of James Hubbard, a native-born

admiralty court judge, recounted that her husband refused
"all the intoxicating seductions of wealth and power" from
the rebels and "submitted to pine for years in honest indi-
gince, secluded from Society, exposed to obloquay," and
finally died "a martyr" from the strain, which clearly suggests that Hubbard was running against the tide.[11]

Further indications of weakness are that the punitive
laws against the Loyalists were leniently applied (no person
was executed for treason by order of the Assembly, or any
court),[12] and that there was a movement, led by Patrick
Henry, favoring the return of the Loyalists after the war.

Also, the testimony of the claimants refers infrequently
to persecution. Anthony Warwick maintained that he was
the only person tarred and feathered in Virginia, but John
Crammond reported suffering this punishment too. John
Turner said he was hung up three times by the rebels in a
vain effort to extract intelligence from him, and Samuel
Greatrex told of four Virginia Loyalists being summarily
executed at Frederick, Maryland. These events are the
whole extent of the persecution reported to the commissioners. That they are so few comes as no surprise, for civil
war, which Virginia largely escaped, and persecution normally went hand in hand.[13]

In some colonies incipient Loyalism can be detected some
years before the actual beginning of the troubles, often as
far back as the Stamp Act. William Orange was beaten by
a mob for taking the British side in the Stamp Act controversy, and George Mercer, the stamp distributor, resigned
after ill-treatment, but these are the only two references
in the claims testimony to early unpopularity. As one witness put it, "there were no Heats and Troubles in Virginia
till the Blockade of Boston in the year 1775."[14]

The King's Friends

One approach to the problem of the weakness of Loyalism in Virginia is to look further at those few native-born Americans who did claim. Twenty-four are analyzed.

Occupations

Farmers	7
Artisans (carpenters)	2
Merchants and shopkeepers	7
Office-holders (attorney-general, customs official, keeper of "the Military Magazine")	3
Professions (doctor, "studying medicine," lawyer, commander of the militia in the west)	4
Unknown	1

Claims

Up to £500	1
£501 to £1,000	2
£1,001 to £2,000	2
£2,001 to £5,000	6
£5,001 to £10,000	3
Over £10,000	5
Unknown	5

Served in the Armed Forces (14)

In the ranks	2
Officers	10
Probably officers	2

Residence

Norfolk	7
Portsmouth	1
Williamsburg	5
Scattered around tidewater	9
Unknown	2

The American-born claimants tended to be in commerce, were usually wealthy (nearly half claimed over £5,000, and

of the three who claimed less than £1,000 one was a lawyer
and another a ship's captain), and probably lived in towns
(more than half lived in Norfolk, Portsmouth, and Williamsburg). Unlike Massachusetts there is here a distinct
dearth of talent and representatives of leading families.
Admittedly the native Loyalists were active, over half serving in the armed forces, and only two reveal themselves
as equivocal in their behavior, but probably only the following should be singled out for special mention: John Connolly, Richard Corbin, Jr., Thomas Corbin, Jacob Ellegood,
John Randolph Grymes, William Byrd Page, and John
Randolph.

John Connolly, Jacob Ellegood, and John Randolph were
certainly leading figures in the colony. Connolly was in
command of the militia in the west defending the frontier
against the Indians. He claimed he "was intimate with
Genl. Washington before the War" and was offered the
command of a regiment by Congress.[15] He went on to
lead an abortive British expedition against Detroit. Ellegood, a leading planter, raised and commanded the Queen's
Loyal Virginia Regiment. Randolph, attorney-general and
a judge of admiralty, was a member of a leading Virginia
family. However, his son Edmund chose the opposite side
and succeeded his father as attorney-general. This high-
lights the fact that a John Randolph was very much the
isolated exception in Virginia.

Richard Corbin, Jr., and Thomas Corbin were from an
eminent Loyalist family. Their father owned one of the
largest estates in Virginia and was receiver-general and a
member of the council, but because of his advanced age he
remained in the colony where he did not help the Patriots
but had to "conform."[16] John R. Grymes at one time

[185]

commanded the Queen's Rangers, while William Byrd Page was studying medicine in Edinburgh when the rebellion began. In passing, two able Loyalists, Ralph Wormley and William Byrd III, from whom there are no claims records, can be mentioned.[17]

Apart from John Randolph, two other native Americans, Thomas Price and Floyd Pitt, came from families split by the Revolution. Price, whose father was Whig, told the commissioners that his mother refused him his inheritance because of his service in the British navy.[18] Pitt followed his father into exile, but his two brothers chose the opposite course.

This discussion of native Loyalism in Virginia merely emphasizes the weakness of the movement. There is nothing save the commercial element to distinguish these Loyalists from the Whigs. The surprise is that the odd wealthy planter, like Lieutenant Colonel Jacob Ellegood, should be found there instead of among the Patriots with the vast majority of his colleagues. Presumably, as was so often the case throughout the colonies, his was an extremely personal decision, stemming from what welter of motives no one will ever know.

Broadly speaking, economic and blood ties are sufficient to explain the position taken by the majority of Virginia Loyalists, the British traders, who had everything to lose from the Revolution and had suffered ever since the non-importation agreements.[19]

In every colony merchants found profit in trade with the British army. Only four Virginia merchant claimants actually mention such trade—William Hargreaves, Hamilton St. George, Andrew Sprowle, who provided barracks at Gosport, and James Miller, who supplied "planks" to

Virginia

Lord Dunmore—but it is known that when Philadelphia fell to the British over one hundred Scottish merchants from Virginia began to trade there.[20]

The nine claimants who were royal officials are also a self-explanatory group, but only occasionally does a claimant in any colony actually name a specific reason—religious principle, private grudge, economic interest—for his loyalty. Only rarely in the Virginia testimony do motives even begin to be articulated.

Thomas Gwatkin, an Anglican minister and professor of languages at the College of William and Mary, recounted that Richard Henry Lee, Jefferson, and others asked him "to draw up Memorials in Vindication of the proceedings of Congress," but he refused "from a regard to the Oath of Allegiance." Similarly, the Reverend Alexander Cruden could not bring himself to break the oath of allegiance, or his ordination vows.[21] William Hunter, the printer of Dixon and Hunter's *Virginia Gazette*, explained with reckless honesty that he changed from the Patriot to the Loyalist side when he thought "the British . . . would prevail." Bernard Carey said that he advised the people of Williamsburg not to fight the British because it would mean certain defeat, and local taxes would be more oppressive than Parliamentary levies. John Randolph Grymes was more wordy: "That however shackled by the Ties of Consanguinity—however embarrassed by his Attachments in that his Native Country Your Memorialist preferred a Compliance with the Duties of the Citizen to the possession of every private Felicity that humanity can enjoy, and by giving his person to the Service of his King he at once sacrificed patrimonial Affluence and all the political advantage flowing from Rank and Estimation . . ." but in fact he reveals less.[22]

Virginia produced no real Loyalist writer or propagandist. Even the Church of England, so often the nucleus of Toryism, was not so in Virginia. Of the approximately one hundred Anglican clergymen, only nine claimed compensation, and about one-third of the whole body took the Patriot side.[23]

There was considerable opposition to an American bishopric throughout Virginia.[24] Typically of the clergy, the Reverend Thomas Gwatkin, although loyal, had opposed the creation of an American bishopric in a pamphlet written in 1771. Another loyal cleric, William Andrews, knocked down in the street for opposing the Declaration of Independence, prayed for the king "but not to the last," and managed to remain in Virginia through the influence of the family of his wife who "was remarkably rebelliously inclined." The Reverend Thomas Fielde was obviously a reluctant Loyalist, his widow reporting that "he wished to have been quiet but he would not take their Oaths and they told him that he must give up his Parish."[25]

In general the congregations were certainly not loyal, and, of course, all the great Virginian Revolutionary leaders such as Washington, Henry, Madison, Pendleton, and even Jefferson were Anglicans of one stamp or another. Political power was bound up with the Anglican church because the parish, administered by a self-perpetuating vestry, was the key unit of local government. Washington, it has been remarked, never missed a vestry meeting. The decentralized church left power firmly in the hands of the vestry, which hired and fired the clergy. The situation was laconically summed up by the Reverend Alexander Cruden, who told the commissioners, "The Vestry are the Patrons of the

Parishes in Virginia." [26] In many ways Virginian Anglicanism was a kind of Congregationalism. [27]

Not one member of the Virginia Assembly or council made a claim, although the Reverend John Camm, Ralph Wormley, Richard Corbin, Garvin Corbin, and William Byrd were undoubtedly Loyalists who had been council members. In June, 1775, the governor could list only five persons prominent in government whom he could trust. Two members of Dunmore's council, John Page and William Nelson, took the Whig side. [28] No graduate of the College of William and Mary is revealed in the claims commissioners' reports, and Harrell notes that only two or three were Loyalists. [29] This is in strong contrast to the contribution of Harvard to the loyal ranks. On the other hand the William and Mary faculty was not all Patriot, although three professors joined the rebel army when the war began. [30] Two members, the Reverend Samuel Henley and the Reverend Thomas Gwatkin, made claims, and the Reverend John Camm, the president, was also loyal.

Hardly any of the Virginia political leadership claimed. Only four local officials are recorded, all magistrates, one of whom, George Logan, was also high sheriff of Bedford County. Thomas Jack told the commissioners that he was the only magistrate in Nansemond County who supported the British. [31]

As far as the central and local political leadership is concerned, one is clearly faced with a remarkably unanimous Whig Virginia. The question is why.

Lord Dunmore, it is generally agreed, was the wrong sort of governor to create or attract a strong government party. His great virtue was that he was active and tried to stem the tide, but he did not act wisely, and his proclamation freeing rebels' slaves who would fight for the British had a very ill effect. As Richard Henry Lee put it at the time, the governor's "unparalleled conduct . . . has, a few Scotch excepted, united every man . . ."[32] Fear of the Negro was probably already welding a "solid" Virginia. Another factor may have been the chronic indebtedness of Virginia planters to British creditors.[33] Although Virginia was overwhelmingly a planters' colony, only sixteen claimants are classified as farmers, and of these only six were substantial planters with claims ranging from £5,000 to over £20,000 and losses of between ten and sixty Negroes.

How far British military failure inhibited Virginia Loyalism will never be known, but its effect must have been considerable. This is shown not only by the obvious connection between British arms and Loyalism in other colonies, but also by the fact that Dunmore's victory at Kemp's Landing in 1775 and Cornwallis' presence in 1780, before the surrender at Yorktown, gave a tremendous if evanescent fillip to Loyalism. This kind of halting, timid Loyalism, like its Whig counterpart, depended on success. After his defeat at Great Bridge much of Dunmore's "loyal" support rapidly vanished.[34]

The weakness of Loyalism in Virginia may not be a paradox at all. Virginia was a homogeneous society in the sense of being free from serious internal divisions. There was no equivalent of the Hutchinson and Oliver—Adams and Otis split in Massachusetts. The traders comprised a tiny minority of the population and had no political power. An aristocracy governed on a practically hereditary basis; yet, because of a wide franchise, it took notice of public opinion: the people followed their leaders, perhaps too blindly, as the

Marquis de Chastellux's often-quoted anecdote suggests. He was told that when the Virginia delegates to Congress, Harrison, Lee, and Jefferson, were about to set out for Philadelphia, ". . . a number of respectable, but uninformed inhabitants, waited upon, and addressed them as follows: 'You assert that there is a fixed intention to invade our rights and privileges; we own that we do not see this clearly but since you assure us that it is so, we believe the fact.' " They added that "[we] are ready to support you in every measure you shall think proper to adopt." It is this extraordinary "confidence they reposed in their leaders" which does much to explain the Virginians' comparative unanimity.[35]

Thus, whichever way Virginians went in the Revolutionary struggle, the great majority would all go the same way. And it was clear that it would be the Patriot way. Virginia was virtually a self-governing dominion (this is what Chastellux had in mind when he named "pride" as possibly being the clue to Virginia's actions).[36] British constitutional, fiscal, and land policies made it seem that the colony had everything to lose by submitting to British encroachments and maintaining the imperial link. If every colony had been like Virginia, Loyalism would have been a negligible force.[37]

XI. NORTH CAROLINA

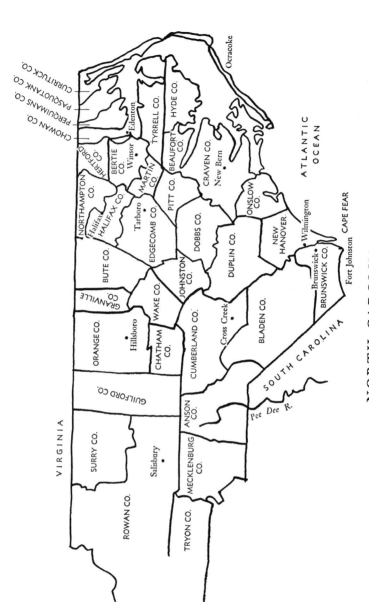

NORTH CAROLINA

ATLANTIC OCEAN

VIRGINIA

SOUTH CAROLINA

CURRITUCK CO.
PASQUOTANK CO.
PERQUIMANS CO.
CHOWAN CO.
HERTFORD CO.
BERTIE CO.
Winsor
Edenton
TYRRELL CO.
HYDE CO.
Ocracoke
MARTIN CO.
BEAUFORT CO.
CRAVEN CO.
New Bern
NORTHAMPTON CO.
Halifax
HALIFAX CO.
Tarboro
PITT CO.
EDGECOMB CO.
DOBBS CO.
ONSLOW CO.
BUTE CO.
DUPLIN CO.
NEW HANOVER
Wilmington
CAPE FEAR
Fort Johnston
GRANVILLE CO.
WAKE CO.
JOHNSTON CO.
Brunswick
BRUNSWICK CO.
ORANGE CO.
Hillsboro
CHATHAM CO.
CUMBERLAND CO.
Cross Creek
BLADEN CO.
GUILFORD CO.
ANSON CO.
Pee Dee R.
SURRY CO.
Salisbury
MECKLENBURG CO.
ROWAN CO.
TRYON CO.

THERE is some doubt about the strength of North Carolina Loyalists. Their historian, Robert O. DeMond, maintained that the colony probably had a higher proportion of Tories than any other province.[1] Governor Josiah Martin was sanguine. On November 4, 1774, he wrote to the Earl of Dartmouth that "my short sojourn [in North Carolina] . . . has led me to conclude that the spirit of Loyalty runs higher here than in any other Colony . . . and that there are in it more friends to Government from principle . . ." However, Martin admitted that the Loyalists lacked confidence, "material support," "assurance of their principles," and an able leader. Further, they could not control the mob, a "Monster" which "people of consideration" had foolishly raised at the time of the Stamp Act, and against which troops should now be sent so that the Loyalists could show themselves.[2]

By 1775 Martin had fewer reservations, informing General Gage on March 16 that he believed the inhabitants of the western counties (the most populous in the colony) would support the government aided by the undoubtedly loyal Highlanders of the middle counties, provided arms were supplied, in which case "I will be answerable to maintain the Sovereignty of this Count[r]y to his Majesty."[3] Later, in June, he thought 20,000 Tories would fight, and on January 10, 1776, he called upon them to gather at Brunswick. Only 1,500 actually assembled, promised British aid did not materialize, and on February 27 at the battle of Moores Creek Bridge the Loyalists were routed.[4] The battle lasted three minutes. "This," commented a contemporary newspaper, "we think, will effectually put a stop to Toryism in North Carolina."[5]

And so it did. The Loyalists were never again a serious threat. Captain Eli Branson, a Virginian, who commanded a company at Moores Creek, noted that he and the other participants "were greatly disappointed discomfitted and finally dispersed and an Endless scene of misery pursued the undertakers of that unfortunate Enterprize." [6] Had the crucial three minutes at Moores Creek Bridge gone the other way, the strength of the Tories would probably have been an entirely different matter.

Further, North Carolina lacked a dominant town, such as Boston, to be occupied by the British and made a Loyalist center. Apart from some guerrilla warfare there was not much more action within the Tar Heel State after Moores Creek until the year of fighting in 1780–1781 when Cornwallis retreated through North Carolina to Virginia with a costly victory at Guilford Courthouse, a stop at Wilmington, and his final surrender at Yorktown. Throughout his retreat little Tory support had manifested itself, especially as it was clear that the British were a losing side. [7] Beyond this, on the American side North Carolina troops had been very active—in Virginia against Dunmore, at home against the Cherokees in 1776, with Washington in New Jersey, and in South Carolina against the Tories at the battle of Kings Mountain.

There are 154 (153 analyzed) North Carolina claimants, about 0.09 per cent of the white population of 1776, [8] which suggests that Loyalist strength was middling compared with other colonies, more than in Pennsylvania and Connecticut, much less than in such strongholds as Georgia and New York.

Van Tyne classifies the laws against the North Carolina Tories as "light," [9] but there were the usual imprisonments, trials, confiscations, and exiles. With the peace many conservatives such as William Hooper, an aristocratic signer of the Declaration of Independence, urged moderation, and in 1783 many of the less notorious Loyalists were pardoned, but the sale of Tory estates continued until 1790.[10] Less evidence of persecution is found in the claims commission testimony than for any other colony: no tarring and feathering, no rail riding, no mob brutalities were mentioned. A partial explanation for this mildness may be North Carolina's lack of a large town where a substantial mob could be recruited and organized. The only atrocity mentioned is in the case (presented by his sisters) of Mathew Colville, a rich Irish planter. Colville was allegedly murdered in 1781 while entertaining some of his neighbors with a view to giving them commissions in the regiment he had just been given by Cornwallis. A year later his nephew was attacked and nearly killed while attempting to recover his uncle's property.[11]

The treatment of the Tory prisoners after the defeat at Moores Creek Bridge in 1776 supports the general picture of moderation in North Carolina. The prisoners were exiled, but committees were appointed to see to the welfare of the women and children left behind.[12] For months after the battle pardon was offered to anyone who would take the oath of allegiance although "few or none" did.[13]

Yet it would be incorrect to leave the impression of a complete lack of bitterness in North Carolina. A state of civil war existed at times. In particular the cruel raids of Colonel Edmund Fanning must be recalled. Also, Colonel John Hamilton was very active in the backlands of the two Carolinas and Georgia. In 1779 a number of North Carolina Loyalists, embodied under a Colonel Boyd, were defeated by Colonel Pickens at Kettle Creek, South Carolina. Boyd and many others were killed, but seventy Tory prisoners were tried and convicted of treason, and five were actually hanged.[14] This occurred in South Carolina, but there were many murders and atrocities in North Carolina, mainly connected with the guerrilla war.[15]

The tables[16] show that the largest single occupation category is the farmers, with 46.5 per cent of the whole. Then come the merchants and shopkeepers with 29.5 per cent, the office-holders with over 11 per cent, and the professional people with 3.5 per cent. The combined commercial element is 39 per cent. At least 95 per cent of the inhabitants of North Carolina were farmers; therefore it is clear that a relatively small proportion were Loyalists as compared with the proportion of merchants, shopkeepers, and the rest.

These farmers who were loyal were mostly yeomen, few owned slaves, very few claimed more than £2,000, and the great majority claimed £1,000 or less. Only one can be classified as a great planter—Mathew Colville, who claimed £12,350 losses which included sixty Negroes and over 5,000 acres. Of the fifty-seven farmers whose birthplaces are known, 79 per cent were British (58 per cent Scottish), and 21 per cent American. Thus the question of the motives of the farmers primarily concerns the Scots.

The merchants submitted some of the largest claims—eleven, well over half the claims for more than £10,000. Colonel John Hamilton, a Scottish merchant from Halifax who claimed more than £50,000 (his trading house was the largest in the colony), combined wealth with great usefulness to the British. He raised and commanded the North Carolina Regiment and led them on missions in the Carolinas and Georgia, during which he was wounded three times.[17] Charles Stedman wrote, "The British nation owed more, perhaps, to Colonel Hamilton, . . . than to any other individual Loyalist in the British service."[18] Hamilton retained respect in America and after the war became British consul in Virginia.[19]

The table of claims reveals a fairly even distribution, 21 per cent for £500 or less, 14.5 per cent for more than £10,000. Forty per cent claimed for sums of £1,000 or less, 65 per cent for less than £2,000, so there is a very slight trend towards rather modest wealth, but all levels are represented.

Seventy-nine per cent of the claimants were immigrants from the British Isles; of these a handful were from Ireland and England, but the great bulk were Scots—over 54 per cent of the total claimants, a figure which is almost certainly somewhat higher because at least some of the individuals listed in the tables as from Great Britain, or unknown, had Scottish names. In 1790 only 14.8 per cent of the North Carolina population was Scottish or of Scottish descent.[20] Native Americans account for only about 20 per cent of the claimants. Not one German is found, which suggests that this element in the population was solidly Whig.[21]

Chief Areas of Residence

County	Claimants
Cumberland	35 (13 at Cross Creek)
Anson	18
New Hanover	14 (13 at Wilmington)
Bladen	10
Halifax	7 (6 at Halifax)
Brunswick	7 (4 at Cape Fear)
Craven	6 (all at New Bern)
Rowan	5 (4 at Salisbury)

The King's Friends

Claimants are found in twenty of the approximately thirty counties which existed in 1776, and Loyalists are found scattered around most parts of the colony, but several concentrations stand out. Cumberland, a middle inland county with thirty-five claimants (thirteen of whom lived at Cross Creek), leads with about 28 per cent of the total. Add the neighboring counties, Anson and Bladen, and over 52 per cent are accounted for. Add another middle county, Halifax, and the frontier county, Rowan, and over 62 per cent are covered. This distribution reflects the Scots element in North Carolina Loyalism, because the great bulk were Scottish immigrant farmers.

The next most noticeable concentration of Loyalists are the thirteen who lived at Wilmington, New Hanover County. Wilmington was the commercial center of the Cape Fear area and chief port of the entire colony. Seven of the claimants were merchants, one owned a salt works, two were doctors, one a royal official, and one unknown. Only three were natives of America.

Apart from Wilmington the only coastal pockets of Loyalists are represented by the seven claimants from Brunswick County (four of whom lived at Cape Fear, two at Brunswick, and one at Fort Johnston), and the six from Craven County (all of whom lived at New Bern, the seat of the governor and the legislature). Only one claimant in each of the two areas was American born, and most were either merchants or office-holders. New Bern had three merchants and three officials (including the governor), Brunswick County three merchants, two officials, and two farmers.

Finally the six claimants from Halifax, an important inland trading town on the Roanoke River, should be noted. All were British merchants, including some of the richest in the colony. However, the town was clearly deeply divided over the Revolution. Governor Martin, as a witness for Andrew Miller, a wealthy Halifax trader, testified that Miller had been asked in vain to take the rebel part with his friends, friends to whom he was attached "by long habits of intimacy."[22]

A study of estates confiscated between 1784 and 1787 reveals sales in twenty-nine counties with Orange, Bladen, and Rowan topping the list. The conclusion is that loyal planters were found in almost all parts of the state.[23]

The Whigs were strong in all areas, but especially in the eastern tidewater, the area which controlled the solidly Whig Assembly.

Take away the British (particularly Scottish) farmers and merchants, and the few royal officials, and there is little left of the North Carolina Loyalist movement as described by the claimants. This is illustrated by the fact that although six members of the royally appointed council were claimants, only one Assembly member and seven local officials (one sheriff and six justices of the peace) filed claims. In 1772 Henry McCulloch lost his position as colonial agent because of "his principles in favor of Government which did not accord with the prejudices of the Inhabitants."[24] In April, 1775, all but one of the members of the Assembly which met at New Bern were also members of the illegal provincial convention which convened concurrently. As early as 1774 power passed to the Whigs in North Carolina without a struggle. Governor Martin, though an able man, was an impotent bystander. After Lexington he had to flee to Fort Johnston and thence to a British ship on the Cape Fear River. Since becoming governor in 1771, Martin had been at loggerheads with the Assembly, which was controlled by eastern planters and merchants. The ruling class, like its counterpart in Virginia, remained solidly Whig when the Revolution came and fought to retain power and autonomy. Only one claimant can be classed as a great planter and he was Irish. Only twenty-eight (21 per cent) of the claimants were American born, and only five of these claimed more than £2,000. Of these only Samuel Cornell, a member of the council who claimed over £60,000, was a member of the great merchant class. Thus the claims commission evidence points strongly to a very patriotic native-born upper class, especially within the ranks of the very large planters and merchants.[25]

In summary, the tables show that a North Carolina Loyalist claimant was most likely a Scottish immigrant farmer living in an inland county (especially Cumberland or Anson), or less probably a British merchant or office-holder living around the Cape Fear estuary, or in New Bern. If in the former group, the Loyalist was probably much less wealthy than if in the latter.

Between 1768 and 1771 North Carolina was racked by a revolt of the back-country farmers against the tidewater aristocracy, a quarrel stemming from class and geographical divisions. The Regulator movement, as it was called, was directed against the inefficiency and corruption of local government, especially the courts, and was finally crushed by Governor Tryon at the battle of Alamance in 1771.

There is some contemporary evidence, seemingly rather misinformed, that the Regulators and the Tories were linked. John Adams was certainly of this view.[26] On April 20, 1775, Governor Martin wrote to the Earl of Dartmouth that he expected and trusted the loyalty of the ex-Regulators who "remember very properly the correction they received for their offences from Governor Tryon and the solemn Oath of Allegiance they took at that time . . ." [27] After the battle of Moores Creek Bridge, the provincial council resolved that the Patriot commander and his men be thanked for suppressing the "dangerous insurrection of the Highlanders and Regulators . . ." [28]

The claims commission testimony gives no indication that any Regulators (or "Banditti" as Governor Tryon called them) [29] were Loyalists. In fact, the evidence points the other way—several persons, such as Colonel Edmund Fanning (who later moved to New York), Robert Palmer, an important royal official, and Richard Wilson, an Irish veteran of the Seven Years War, mentioned their part in suppressing the Regulator revolt, presumably as evidence of their loyalty. [30] Thomas McKnight invoked his opposition to the Regulators as "an early instance of his attachment to his Country." [31] Lewis Henry De Rossett pointed out that he was Governor Tryon's adjutant at the battle of Alamance in 1771. [32] Jonas Bedford, an American-born farmer, marched a body of men 220 miles to join Tryon at Hillsboro in 1768, and Arthur Benning, the Irish owner of a salt works, led 120 Light Horse Volunteers from Wilmington to help the governor in 1771. [33] Ann Hulton noted in Boston on January 31, 1774, that Jonathan Malcolm, a customs official, had just been tarred and feathered for the second time, a fate she attributed to a grudge owed him because "he was of great servise" to Tryon against the Regulators. [34]

Anson, Rowan, and Orange Counties were the chief areas of Regulator influence. Only seven claimants are found in the latter two counties, but Anson supplied eighteen. But thirteen of the total of twenty-five claimants from the three counties did not arrive in America until the Regulator movement was over, and there is no evidence that the remaining twelve had anything to do with it. Granville, Guilford, and Surry Counties were three further areas of Regulator strength. Granville had one claimant, the latter two had none.

This lack of evidence of any Regulator influence in North Carolina Loyalism is in accord with the trend of modern scholarship. A recent history of North Carolina shows that of 883 known Regulators 289 were Whigs, thirty-four Tories, and the rest unknown.[35] Herman Husband, the Regulator leader, was not a Tory.

The conclusion must be that some Regulators, a small minority, were Tories. The motives of these few probably stem from the fair treatment they received from Tryon's successor, Martin; dislike of the ruling eastern seaboard gentry, who were responsible for their grievances in the first place; and, connected with this, the opportunity for revenge (a point made by John Adams). The oath of allegiance they had had to take after the defeat at Alamance was also a factor.[36] In August, 1775, one Samuel Williams reported to the British that at a public meeting in Anson County, Colonel Samuel Spencer, while trying to get support for the Association, was asked by some about the oath of allegiance they had taken. Spencer replied that they were absolved because George III had broken his coronation oath. Later, Williams believed that the Patriots had enlisted "vast numbers."[37]

The Church of England was not established in North Carolina until 1765,[38] but its influence in binding the colony to the homeland was fully realized. In 1771 the Reverend

Dr. George Micklejohn preached a sermon to the troops mustered against the Regulators entitled "On the important Duty of Subjection to the Civil Powers." [39]

On November 4, 1774, Governor Martin, writing to the Earl of Dartmouth, noted the "congeniality of the principles of the Church of England with our form of Government." He also pointed out that the loyal part of the population was Anglican and the disloyal part Presbyterian, and therefore, rather belatedly, appealed on political grounds for an increase in the number of Anglican clergy.[40] On the eve of the Revolution the church was extremely weak in North Carolina (the whole of Granville County had only one clergyman), and although that important segment of the Loyalists, the royal officials, was Anglican, the church did not play an important part in the Loyalist movement. Only one cleric, the Reverend William Mackenzie (a Scot), rector of Granville Parish, submitted a claim.[41] At least three ministers actually remained at their jobs throughout the war —Charles Pettigrew, who married a rebel's daughter, Daniel Earl, of Edenton,[42] and George Micklejohn. Micklejohn's actions illustrate that Vicar-of-Brayism which was so common in the south. He was captured at Moores Creek Bridge and paroled, but later took the oath to the new regime and followed a successful ecclesiastical career in North Carolina and later in Virginia.[43]

Although the claims commission testimony only rarely mentions it, most of the Scots, the main body of the claimants, were Highlanders. The question is, why should these traditional opponents of the House of Hanover, with bitter memories of 1715 and 1745, fight for their erstwhile enemy? One reason is that over half were very recent immigrants; at least forty-one of the seventy-five Scottish claimants had arrived in 1771 or later, and most of the others had come in 1770 or the late 1760's. Thus the Scots had little chance of becoming Americanized (especially as they continued to live in clans), were unaffected by most of the issues of the Revolution, and were grateful to the British government which had allowed them a fresh start and land in the New World. Alexander Morrison noted that he left Scotland in 1772 with 300 emigrants because his rent had been raised five times. Significantly, he claimed to have lost a plantation of 1,100 acres in North Carolina.[44]

A recent student of North Carolina Highland Scots gives four general reasons for their loyalty:[45]

(1) The English knack in the eighteenth century of making friends of former enemies, such as the French Canadians. The Highlanders had been successfully pacified since 1745 and the clansmen had served England well during the Seven Years War. Also, many Scots were from Argyll-shire where the Campbells were traditionally loyal to Hanover (only one person named Campbell submitted a claim, however).

(2) The threats by Governor Martin and others of punishment (including loss of property) for rebellion. Highlanders remembered 1715 and 1745, and, as another scholar has suggested, did not want to lose a third time.[46]

(3) Governor Martin had been generous with land grants in 1775. Allied to this was the fact that many who had received land had taken loyalty oaths. Even if oaths might be disregarded, the fear of losing land could not—there was even the danger of losing property still owned in Scotland.

(4) Highlanders who were retired officers (on half-pay), such as Flora McDonald's husband, Allan, gave immediate

loyal leadership (however, no Scottish claimant identified himself as a former officer).

This final point concerning leadership deserves emphasizing. The Highlanders stuck together and were loyal to their leaders. A witness in the case of Major Alexander McLeod perhaps hinted as much, noting that McLeod raised a company in the area where he lived and therefore must have been wealthy, because no one "would follow any Man as a Leader unless he was possessed of Property." [47] Alexander Schaw, a visiting Scot, ascribed the Highlanders' loyalty to the "gentlemen . . . several of whom have been officers . . . [who] still retain their influence among the people." He also mentioned Governor Martin's kindly behavior.[48]

Contemporary evidence confirms the suggestion of the claims analysis that most of the Scots were Loyalists. Governor Martin wrote to Major Alexander McLeod in July, 1775, of "the good dispositions that are manifested by the Highlanders throughout the Province in this time of unnatural revolt . . ." [49] A witness told the claims commissioners that he believed that the North Carolina Highlanders were generally loyal.[50]

They were also exceptionally active. Fifty-nine of the seventy-five Scottish claimants served in the armed forces, nearly all in the North Carolina Highlanders, and at least forty-three of these were at the disastrous battle of Moores Creek Bridge. This commitment may be partly a reason for, as well as a sign of, Loyalism. The Highlanders had been organized before the defeat and thus, unlike some potential Loyalists, had a chance to show themselves. Alexander McDonald, a loyal New York Highlander, told the claims commissioners that while organizing the Mohawk Scots he sent an officer to North Carolina disguised as a peddler "to inform by word of Mouth several hundred Highlanders" because "he durst not venture to write." Later the North Carolina Highlanders were defeated because they were ill-armed and British help did not arrive.[51]

Together with the back-country Scottish farmers, the merchants constitute the most important element in the North Carolina Loyalist movement. Forty-five of the sixty-eight people named in the North Carolina Confiscation Act of 1779 were merchants.[52] A. M. Schlesinger has demonstrated the sluggishness of the merchants in the early Revolutionary movement.[53] Although there were many conspicuous exceptions, especially in the Cape Fear region, the majority of the North Carolina merchants were loyal.[54]

Forty-two merchants and shopkeepers (more than 29 per cent of those whose occupations are known) submitted claims. The total is increased to forty-four if two office-holders who were also merchants are included. Only six of these can be identified as American born; the rest were from the British Isles, mostly Scotland. The majority had arrived after 1763. Quite apart from their nativity and recent arrival, matters of trade inclined the merchants toward Loyalism. The North Carolina test act of May, 1777, admitted as much because it was directed particularly against those who had "traded immediately to Great Britain or Ireland within ten years last past, in their own Right, or acted as Factors, Storekeepers, or Agents" for British merchants.[55] Many merchant Loyalists were factors of British houses,[56] and three claimants positively identify themselves as connected with British firms. The large merchants' trade was mainly with Britain and the West Indies. Naval stores were subsidized by Britain. John Rutherford, who claimed over

£20,000 in losses, sent tar and turpentine to the home country and shingles (from a mill that cut 20,000 feet of lumber a week) to the West Indies.[57] Some of the large houses depended upon British credit.[58] There was also the allure of trade with the British army, in which activity Colin Clarke, a hard-drinking British merchant from Windsor, Bertie County, was engaged for most of the war.[59] Connor Dowd, an illiterate Irishman and ex-peddler, supplied the British with provisions.[60]

After farmers and merchants the biggest category of Loyalist claimants is the royal office-holders. Little need be said about their motives. Jonas Bedford, in his memorial to the commissioners, claimed to quote himself in reply to a rebel officer: "I have been Sworn as an Officer and Magistrate under my lawful Sovereign. I never will turn my back to my King's cause and perjure myself. I shall remain a loyal Honest Subject during my life to my King and Country."[61] Throughout the colonies office-holders seem to have taken their oaths of allegiance seriously. The rest of the population seldom had to take a formal oath (the Highlanders were a rare exception).

American-born Loyalists, the hardest to explain, comprised only about one in five of the North Carolina claimants. An analysis of these twenty-eight claimants reveals no features to distinguish them from the rest in North Carolina (except that a very slightly greater proportion were farmers). Two were royal officials, seven were merchants, one was a miller, and eleven were farmers. The claimants' testimony tells us almost nothing about motives. Presumably in each case it was a very personal matter, as is suggested by the fact that James Pemberton, a loyal Bladen County farmer, had a rebel brother.

In Colonel David Fanning the American-born supplied one of the most notorious and ferocious of all Loyalists. He admitted to the commissioners that he had served for a year in the rebel militia before going over to the British for whom, as an understating witness put it, he "commanded a number of free-booters who were much feared by the Rebels." His exploits included the capture of the governor of North Carolina, Thomas Burke, and his council.[62] It has been suggested that the reason for Fanning's change of allegiance was that he suffered at the hands of an allegedly Whig gang, and his unstable cruel character may have been partly caused by a physical deformity—a scalded head which he always kept covered with a silk cap.[63]

XII. SOUTH CAROLINA

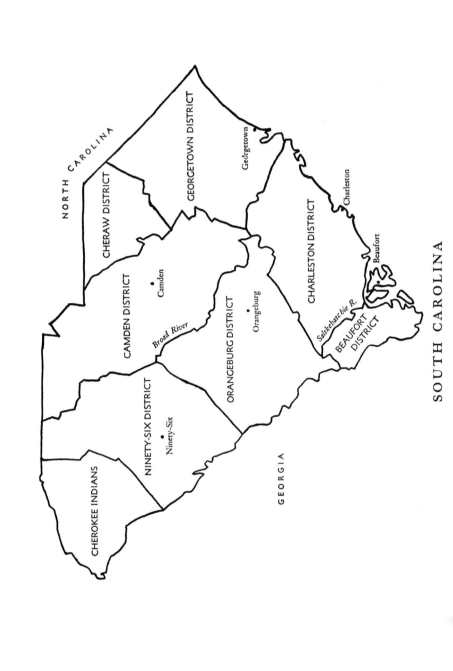

SOUTH CAROLINA

NORTH CAROLINA

CHERAW DISTRICT

GEORGETOWN DISTRICT

Georgetown

CHARLESTON DISTRICT

Charleston

Beaufort

CAMDEN DISTRICT

Camden

Broad River

ORANGEBURG DISTRICT

Orangeburg

Salkehatchie R.

BEAUFORT DISTRICT

NINETY-SIX DISTRICT

Ninety-Six

CHEROKEE INDIANS

GEORGIA

SOUTH CAROLINA possessed in Charleston the only real city of the South, a city which was the focus of the Low Country, Anglican, slave-holding, rice- and indigo-growing aristocracy who largely ruled the colony. Between 1765 and 1770 South Carolina experienced a bitter Regulator movement which, like the one in North Carolina, was an upcountry revolt of noncon-formist small farmers against lawlessness, lack of local government, and underrepresentation in the tidewater dominated Assembly.

This sectional conflict did not prevent the colony (apart from a small clique around the royal governor) from offer-ing strong united opposition to British policy, from the Stamp Act crisis of 1765 until the Revolution. In January, 1775, a provincial congress met at Charleston and royal government rapidly disappeared with hardly any protest.

In June, 1776, the Patriots beat off a British attack on Charleston and at the same time defeated the pro-British Cherokees on the border. The South remained secure for nearly three years until May, 1780, when General Clinton captured Charleston. In August the British beat the Patriot force under General Gates at the battle of Camden and secured the upcountry. But partisans continued to harass the British and Tories in bitter civil war, and finally the Patriot victory at Kings Mountain in October, 1780, turned the tide, although it was not until December, 1782, that Charleston was evacuated.

There are 328 claimants (320 of whom are analyzed in the tables) from South Carolina. This is 0.47 per cent of the white population of 69,426 in 1776,[1] almost as high as the proportion for New York and much higher than in any other colony, north or south, except Georgia. Charleston, with 2.17 per cent of the white population of 6,000 in 1775 as claimants, stands forth as the most strongly loyal city in all America, more than twice as strong as Boston, and more than four times as strong as New York City. When the British evacuated Charleston in 1782, nearly 4,000 whites (not all residents of Charleston, or even of South Carolina), sailed with them, compared with 1,100 who departed from Boston in similar circumstances.[2]

Van Tyne considers South Carolina and New York the two states which enacted the harshest anti-Loyalist legislation.[3] This reflects the great Tory strength in the two areas, although South Carolina did not act decisively until 1781, by which time the harsh British occupation and the civil war had caused great bitterness. However, in spite of some articulate radical opposition in Charleston and general agreement that British debts should not be paid, South Carolina under conservative leadership dealt very leniently with the Loyalists after the peace treaty; many of the banished returned, and by 1786 most confiscated estates had been restored.[4] Patrick Cunningham, a notable Loyalist soldier, returned to Charleston in early 1785 and successfully petitioned to be allowed to remain, although he was fined 12 per cent of his property and denied political rights for seven years. (In fact, he served two terms in the legislature during this time.)[5] His seems to have been a more typical case than that of one Love, a participator in a massacre, who was lynched in 1785 at Ninety-Six after having been acquitted by the court.[6]

The South Carolina claimants mention three mobbings, one whipping, and one tarring and feathering. George

Walker, the English gunner at Fort Johnson (by Charleston), has left a vivid account of this latter experience.

> On the 12th of August 1775 went on board a Brigantine to Charlestown from Philadelphia the Master whose name was Workman desired a clearance . . . the Master asked him to drink damnation to King Geo. the 3d and all the rascalls about him. Witness refused and as soon as he conveniently could retired on Shore. Soon afterwards he was met by a mob consisting of 500 people who seized and carried him to the Royal Exchange where he underwent a sham Trial at which Dr Budd and Mr Ferguson presided and was condemned for a Tory and an Enemy to the Country—he was sentenced to be put into a cart, Stripp'd naked, Tarred and Feathered all over his body and pelted with whatever might be found in the Street and in that condition to remain 5 hours at the expiration whereof to be put under a pump and pumped upon one hour and finally be thrown over the end of Col. Beals Wharf into the River. The whole of this Sentence was immediately and punctually carried into Execution—by the fall from the Wharf two of his ribs were broken and he received other wounds in different parts of his Body—and in consequence of the Tar has nearly lost the Sight of his left Eye. His Life was preserved by his boat happening to be near the place of his fall by which he was taken up and conveyed to the Fort.[7]

Ten unspecified "murders" and a further ten executions, usually following capture in a military engagement, were mentioned to the claims commissioners. They reflect the fury of the internecine war in the back country. After the Tory defeat at Kings Mountain nine prisoners, followers of the hated Patrick Ferguson, were summarily executed.[8] As in other colonies there were also mental victims. The widow of Dr. Robert Gibbs recounted that the prospect of the loss of his property "so preyed upon his Spirits" that he died.[9] A witness in the case of Alexander Harvey, a

Charleston lawyer, testified that Harvey was in a private madhouse having been "driven to Distraction" by his loyalty.[10]

A general reason for the great strength of Loyalism in South Carolina was fear of British power, especially in view of the dangers of the large number of slaves, the Cherokee threat on the frontier, and the long stretch of unprotected seacoast.[11] This fear was realized when the British occupied Charleston from May, 1781, until December, 1782.

Even the besieging of the city before its capitulation gave the Loyalists "strength and Courage," according to James Alexander. It also provided an opportunity to pay off old scores—Alexander and others sought out a Captain John Felder who "had for some years cruelly oppressed the Loyalists," surrounded his house, set it on fire, and shot the unfortunate occupant.[12] And there was always the temptation to deal with the British for profit.[13] The British occupation resulted in many Loyalists' at last getting the freedom to show themselves, while many other neutrals and even Whigs bent with the wind and temporarily became Loyalists.

Charleston was the metropolis and entrepôt of the state, and thus when it fell the whole state fell. The British rapidly established complete, if rather shortlived, control of the entire back country. It must be mentioned, however, that early British failure to capture Charleston (under Sir Henry Clinton in June, 1776) had been a great blow to the Loyalists at the beginning of the rebellion and had helped the Whigs to become firmly entrenched. What one witness said of two claimants was doubtless widely true, that they "were liable to be swayed by the prevailing Party." [14] The Whig commander at Ninety-Six, General Andrew Williamson, not only surrendered but became a Loyalist.[15] Robert Gray, a Loyalist colonel, noted that with the British occupation "the Whigs and Tories seemed to vie with each other in giving proof of the sincerity of their submission . . ." [16]

The arrival of the British was a blessing for the Loyalists. The British encouragement of the Cherokees to attack the back country alienated many Tories.[17] One claimant's entire losses were damages caused by the British troops,[18] while William Wragg, a very prominent Loyalist and member of the council (and incidentally one of the few Americans commemorated in Westminster Abbey), lamented being "exposed to the alternate depredations of both Parties." [19] James Simpson, the attorney-general, reported to Lord Germain on August 28, 1779, that a recent British raiding force in South Carolina had "shamefully plundered" loyal inhabitants "in return for their hospitality." [20] Colonel Gray placed abuses such as "taking the peoples Horses, Cattle and provisions in many cases without paying for them" as second only to "the disaffection of the Whigs" in ending the brief tranquillity which followed the British occupation.[21]

Strong as the Tories were in South Carolina, they were a minority. David Ramsay was sure that the Whigs were a solid majority "great in number, and in weight and influence greater still," [22] a conclusion borne out by contemporary Loyalist witnesses. Angus Macaulay arrived in the colony in 1773 and at once "clearly perceived from the Humour of the people and the Temper of the Times that the only road to popularity and Fortune in that Province was to join in the cry for what they called Liberty and to exclaim against every Measure of Government."[23]

Paul Hamilton fled at the beginning of the troubles because it was "dangerous, nay Madness longer to oppose" the Whigs.[24] Another claimant remarked that in Charleston (the Tory stronghold) the "Generality of Gentlemen were Whigs."[25] Thomas Irving said that "although many persons continued friendly to the British Government yet with such violence were the measures of the disaffected carried on that few besides the Officers of the Crown dared to oppose the measures of the leading party or even avow their Sentiments."[26]

George Ogilvie admitted that without British support "active exertions of Loyalty were impossible."[27] Many claimants mention having either to flee into the countryside or remain in Charleston and submit to the rebels. Governor Bull had to retreat in the autumn of 1775 to avoid the "insults of the people."[28] Colonel Robert Gray wrote, "The loyal part of the inhabitants being about one third part of the whole and these by no means the wealthiest . . ."[29]

The Patriots assumed power with barely any opposition, and even the able native-born governor, William Bull, was powerless to influence events. When Lord William Campbell arrived to replace Bull in 1775, royal government was, in the words of Chief Justice Thomas Knox Gordon, an "empty name" and a "Mockery."[30] The ruling class was quite solidly Whig—no members of the Commons House of Assembly and only five justices of the peace and four councilors submitted claims. Nearly half the councilors, led by William Henry Drayton, were Whigs, and colonial upper houses were invariably more loyal than the lower.[31]

There are no early divisions dating back to the Stamp Act and other crises which presage the Whig-Tory split. Chief Justice Gordon, for example, told the commissioners that until the troubles began he was perfectly able to please both the people and his superiors equally well.[32]

The solid Whig front of the South Carolina ruling class (especially if native born or planter) requires some explanation. Motives were probably similar to those of the Virginia aristocrats: power was firmly in their hands and they were not disposed to brook interference from Britain, back-country Regulators, or anyone else.

Loyalism in South Carolina was largely an immigrant phenomenon; only about one in five of the claimants was native born. Irishmen (generally Scotch-Irish) make up 25 per cent, Scotsmen more than 19, and Englishmen about 16 per cent of the claimants. The total for the British Isles is 70 per cent. Finally, the twenty-three Germans, about 8 per cent of the whole, comprise a significant minority.[33] Twice as many immigrants had arrived after 1763 as before.

Most economic levels and occupations are found in the tables. The largest single occupation group is the farmers (45 per cent). Taking a claim of £2,000 or more as the criterion for a planter, or large farmer, 24 per cent fall into that category, and 76 per cent appear as small farmers. (It must be remembered also that several rich officials, professional men, and merchants also owned plantations.) More than 20 per cent of the claimants were merchants and shopkeepers (mainly Scots and English), more than 9 per cent artisans (the combined commercial element is over 31 per cent), while office-holders and professional men contributed over 11 per cent each.

Almost as many Loyalists claimed £5,000 or more as

claimed £500 or less (a majority of these poorer Loyalists were Irish and Germans). Nearly 60 per cent claimed £2,000 or less so there is a slight tendency towards moderate wealth. However, thirty-four claimants, nearly one in nine (including ten Americans, nine Scots, and seven English), claimed amounts of £10,000 or more, a proportion much higher than the proportion of very wealthy to the whole population. As most of the population were farmers and very few were worth even £2,000, the conclusion must be that the wealthy, the planters, the traders, the office-holders, and the professional men contributed most heavily to the Loyalist ranks as reflected by the claimants.

Claimants are found in all seven districts of South Carolina, but only in insignificant numbers in Cheraw, Beaufort, Orangebury, and Georgetown. The concentrations of Loyalists are in Camden (over 11 per cent of the claimants, mainly Irish and American), Ninety-Six (30 per cent, usually Irish, but to a lesser extent Germans and Americans), and Charleston (50 per cent—about 6 per cent in the district, and 44 per cent in the city, about equal numbers of Scots and English, followed quite closely by a solid minority of Americans, and a handful of Irish and Germans). These three areas account for over 90 per cent of the claimants. The Loyalist strength in South Carolina lay along a central band stretching from Charleston inland to Ninety-Six, while the northern and southern flanks were very weak. Charleston emerges as clearly the most important Loyalist center—especially when it is noted that most of the claimants for Charleston district lived close by the city. The highest proportion of Loyalists may have been in the Ninety-Six district in the fork between the Broad and the Saluda Rivers which, according to David Ramsay, was the only part of the colony where the Tories were in a majority.[34] Colonel Gray believed that "about one half" of the people in the district were loyal.[35] However, in terms of actual claimants Charleston emerges as the most strongly Loyalist area in the colony.

An analysis of the Charleston claimants shows that they made up the great bulk of the artisans, the traders, the royal officials, and the professional men. Also, there was a striking trend towards great wealth; nearly twice as many claimed for more than £2,000 as for less, and the claims for over £10,000 or more (twenty-four of the total of thirty-four for the whole colony) are the second largest category. Only nine Loyalists claimed for sums of £500 or less. The proportion of immigrants is even higher in Charleston than for the colony, but English and Scottish predominate rather than the Irish.[36]

Analysis of claimants by nationality is interesting. Apart from a sprinkling of artisans and traders, the Irish were mainly poor or moderately prosperous farmers living in the Camden or, more usually, the Ninety-Six district. By contrast the Scots were a remarkably wealthy group—only one individual claimed £500 or less and most claimed £2,000 or more—and presented a complete cross-section of occupations, but with rich merchants and planters most important. Almost all the Scots lived in Charleston or nearby (a very few at Ninety-Six), and the majority had arrived before 1763, thus having had time to settle down and accumulate wealth. Of the 109 members of the St. Andrew's Club in Charleston when the war began thirty-two were Loyalists, fifteen Whigs, and the rest unknown.[37]

The English were very similar to the Scots although somewhat less uniformly prosperous and more predominantly traders (only four farmers claimed). Also the concentration in Charleston was more pronounced. The only striking contrast is that most of the English arrived after 1763.

Apart from three merchants and an artisan living in Charleston, all the German claimants were poor farmers from the Ninety-Six district. A very slight majority had arrived after 1763. The poverty of the Germans and the Irish is reflected by the fact that almost all the former and two-fifths of the latter went to Canada after the war. Conversely, most of the English and Scots returned to Great Britain.

Nativity and, in many cases, wealth and recent arrival may be sufficient to explain the loyalty of immigrants from the British Isles. The native-born claimants present more of a problem. They were overwhelmingly farmers and generally lived in three districts—Charleston, Ninety-Six, and Camden. All levels of wealth are found, and great riches are not the clue to the loyalty of the majority of American claimants; rather there is a slight tendency to moderate wealth. But in some cases riches may offer a partial explanation. William Gist was a farmer, surveyor, and justice of the peace in the Ninety-Six district, and, as a witness put it to the commissioners, only two or three were better off in the back parts of South Carolina.[38] Gist's loyalty may well be the result of a fear of losing his respectable position, and memories of the fate of the neighboring Regulators may also have been vividly in his mind.

A connection with officialdom provides plausible motives for a further eight Americans: five were royal officials, one was a member of the council, one was the son of a councilor, and at least one had recently been educated in England.

Apart from pecuniary considerations, an official might well find himself like John Bremar, surveyor-general of the king's lands, "obnoxious to the populace from his Office." [39] George Hartley, organist at St. Michael's Church and previously in the same position at King's Chapel, Boston, is another whose background probably led him inevitably to Loyalism.[40]

As in other colonies one is obliged to say that the decision to be a Loyalist must have been an intensely personal matter with many, especially the native-born. Split families always suggest this—Robert Cooper's brother Samuel was a Whig captain, and Henry Peronneau, a leading South Carolinian, came from a famous Patriot family. A few more examples concern immigrant claimants. Alexander Harvey, a Charleston lawyer, had a Whig father; Janet Cumming, a midwife, had a rebel son, as did Dr. Alexander Garden (the able naturalist after whom gardenias are named); Elizabeth Henry of the Ninety-Six district, who later carried intelligence for the British, was turned out of the house by her French-born Whig husband; and most conspicuously of all, Governor Bull was opposed by his nephew, Stephen.[41]

There is much evidence that many Loyalists were timid, particularly the American-born South Carolina claimants, twenty-three (more than one-third) of whom admitted equivocal actions to the claims commissioners. The twenty-three included six who took the rebel oath and eight who served in the rebel militia, one of whom ascribed his action to "fear." [42] Elizabeth Barkesdale, a planter's widow, admitted forthrightly that her husband had taken part neither for nor against Great Britain.[43] Several others left the colony at the first whiff of danger, as did John Bremar, who fled in May, 1775.[44]

David Ramsay wrote that "men of ardor" were usually Whigs while the Tories were "the ignorant, the selfish, and the timid." This may be an exaggeration,[45] but it is a fact that in general the Whigs acted vigorously, the Tories "feebly."[46] Indeed, they were encouraged in this because Lord William Campbell, the last governor, "uniformly recommended the royalists to remain quiet" until the British forces arrived; meanwhile the Whigs took over.[47]

However, one cannot always equate inconstancy with timorousness. William Cunningham, after early Whiggish activities, turned Loyalist and, under the nickname "Bloody Bill," became the personification of boldness by his partisan exploits in the back country.[48] The conduct of William Powell, a rich Charlestonian merchant, was considered by the commissioners to "stand as high as that of any Man from the Continent of America," although he had attended the provincial congress a few times in 1776.[49] Finally, the several examples of native-born claimants who endured imprisonment and worse rather than take the oath or serve in the militia must be remembered. James Boisseau, a wealthy planter, resisted the pleas of his friends, family (all Whigs, including his mother), and even Governor Rutledge's offer of a pardon and release from prison to preserve his loyalty.[50]

A contemporary Patriot manuscript entitled "Loyalists reasons for refusing to unite with the Whigs" has survived and has some interest. Most of the Tories questioned ascribed their stand to one of principle and, in the case of office-holders, to their oaths. The entry for Mark Walkman (from whom there is no claim) reads, "Holds a small office under the Crown in the Customs, fears loss of his Bread—desires not to offend either his Superiours or his Countrymen but persists." Chief Justice Thomas Knox Gordon, an Irish claimant, would not join the Whigs because it would not be consistent with "principles of Liberty"; it would be "contrary to Allegiance to the Crown," and, so typically of many sensitive Loyalists, it would be "Ingratitude—But no Man wishes better to the Liberties of the Colonies." [51]

The vast majority of farmers in South Carolina were not Loyalists, yet farmers (mainly of modest wealth) are the largest single group found among the claimants. They were mainly, in descending order of importance, Scotch-Irish, Americans, Germans, and Scots. David Ramsay drew attention to this upcountry Loyalism. He ascribed it to Regulator influence, a fear (on the part of the immigrants) of losing land titles, Governor Campbell's argument that the whole dispute was over "a trifling tax on tea" which the upcountry farmers did not use anyway, and finally the apathy and remoteness of the farmers who were contented and undisturbed by "distant evils" in Massachusetts and the British Parliament.[52]

South Carolina had had serious sectional problems which were focused in the Regulator movement (concurrent, but unconnected, with the North Carolina phenomenon from which it differed in many important ways). One recent scholar of the Regulator revolt concludes that it "contributed greatly to Backcountry Loyalism." [53] In July, 1775, the council of safety sent the Reverend William Tennent and William Henry Drayton into the interior to win the people over. They were by no means successful and discovered a deep distrust of Charleston and the seaboard.[54] John R. Alden, however, doubts that the majority of Regulators became Tories and points out, with force, that "in the end it was the Upcountry that offered determined, desperate resistance to British arms." [55] The claims commission testimony shows no particular connection between Loyalism and the Regulators. [56] More relevant than the Regulators is the fact that Camden and Ninety-Six, the two chief British inland military strongholds, were also the chief centers of Tory power, apart from Charleston.

Many German farmers had every reason to be grateful to the British government. Adam Bowers recalled leaving Germany in 1762 with many others for London where the party was given bounty and three ships to carry them to Charleston. There they were provided with wagon transport to the Ninety-Six district. [57] Once settled they feared that joining the Whigs (whose political arguments they did not understand) would mean the loss of their lands: Drayton wrote back to the council of safety, "the Dutch are not with us." [58]

David Ramsay charged that the Loyalists in South Carolina were "the selfish, among the merchants and planters whose gains were lessened by the cessation of trade . . ." [59] Certainly a significant segment of the Loyalists were merchants and shopkeepers (although a minority of that class as a whole). Some like John Hopton and Colin Campbell, of Charleston, had close connections with British houses. [60] Others, such as Thomas Hopper, were tempted by British gold to supply the troops during the occupation. [61] A recent scholar has discovered that this was the case with the Charleston artisans, a minority of whom were Tories. Of the thirty-two mechanics who signed addresses of welcome to the British invaders, twenty-four seemed to depend on British trade for a living. [62] The claims testimony reveals such examples as two bakers, Thomas Mergath and Thomas Creighton, who baked for the army during the occupation, and James Moore, who drove cattle.⁶³ Any glib economic explanation falls down when the number of merchants whose partners were rebels is considered. In Charleston there were partners of Walter Mansell and of Charles Atkin and the two associates of John Douglas, a distiller; at Ninety-Six Evan MacLaurin's partner, William Currie, was a Whig.⁶⁴ Ramsay concluded that a majority of merchants and planters were patriotic against their economic interest because "they believed their liberties to be in danger." ⁶⁵

The Church of England was established in South Carolina, but the Society for the Propagation of the Gospel had withdrawn in 1759.⁶⁶ The situation was similar to Virginia's in that the church was largely autonomous and the power of the vestries resulted in a kind of Congregationalism. Thus only six of the twenty Anglican clergymen were loyal.⁶⁷ All were claimants and British; five lived in Charleston, the other in Georgetown.

The seaboard aristocrats were Anglican, but generally Whig, and Anglican congregations were mostly Patriot; thus when the Reverend John Bulman, assistant minister at St. Michael's, Charleston, preached a sermon "on the Christian Duty of Peaceableness" in August, 1774, he was dismissed by the vestry.⁶⁸ His superior, the Reverend Robert Cooper, after a more equivocal career—he signed the Association, but with a "reservation"—suffered the same fate in April, 1777, after he refused to take the oath of allegiance to the new state.⁶⁹

Dissenters were a majority everywhere in South Carolina, and James Simpson told the claims commissioners that Henry Peronneau "was almost a nigh [i.e. only] Instance of a person being of the Sect of Independants [*sic*] who did not take part against the British government." ⁷⁰ The Scotch-

Irish claimants were probably mainly Presbyterians (the minister of the Scotch Presbyterian Society in Charleston, the Reverend Alexander Hewett, was a claimant); one Irish Catholic and one English Quaker are revealed in the claims testimony; and there is evidence that most Huguenots were Patriots;[71] but the conclusion must be that religion was not a basic factor in deciding allegiance in South Carolina.

In spite of the large number of Tory exiles, South Carolina was not seriously weakened or disrupted. It simply sloughed off a largely immigrant group and was deprived of only isolated talent like that of Dr. Alexander Garden, or Robert Wells, who owned a very fine bookshop in Charleston. South Carolina Whigs and Tories alike leave the impression of being moderate, equivocal, undynamic, and timid. This is suggested by the ease of the Patriot take-over, the equally easy British recapture, and the large numbers who changed allegiance each time. Or perhaps most South Carolinians simply had good sense, wanted business as usual as soon as possible, and realized that it did not matter which side won the war.

XIII. GEORGIA

GEORGIA

THE GEORGIA Loyalist claims figures[1] reveal that the great bulk of claimants were wealthy planters, professional men, or office-holders living mainly in Savannah, which the British captured. The total of planters, merchants, lawyers, physicians, ministers, and office-holders is sixty-two out of ninety-one whose occupations are known. Not surprisingly, the biggest single category is that of office-holders with a total of twenty-two.

In a report of September 20, 1773, to the Earl of Dartmouth, Sir James Wright, the governor, listed the principal office-holders of the colony.[2] Of the twenty named, twelve, including most of the major officers, were clearly loyal, eleven of them later submitting claims (the twelfth, James Habersham, a prominent Loyalist, had died). Of the remaining eight one was an absentee in England, three held petty positions, and only two, Sir Patrick Houston and Andrew Elton Wells, were Whigs.

In spite of the preponderance of the wealthy in the figures the whole economic gamut is present, from Sir James Wright, the former governor and a member of a distinguished English family, with his claim for £97,773.11.8, including 522 Negroes and thousands of acres, to William Reid (or Reed), an Irish immigrant who claimed £183.10.0 for his few acres and livestock.

Although thirty claims were for over £5,000, including those by most of the wealthiest men in the colony, forty were for less than £2,000, twenty-five for less than £1,000, and thirteen for less than £500. The presence of these more modest claims and the fact that six artisans claimed suggest a substantial number of Loyalists from the middling sort and lower in the scale. The conclusion must be that the Loyalists came from all economic sections of the community in Georgia.

Scotland was the homeland of the largest single group of Loyalists, and the British Isles contributed fifty-one out of a known total of sixty-nine. Only fifteen were native born. But the number is sufficiently great to suggest that many native-born Georgians remained loyal. It must be remembered that Georgia was such a young colony that a large proportion of the population was necessarily immigrant. The white population was about 7,000 in 1760, 10,000 in 1766, and nearly 20,000 in 1776.[3] In general the English tended to supply the large office-holders, the Scots the merchants and professional men, and the Irish the small farmers. A majority of the Loyalists, and indeed of the entire population, had arrived in Georgia after 1763 and thus had little time to become Americanized or lose their allegiance to the homeland.

Most Georgia Loyalists were from Savannah (60 per cent), and most of the remainder lived in the northern part of Georgia, in parishes between the Savannah River and the Ogeechee Valley. Savannah, the colony's chief port and town, center of the royal administration and later of the occupying army, was the natural focus of Loyalism. Of the city's white population 5.72 per cent submitted claims, easily the highest figure for any colonial town.[4]

Some of the factors inclining Georgians towards Loyalism will be mentioned later, and the general strength of Toryism in the colony comes as no surprise. Now to discuss the particular motives of certain groups and individuals.

Office-holders and royal officials are the easiest class to explain. They were usually Englishmen or at least from the

British Isles, they were usually quite recent arrivals, they had taken oaths, they depended upon the crown for their livelihood. In short, they constituted the group most committed to the mother country.

There is a distinct upper-class tinge to Loyalism in Georgia, partly borne out by a native Georgian lady's remark that with the Revolution "everywhere the scum rose to the top."[5] Some wealthy planters, merchants, and professional men were naturally conservative and inclined to Toryism, and the loyalty of a wealthy office-holder, an Anglican clergyman, or an Indian trader is quite understandable, but it must always be remembered that this group also provided a good deal of the Whig leadership.[6] The humbler Loyalists and those who were natives of America present more of a problem.

The American claimants were all wealthy and men of position (except one), the richest claim being James Butler's for £25,470.[7] Josiah Tatnall, born in South Carolina, claimed nearly £8,000 and had been a rich planter and lawyer and a member of the council.[8]

Henry Yonge, the surveyor-general of Georgia and brother of the Bishop of Norwich, was a Loyalist who died in 1778 leaving property worth over £10,000.[9] His two sons and his daughter, all born in America, put in claims because they never inherited their father's property. Henry Junior, a Savannah lawyer making £1,000 per annum, had worked for the law establishing the Anglican church in Georgia.[10] William, the other son, had been in England from 1769 to 1774 studying medicine and had returned with a rich English bride.[11]

The two sons of Alexander Wylly were native-born Georgian claimants. Wylly had been speaker of the house, and was a long-time Whig before he finally ended up in the Loyalist camp. His two sons' loyalty may be partially explained by the fact that they were both in England being educated when the Revolution broke out.[12]

Martin Weatherford is probably typical of native-born Georgia claimants in his equivocal behavior. He stated that he "remained quiet till 1779," paid fines to avoid serving in the rebel militia, and took the oath of allegiance. He joined the British when they regained control of Georgia. Such unspectacular conduct was all designed, as one witness put it, to save Weatherford's property worth £1,692. This is the kind of person who accounts for the Loyalists' failures.[13]

One other native Loyalist, although he made no claim on the British government, deserves to be mentioned. Lachlan McGillivray is the sort of Loyalist who put the issue of the War for Independence in doubt. His father was Scottish, his mother a half-breed Creek. McGillivray preferred the Creeks to a counting house in Savannah where he was apprenticed and with the aid of his more famous son, Alexander, helped keep the Creeks on the British side.[14]

All the Americans claimed over £1,000 except William Ring, who was apparently native born and the only one who could really be described as humble. The amount of his losses was not given, but he said he served an apprenticeship to a merchant in Savannah, and his award for Temporary Support was small, suggesting humble circumstances.[15] It must be noted that Ring was a mere boy (born in 1760) when the Revolution began and that his elder brother joined the rebels and gained their father's property.

However, the names of really humble Loyalists with small claims, mainly Irish immigrants, do stand out in the records: Samuel Montgomery, farmer (£100), Hugh Steel,

farmer (£354), William Thompson, spinning wheelwright
and farmer (£248).[16] The reasons for their loyalty, probably extremely personal, will presumably never be known.
They were certainly not typical of their nationality in
Georgia.[17]

The artisans who claimed, though following rather humble callings, were often quite wealthy, and their success in
Georgia may well have inclined them to loyalty. For example, William Harding left Ireland in 1760 and came to
America as a carpenter, but was able to claim losses of
£1,465 in 1784 and had been a justice of the peace.[18] James
Harriott, a cooper who became a wine and spirits merchant,
claimed £2,000, and Charles Watts, a ship's carpenter,
£1,990.[19]

Most wars provide unusual opportunities for advancement. Georgia supplies one such interesting case. In their
decisions the commissioners reported that Richard Davis, a
baker, went out to Georgia "only two or three Years before
the troubles, where (instead of suffering by the war) he
got into Situations created by the War which he had no
right at any time to have expected." These "situations" were
clerk of market at £80 per annum and clerk to the chief
justice at £50 per annum. The commissioners continued
that "he comes with a very bad grace" to claim for the loss
of offices and observed finally, "He probably will be able
to get his bread in this Country by following his old trade
of Baker which is much more fit than to be Clerk to a Chief
Justice."[20] One wonders whether Davis wished he had
chosen the other side and remained in America.

As elsewhere, families split between loyalty and rebellion
show the personal nature of a man's allegiance. William
Ring was a Loyalist like his father, but his elder brother was

a Whig.[21] Charles Price, an office-holder in Savannah, had a son killed in the American army.[22] Edward Telfair was a leading Whig, while his brother William was ultimately loyal.[23] John Habersham, a former acting governor, and Noble Jones, a leading Loyalist, both had sons who were Patriot leaders.[24] Most of these examples lend weight to the suggestion[25] that in split families the younger generation was usually Whig, but they also show that brother could be against brother.

Sixty-two per cent of the immigrant Georgia Loyalists had arrived in the New World after 1763. Probably a more lengthy stay in the colonies made for a degree of Americanization and inclined people to Whiggery, but not always. George Johnston claimed a loss of about £800 for a mill, a still, land, and livestock. He had come from Ireland to Pennsylvania as a boy, and later went to Georgia where he remained loyal. There is no clue to why.[26] Similarly, Edward Crawford, who had come out with his parents about 1752, claimed for a fairly modest farm (including one slave) worth about £650.[27] Robert Correy, another Irish immigrant, had arrived when he was very young yet claimed £761 losses. The clue to his loyalty may be that he was employed in the Commissary General's Department.[28] More understandable still is the case of James Habersham, who was born in England in 1712 and went with Whitfield to Savannah in 1738 as a schoolteacher for orphans. In 1774 he formed the first commercial partnership in Georgia, and by the time of the Revolution he was a council member, one of the richest men in the colony.[29] Habersham's success and prosperity probably inclined him to Toryism.

An interesting approach to Loyalism is through religion and national origin, which are often closely linked. Anglicans made up a majority of the population. Two of the five Anglican clergymen in the colony became Whigs; William Piercy, the superintendent of the Bethesda Orphanage, and John Holmes of St. George's Parish.[30] The other three, John Renny, James Seymour (by his widow), and Haddon Smith put in claims to the commissioners.[31] If the clergy were divided the congregations certainly were. A good many of the leading Loyalists were Anglican, including the governer and the royal officials. But many leading Whigs were Anglican, such as Joseph Clay and George Walton. Reba C. Strickland concludes that probably a larger proportion of Loyalists can be found among Anglicans than any other religious group, but not a majority. Further, the division tended to be between the old and the young—American-born Anglicans such as James Habersham and Noble Wymberly Jones being Whigs.[32]

The tables reveal that the Scots, mainly Presbyterian, were the largest single national element to put in claims, but as a group the majority seem to have been Whigs. Darien in St. Andrew's Parish was the center of the Scottish Highlanders, who, under the leadership of Lachlan McIntosh, took a leading part in the Whig cause.[33] Many of the Patriot leaders such as Edward Telfair (representing the more newly arrived Scots in the towns), Archibald Bullock, and Jonathan Bryan were Scottish.[34] The most explainable Scottish Loyalist group was the Indian traders, whose livelihood depended upon the British.[35] For example, John Brown, a tinworker in the Indian trade, who had arrived in Georgia in 1744, put in a claim for £185.5.0.[36] The rest of the Scottish Loyalists were planters, office-holders, and professional men.

Next to the Scots in sheer numbers came the Irish, who

were mainly Presbyterian Scotch-Irish, settled around Queensborough. As with the Scots, the majority were probably Whig. Many Irish on the frontier were alienated when the Indians attacked as a result of British policy.[37] Janet Russell, who claimed for her late husband, David Russell, said that most of Queensborough "went into rebellion" and that he "was one of the very few who preserved his loyalty."[38] The conclusion must be that a majority of Presbyterians, Scottish or Scotch-Irish, were probably Patriot.[39]

The largest national element in the population was the English, but they have many fewer claimants than either the Scots or the Scotch-Irish. English birth seems to have had little direct effect in deciding allegiance.[40]

The Germans, the most numerous foreign group, were centered in Ebenezer. These Lutherans, having gained religious freedom and prosperity in Georgia, could not be expected to exhibit much loyalty to the remote crown and because of the language barrier were rather outside the quarrel. Only two Germans made claims; one of them, Jacob Behler, a storekeeper at Ebenezer, claimed a modest loss of £440 and said he was one of the twenty-one Germans who refused to take the rebel oath or sign the Association.[41] This backs up the general impression that a slight majority of the Germans in Georgia were Whig,[42] although interestingly enough the minister at Ebenezer, Christopher Frederick Triebner, was that great exception, a loyal dissenting clergyman.[43] In 1779 Triebner welcomed the British to the town, but his hospitality seems to have been abused; the town suffered, and the Jerusalem Church was used as a hospital, a move unlikely to win friends among the Lutherans.[44] It is impossible to say why Triebner was loyal, but it may be significant that he was quite rich, claiming a property loss of £2,337 and an annual salary of £90 per annum, £50 of which was supplied by the Society for the Propagation of Christian Knowledge.[45]

The most nearly unanimous religious group was the solidly Whig Congregationalists of Midway, St. John's Parish. They had come from New England, via South Carolina, and made the parish the radical center of Georgia.[46] The Baptists of the back country seem to have been mainly Patriot—certainly no recognizable Baptist put in a claim.[47]

The Quakers were centered in Wrightsborough and had had good treatment from Governor Wright. According to Strickland, they were usually loyal.[48] If this is so, it is curious that only one identified Quaker, William Manson, put in any claim to the commissioners.[49] His brother also claimed, but he was not noted as a Quaker, and certainly bore arms.[50]

The Jews are generally held to have been mainly Whig, but three were banished as Loyalists, and one, John Charles Lucena, put in a claim.[51] Lucena was a Portuguese who went to Rhode Island in 1761 with his father, a merchant. A few years later they went into partnership in Savannah, and in 1775 Lucena became a planter. The two Lucenas were apparently very rich men. At the time of his claim, which was disallowed, Lucena was consul-general of Portugal in London.[52]

Oaths were taken seriously in the eighteenth century, and a reluctance to break their oaths was a definite factor in keeping such groups as office-holders loyal.[53]

Many Loyalists took the oath to the rebels at one time or another, but as James Simpson, a former attorney-general of South Carolina, testified, "A temporary Submission to the

authority of the usurped Government does not prove
Approbation . . . the Government of this Country had lost
its energy, and the system adopted by the Americans was
introduced with such sudden violence, it would have been
fatal as well as ineffectual to have opposed it, many well
disposed people were obliged to go down with the Stream
. . ." [54]

One Georgian claimed that he had taken the oath at
bayonet point, but the usual story was that it was the only
way to save one's property. [55]

Tendering the oath of allegiance was a favorite method
of the Whigs for putting pressure on the Loyalists. As John
Starr testified, "The Oath was only press'd on those who had
taken the Protection of the British Government After the
Declaration of Independence." [56] The commissioners did not
consider that the taking of the oath prevented classification
as a Loyalist, although they agreed with the claimant who
"thinks he is not so good a Subject as the man who took no
Oath." [57]

William Goodgion took the oath of allegiance to both
sides, served in the rebel Assembly in 1776, later joined the
British troops, and was finally tried by the Whigs and sentenced to death. The commissioners were aghast at his story,
declared that he deserved to be tried by the rebels, deemed
him "guilty of impartial treachery to both Countries," and
gave him no award. [58]

The exact number of Georgia Loyalists will never be
known, but some indications can be made. According to
Van Tyne [59] 129 Loyalists claimed from the British government, but if the claims for Temporary Support are added the
number is more like 140. This is about 0.7 per cent (the
highest for any colony) of the white population of 20,000

in 1776.[60] If, as is usual, the claimants were heads of Loyalist families, and families averaged six persons, then the percentage is increased five times to 3.5 per cent. It seems certain that the claimants were a minority of the whole body of Loyalists. One indication of this is that thirty-five probable officers made claims as against only eight rank and file. Another is that as many as 3,100 (or 15 per cent of the population in 1776) fled from Savannah when the British evacuated in 1782.

The Loyalists themselves, however, usually claimed that they had been a majority. A possible corroboration of this view is that the Georgia state legislature banished 279 Loyalists in 1782 while the British could find only 161 rebels to disqualify in 1780.[61] Thus the great strength of Loyalism in Georgia becomes clear. Only New York could rival it (in terms of the *proportion* of the population loyal).

General reasons for the power of Loyalism in Georgia can easily be given: the comparatively late growth of the colony which meant that most people were recent immigrants and had not become Americanized, the lack of real grievances, the British financial and military support which was considered necessary for the colony's stability, economic prosperity, fear of Indian attack, and the presence of the British garrison at St. Augustine.[62] During the Revolutionary War Savannah was occupied by the British from December, 1778, to July, 1782, and in spite of the severe civil war, the rest of Georgia was in British hands during much of this period. As always the British military presence was a powerful stimulant to the Loyalists, and Governor Wright and all the apparatus of royal government were restored.

The Loyalists generally blamed the Whig success on outside pressures and the lack of proper British support. In his memorial to the claims commissioners Sir James Wright explained,

In Georgia we resisted the Rebellion a long while and for many Months there were only twelve United States . . . and if we could have had or got any support or assistance who [we] should have kept that province out of rebellion . . . our misfortune was in . . . being the next province to So. Carolina, and only separated by a narrow River, so that the Rebels from thence, together with the Rebels in Georgia at length intimidated some, cajoled and prevailed upon others, and then overpowered the rest of the Loyalists. But had it not been for the assistance and force of our Neighbours in Carolina who had Emisaries continually going about Georgia to stir them up the King's Officers and other Loyalists . . . would have been sufficient to have kept the Rebel Party under.[63]

John Simpson, a wealthy council member, agreed with Wright, telling the commissioners that only the interference of South Carolina put Georgia into the Whig camp.[64] Wright and Simpson, of course, were hardly unbiased, but the crucial influence of other colonies, and South Carolina in particular, is recognized by historians.[65] The strength of Georgia's Loyalism is well attested by the colony's late entry into the Revolution and by the extremely bitter civil war which followed. But against this it must be remembered that by July, 1775, royal government had collapsed. If the Tories were a majority they were not an effective one. Further, they were fatally weakened because many subsequent Loyalists were Whig at this stage, and only changed sides when independence was the issue.

Governor Wright's complaint of British neglect was echoed to the claims commissioners by other Georgia Loyalists. Jermyn Wright, the governor's brother, recounted how he built a fort, at his own expense, on the St. Marys River by the pass into Florida. He then asked British troops under the command of Major Graham, on the Florida side of the river, to occupy it. Major Graham approved, "provided he could obtain Orders and recommend the Case to the Commander of the Forces at Saint Augustine, but could get no Orders, by which your Memorialist was sacrificed to the Brutal fury of the Revolters." [66]

As in other colonies the British not only neglected the Loyalists but actually harassed them. Many a supercilious British officer simply equated Americans with rebels. Thomas Stringer gave an example of this to the commissioners. In December, 1775, he loaded a brig bound for London with indigo; it was captured by "Carolineans" just outside the bar of Savannah. A few days later four royal ships arrived commanded by a Captain Stanhope to whom Stringer appealed for help in recapturing the brig. The "answer I received we were all Rebels (There Sir take that Proclamation) and give it to your Governor. That he had orders to burn and destroy the Town, he would give me no assistance. This Proclamation actually drove the Province into the resolve with the other Provinces sooner than they would have been, as we were importing and Exporting without any Molestation but what we received from the Carolineans." Later Stringer chartered the "Nelly" and would have sent her to Liverpool with a cargo of rice and indigo "but for His Majesty's troops taking possession of her" and burning "all your Memorialist's Books, Papers, Clothes and Household Furniture." The apparently sore-tried merchant added, possibly ironically, that "Your Memorialist not chusing to join in the Rebel party went and joined His Majesty's troops . . ." [67]

Many cases bear out the witness who told of plundering by both sides: "What the one left the other gleaned—it was the Man's misfortune, and was no uncommon thing." [68]

Georgia may well have had the largest proportion of Loyalists of all the colonies; yet by mid-1775 royal power had collapsed. The answer to this apparent paradox is only partly that the Loyalists were cautious and conservative, defending the status quo while the initiative lay with the aggressive Whigs, or that the British were incompetent. The great weakness of the Loyalists (and this was general throughout the colonies) was that so many were timid or equivocal at first, while others (often the ablest) were sympathetic to, and even took the lead in, the Whig cause until it became a question of independence. (It was not, of course, illogical or reprehensible to change sides at this point.)

One of the leading Georgia Loyalists was the Swiss Presbyterian clergyman, John Joachim Zubly, but he was a consistent Whig until actual independence was the issue. He was Georgia's leading Whig pamphleteer and finally a delegate to the Second Continental Congress where he impressed John Adams profoundly. He left the Congress when it was clear independence was coming[69] and returned to Georgia a Loyalist. Zubly may well illustrate the Loyalists' fatal weakness: too many worked against the essential Loyalist cause, and when opposition to grievances became a movement for independence, it was too late.

Also, David Zubly, who seems to have been a brother of the Reverend John J. Zubly, was an able native-born Georgia Loyalist, but significantly, like his brother, he was initially active in the Whig cause, serving in the rebel militia, and not resigning until April, 1776, because "he thought Great Britain had no right to Tax America, but he did not approve of Opposition by force of Arms, neither did he wish for Independence."⁷⁰

In a showdown one was either a Tory or a Whig, but most people preferred to avoid a decision. As the commissioners remarked of John Murray, "He says he took no part at all but kept out of the Way as much as possible." Many others wavered. These waverers are very interesting because they illustrate the subtleties of the situation. Alexander Wylly, speaker of the House of Assembly for many years, and Robert Baillie, a rich planter who later claimed a loss of about £15,000, were both members of the liberty faction in the 1760's but were loyal when it became a matter of rebellion.⁷¹

Basil Cowper, who claimed a loss of over £30,000, was actually chosen as a member of the Georgia provincial congress in July, 1775, where he claimed that he acted "in behalf of moderation and the Mercantile Interest and did his utmost to keep open Exportation for the payment of British debts."⁷²

James Gordon stated, somewhat plaintively, that his partner in a land scheme, Thomas Brown, "being Young and Active and Violent against the Rebel Measures used to attend their Meetings and oppose their measures. Claimant had the same Sentiments, but did not declare them with so much warmth." Brown became the victim of the "most famous tarring and feathering" in Augusta and had to flee, while Gordon stayed on to look after the property.⁷³

The practice of trying to keep a foot in both camps, either by leaving one's wife in America, or by business partners' splitting up, was common throughout the colonies. The above-mentioned merchant, Basil Cowper's partner,

Mr. Telfair, went to England while Cowper stayed on in Georgia. The commissioners asked Cowper "if there was no Agreement between them that one should take one side and the other the other. He replies there is not." [74] Lieutenant-Governor Graham, giving evidence in John Murray's case, observed dryly that Murray "would have sacrificed a little principle to preserve his property in America." [75]

To sum up, Loyalism in Georgia conforms quite well to the traditional view of it as a movement weighted toward wealth and privilege, recent immigration, and the towns of the seaboard, and fatally weakened by equivocal or timid leadership (except for that of Governor Wright) and by British neglect.

XIV. CONCLUSION

THE PRECEDING thirteen chapters have demonstrated that the Loyalist movement in each colony was unique. But it is worth surveying the Tories as a whole and making comparisons between different areas and groups. First there is the question of the number of Loyalists.

The Loyalists are important in the history of the American Revolution if only because of their number. In 1814 Thomas McKean, the Pennsylvania Patriot and statesman, agreed with John Adams that about one-third of the colonists had been opposed to the Revolution.[1] The usual estimate of Loyalist exiles (first propounded by the Pennsylvania Tory and British consul, Phineas Bond) is 100,000 out of a total population of approximately 2,500,000 (2,100,000 of whom were white),[2] and R. R. Palmer has suggested, on the basis of a lower estimate, that the American Revolution produced twenty-four émigrés per thousand of the population compared with only five per thousand in the French Revolution. (He also calculated that the American confiscation of property was proportionately almost as great as the French.)[3] Between 30,000 and 50,000 Loyalists fought in the regular army for the king at some time between 1775 and 1783, and many more served in the militia or engaged in guerrilla warfare. In 1780, 8,000 Loyalists were in the regular army, at a time when Washington's army numbered only about 9,000.[4]

A fresh attempt at guessing the number of active Loyalists and exiles can be made on the basis of the claims. Esther Clark Wright has shown that in New Brunswick 8 per cent of the male Loyalists submitted claims.[5] There is some reason to suppose that this is a constant percentage of the exiles. It has been estimated that there were 2,000 male Loyalists in Connecticut, about 1,000 of whom left the state.[6] There were ninety-two Connecticut claimants, which is 9.2 per cent of the exiles, a figure very close to Wright's. In New Jersey 5,000 male Loyalists have been counted.[7] If it is assumed the Connecticut pattern was followed, 2,500 went into exile, and it is a fact that 208 persons, or 8.2 per cent, of the 2,500 put in claims. Thus 100/8 multiplied by the total number of claimants (2,560) should give the number of male exiles, and double that number should give the total number of active male Loyalists. The figures are 32,000 exiles and 64,000 active males respectively. If each man is assumed to have a family of five, 160,000 persons suffered exile; if six, 192,000 were exiled. However, this figure is probably too high for two reasons. First, Wright believes that in New Brunswick, because of the large number of single men, each claimant probably represented two and a half persons.[8] Second, it is likely that a higher proportion of the London exiles claimed because they were generally much wealthier or more sophisticated than their Canadian brethren. Therefore on the basis of two and a half persons per male the number of persons exiled may well have been 80,000 (two and one-half times 32,000), a figure much closer to Phineas Bond's. The exiles were certainly numerous—one of the first modern examples of what have come to be known as "displaced persons."

If it is assumed only half the active Loyalists went into exile, the conclusion is that the complete body totaled between 160,000 (on the basis of 80,000 exiles) and 384,000 (on the basis of 192,000 exiles)—between 6.4 and 15.3 per cent of the total population of 2,500,000 on the eve of the Revolution, or between 7.6 and 18.0 per cent of the *white* population of 2,100,000.[9]

Conclusion

These figures are tentative and represent only active Loyalists. Further, in the special case, New York, which had 941 of the total 2,560 claims, it is certain that less than half the active Loyalists went into exile. Thus the figures should be raised; also, if equivocal and quietist Loyalists were considered, the figures would go up again. However, there is a good indication that Adams' estimate of the total Loyalists (if he meant *active* Loyalists) as one-third of the population is too high, and that Bond's estimate of the exiles is quite accurate.

The overwhelming impression from the claims testimony (and Loyalist writings in general) is that Loyalist strength would have been considerably greater had the British government and army shown more interest and finesse toward their real or potential allies, or at least avoided harassing them. An anonymous witness told the British government in February, 1782, that he believed British shortcomings had strengthened the rebels more than the French alliance and noted dryly that if there were to be any hope for success in America "all the People should experience the Generosity and humanity of an English Government and an English Army which has not been the case hitherto." At the same time an Alsatian Loyalist reported the belief that the British army deliberately prolonged the war to profiteer and finally the Commander-in-Chief had *"made the Friends of England, Yea, the most inimical to England . . ."* It is very clear that the British government was generally woefully negligent in rallying and making use of the Loyalists; a petition of March, 1785, from several leading Loyalists put it nicely when they stated they had remained loyal "as much from inclination as encouragement." [10]

Any discussion of the number of Loyalists faces the insuperable problem of definition. Probably a majority of the colonists, certainly a good many, would have preferred not to have to take a stand on the question of independence and allegiance, especially before it was clear which side would win, and would have echoed the Long Island innkeeper's reply to an interrogator who asked if he were Whig or Tory: "I told him I was for peace."[11] These neutralists, whom John Adams thought to be one-third of the population, and pacifists (such as Quakers) cannot be considered as Loyalists. Conversely persons who went into exile, or who rendered substantial service, military or civil, to the British, or against whom the Whigs took justified legal action, must be classed as Loyalists. Other groups are equivocal. Many colonists changed sides, sometimes more than once and usually according to variations in the fortunes of war, and thus qualified as both Tories and Whigs at different times. Many Loyalists escaped exile, confiscation, and military service, or were quietist, biding their time, merely expressing their loyalty with a secret prayer for the king, a muted curse for the Congress.

Contemporary definitions of the Loyalists include, "A Tory is a thing whose head is in England, and its body in America, and its neck ought to be stretched," and "Every fool is not a Tory, yet every Tory is a fool," but basically Tories were simply those who remained actively or passively loyal to George III and opposed the Declaration of Independence even if they had taken a Whig position earlier, like Joseph Galloway of Pennsylvania and William Smith, last royal chief justice of New York.[12]

The difficulty in discovering and even defining the Tories means that no accurate count can ever be made, and it may well be that the precise number is comparatively unimportant. However, the relative strength of the Tories in different areas can be suggested and certainly is important.

Strength of Loyalists as Reflected by the Claims

Colony	Percentage of the Population who were Claimants[a]
Georgia	0.7
New York	0.54
South Carolina	0.47
New Jersey	0.19
Massachusetts	0.11
Rhode Island	0.10
North Carolina	0.09
Connecticut	0.08
Pennsylvania	0.07
New Hampshire	0.06
Virginia	0.05
Maryland	0.05
Delaware	0.02
Towns	
Savannah, Ga.	5.75
Charleston, S.C.	2.17
Boston, Mass.	0.98
Norfolk, Va.	0.7
Annapolis, Md.	0.56
New York, N.Y.	0.55
Baltimore, Md.	0.52
Portsmouth, N.H.	0.37
Newport, R.I.	0.27
Philadelphia, Pa.	0.26

[a] These figures can be multiplied by five or six to give the over-all percentage. This will not, of course, affect the relative strength which is the point at issue.

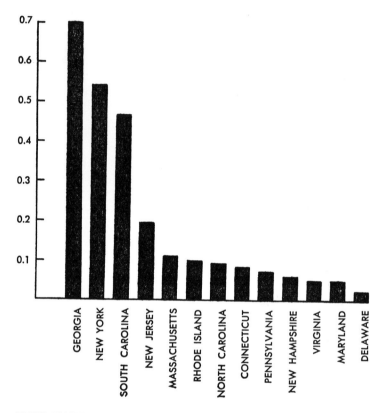

GRAPH SHOWING THE PERCENTAGE OF THE POPULATION WHO WERE
CLAIMANTS IN EACH COLONY

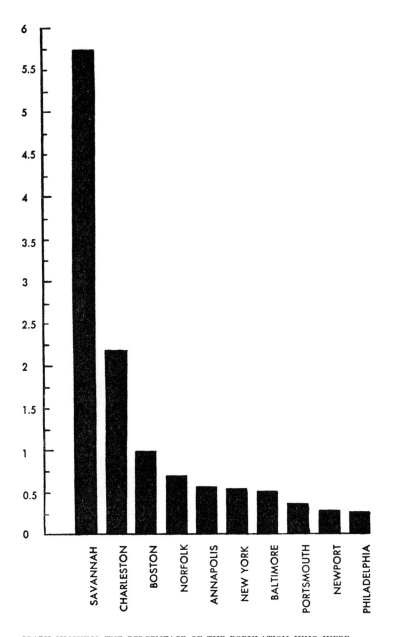

GRAPH SHOWING THE PERCENTAGE OF THE POPULATION WHO WERE
CLAIMANTS IN TOWNS

The strength of Loyalism by colonies falls into several rough sections. Georgia, New York, and South Carolina lead with easily the highest percentages of claimants.[13] Then, strong, but considerably behind, come New Jersey and Massachusetts, followed by Rhode Island, North Carolina, Connecticut, Pennsylvania, and New Hampshire with middling numbers, then, with weak percentages, Virginia and Maryland, and, definitely taking up the rear, Delaware. By towns, Savannah and Charleston are clearly ahead, then come Boston and finally the other leading Loyalist towns well behind. Georgia was a uniquely weak, new, and immigrant colony and was occupied for so long that, not surprisingly, it heads both lists. These lists are fairly true to generally accepted opinions of the strength of Loyalism and to collateral evidence in the preceding thirteen chapters.[14]

But there are three exceptions. First, New York City, as well as the colony, is usually considered a Loyalist stronghold. It has already been suggested, however, that the figures for the city are probably not an accurate reflection of the true strength of the Loyalists because there were simply *too many* to be forced into exile. Second is the relatively powerful showing of the Loyalists in Boston and Massachusetts, and third, the weak showing of Pennsylania and especially Philadelphia. The weakness of Loyalism in the Chesapeake Bay area is amply confirmed, although the contrasting strength in Norfolk, Annapolis, and Baltimore (the first two outrank New York City, and all three outrank Philadelphia and Newport) is perhaps a little at variance with previous estimates.

Apart from relative strength the Loyalists were probably a majority in no colony (certainly never an effective majority), and only in New York, Massachusetts, and to a degree in Georgia, can the ruling class be said to be substantially

Conclusion

represented in the Loyalist ranks. Only in Massachusetts and New York can the Loyalists be said to have included a notable amount of outstanding talent, although Pennsylvania and New Jersey, to a lesser extent Georgia, and (because of a few isolated cases) Maryland and South Carolina can also be mentioned.

In most colonies Loyalism was a distinctly urban and seaboard phenomenon, although the majority of claimants were farmers (but without the New York farmers, the urban-commercial element would be in a huge majority). A glance at the normally much higher figures for the towns compared with the colonies in the above tables graphically illustrates this. Fifty-three per cent of the New Hampshire claimants lived in Portsmouth; 89.8 per cent of Rhode Island's in Newport; 52.5 per cent of Massachusetts' in Boston and nearby towns and 75 per cent along the seaboard in general; 56 per cent of Connecticut's were in the seaboard county of Fairfield, mainly in the small towns of Greenwich, Stamford, Norwalk, Fairfield, and Stratford; New York City housed only 13 per cent of the colony's claimants, but this was a sizable concentration, and a large number compared with most cities; in New Jersey one-third lived at Perth Amboy and the surrounding Raritan Bay and estuary; in Pennsylvania 54 per cent lived in Philadelphia and most of the rest were from the three eastern counties, Bucks, Chester, and Philadelphia; 56 per cent of the Virginia claimants lived in the towns of Norfolk, Portsmouth, Gosport, Williamsburg, and Petersburg, and almost all the rest are found in the tidewater; in Maryland about 60 per cent lived in Baltimore and Annapolis; the area of Charleston, South Carolina, accounts for 44 per cent of that colony's claimants; Savannah contained 60 per cent of Georgia's Loyalists.

The King's Friends

There are major rural, inland pockets of Loyalists only in New York (mainly in Tryon, Albany, Charlotte, Westchester, and Dutchess Counties with 82 per cent of the claimants), and in North Carolina at least 70 per cent were from the back country, particularly Cumberland and Anson Counties (but there was also a small number of urban Loyalists at Wilmington). There were minor rural concentrations in South Carolina at the two inland districts of Camden and Ninety-Six, with about 40 per cent of the claimants between them; in Maryland in the western county of Frederick with 17 per cent of the claimants; and to an extent in Delaware (the few claimants were certainly not urban).

Explanations for the rural Loyalists have already been suggested in the chapters dealing with the relevant colonies, but a word is necessary to explain the generally urban character of the Loyalists. It was in the towns and cities that the royal administrations, the office-holders, the professional men, the commercial segment of the population, and often the most recent immigrants were mainly found. Further, Loyalism was a sophisticated creed; only in the towns was one likely to find that sophistication.

Very slightly (nearly 3 per cent) more Loyalist claimants were immigrants than native born, but as the latter made up a minority of the population, they contributed proportionately more claimants to the Tory ranks. About 90 per cent of the immigrants were from the British Isles with Scotland the major country of origin, while Germany supplied almost all the non-British. The Scots lived chiefly in New York and to a lesser extent in North Carolina, South Carolina, and Virginia; the English were widely spread, but with slight concentrations in New York, South Caro-

Conclusion

lina, and Pennsylvania; the Irish were mainly from New York and South Carolina; the Germans lived almost entirely in New York, South Carolina, and Pennsylvania.

Nationality of Claimants (A)

Country of Birth	Number of Claimants (all colonies combined)	
Great Britain	94	
England	290	
Scotland	470	1144
Ireland	280	
Wales	10	
Germany	117	130
Elsewhere in Europe[a]	13	
Total immigrants	1274	
America	1201	

	% of All Claimants		% of Foreign-born Claimants	
Great Britain	3.8		7.3	
England	11.6		22.8	
Scotland	19.0	46.17	36.8	89.62
Ireland	11.3		21.96	
Wales	0.4		0.76	
Germany	4.7	5.23	9.18	10.27
Elsewhere in Europe	0.53		1.09	
Total immigrants	51.4			
America	48.6			

[a] One from Sweden, Minorca, Alsace, France, and Portugal; two from Switzerland; five from Holland.

Nationality of Claimants (B)

Colony	Total Foreign-born Claimants	Total American-born Claimants
New Hampshire	6	19
Massachusetts	65	203
Rhode Island	12	21
Connecticut	15	75

New York	489	485
New Jersey	49	160
Pennsylvania	103	83
Delaware	4	6
Maryland	56	20
Virginia	88	24
North Carolina	110	28
South Carolina	223	62
Georgia	54	15

In New England and New Jersey the claimants were usually native Americans; in New York, Pennsylvania, and Delaware they were quite evenly divided between native and foreign born; in the South they were usually immigrants.

The subordinate position taken by the Irish relative to the Scots in the tables is supported by contemporary testimony. The Marquis de Chastellux wrote that "an Irishman, the instant he sets foot on American ground becomes, *ipso facto*, an American." [15] In 1777 an English newspaper ascribed American military success partly to the Irish (also to officers experienced in the Seven Years War and to French engineers). [16] By contrast the Scots were uniformly suspect, especially in the South, where as creditors and merchant interlopers they were particularly disliked, and "Our common toast is, a free exportation to *Scotchmen* and Tories." [17] Henry Hulton, writing from Boston, as early as 1770, considered that although "the disease [of opposition to Britain] has been universal thro' the British dominions let me except" Scotland, "her sons have kept free from the general contagion" and "proved themselves good subjects and supporters of Government and order." [18] On August 5, 1782, the Georgia legislature passed an act prohibiting the

Conclusion

immigration of Scots because "the people of Scotland have in General Manifested a decided inimicability to the Civil Liberties of America and have contributed Principally to promote and Continue a Ruinous War . . ." [19]

Now to consider the claimants by occupation. In the tables which follow, the four basic divisions, farmers, commercial people, professionals, and royal officials, make up 100 per cent of the claimants, but the classification "commercial people" is followed by two subdivisions, artisans, and merchants and shopkeepers.

Occupation of Claimants (A)

Colony	No. of Farmers	% of Farmers	No. of Commercial People	% of Commercial People
New Hampshire	11	26.8	10	24.3
Rhode Island	9	20.0	26	58.0
Massachusetts	37	11.5	149	50.0
Connecticut	59	42.8	60	43.4
New York	800	74.7	190	17.7
New Jersey	115	50.1	63	28.0
Pennsylvania	67	33.5	84	42.0
Delaware	3	30.0	4	40.0
Maryland	11	14.2	33	42.0
Virginia	16	12.8	80	64.0
North Carolina	66	46.5	55	39.0
South Carolina	144	45.5	101	31.5
Georgia	30	33.0	28	30.0

Colony	No. of Artisans	% of Artisans	No. of Merchants and Shopkeepers	% of Merchants and Shopkeepers
New Hampshire	3	7.3	5	12.2
Rhode Island	1	2.2	20	44.4
Massachusetts	27	9.1	106	35.5

Connecticut	20	14.5	35	25.3
New York	94	8.9	77	7.3
New Jersey	25	11.0	32	14.0
Pennsylvania	41	20.5	33	16.5
Delaware	0	0.0	2	20.0
Maryland	10	13.0	16	20.5
Virginia	8	6.4	65	52.0
North Carolina	9	6.3	42	29.5
South Carolina	30	9.3	65	20.5
Georgia	6	6.5	19	20.0

Colony	No. of Professional Men	% of Professional Men	No. of Office-Holders	% of Office-Holders
New Hampshire	5	12.2	15	36.6
Rhode Island	5	11.0	5	11.0
Massachusetts	51	17.0	64	21.5
Connecticut	11	8.0	8	5.8
New York	39	3.7	42	3.9
New Jersey	26	11.5	23	10.4
Pennsylvania	23	11.5	26	13.0
Delaware	2	20.0	1	10.0
Maryland	19	24.5	15	19.2
Virginia	20	16.0	9	7.2
North Carolina	5	3.5	16	11.0
South Carolina	36	11.5	36	11.5
Georgia	11	12.0	22	24.0

Only in New York and New Jersey were farmers a majority of the claimants, but in North Carolina, South Carolina, and Georgia they were the largest single category. In Rhode Island and Virginia the commercial element was in a majority, and in Massachusetts, Pennsylvania, Delaware, and Maryland it was the largest single category. (In Connecticut the commercial element slightly outstripped the farmers.) Further, if numbers rather than percentages are considered, in New York, New Jersey, North Carolina,

Conclusion

South Carolina, and Georgia the commercial element is very powerful. The proportion of professional men is quite steady (ranging from 11 per cent to 17 per cent), with the exceptions of Maryland and Delaware, which have higher figures. Looking at numbers rather than percentages, Massachusetts, New York, and South Carolina are clearly the prime areas where office-holders were very significant, and looking at percentages one can add New Hampshire, Maryland, and Georgia.

Occupation of Claimants (B)

Occupation	No. of Claimants	% of Claimants
Farmers	1,368	49.2
Commerce		
(a) Artisans	274	9.8
(b) Merchants and shopkeepers	507	18.2
(c) Miscellaneous innkeepers, seamen, etc.	102	3.7
Combined commerce	881	31.7
Professions		
(a) Lawyers	55	1.97
(b) Teachers and professors	21	0.75
(c) Doctors	81	2.9
(d) Anglican clerics	63	2.3
(e) Other clerics[a]	7	0.25
(f) Miscellaneous	24	0.86
Combined professions	251	9.0
Royal or Proprietary Office-Holders	282	10.1

[a] Includes two Congregationalists, one German Reformed, one Dutch Reformed, one Presbyterian, one Lutheran, and one Roman Catholic.

Almost 50 per cent of the claimants were farmers, nearly 32 per cent were in the commercial line (if artisans are included), about 9 per cent were professional men, and a

little over 10 per cent were royal or proprietary office-
holders. Although farmers are easily the largest group, it
must be concluded that the other three categories contributed proportionately many more Loyalists because at least
90 per cent of the colonial population was on the land. Thus
among farmers only a tiny minority were claimants. Also,
there is no evidence that the next largest group, the commercial element, was anything but a minority—a much
larger minority, however. Only in New York City, Virginia, and North Carolina were a majority of the merchants
clearly Loyalists, and in New York only a small minority
were sent into exile. Over the country as a whole the great
majority of merchants were not Tory. But the conclusion
is that the Loyalist movement had a distinct commercial,
office-holding, and professional bias.

Among the professional claimants doctors easily out-
number all other groups, especially teachers (including all
kinds). Nearly four times as many doctors as teachers submitted claims. (The relative proportions of doctors and
teachers in the population is not clear, but doctors probably slightly outnumbered the teachers.) The proportion
of Loyalist doctors is probably actually much higher because, as Sabine has suggested, doctors were so badly needed
during the Revolution that often their Toryism did not
result in persecution.[20] The reason for the few loyal teachers is obscure. It may be that teachers are inherently more
radical than doctors. The heads of King's College, New
York, and the College of William and Mary, Virginia, were
Loyalists, but faculties were generally Whig, and Loyalist
alumni seem to have been a minority at all colonial colleges.
More than twice as many lawyers as teachers filed claims,
and lawyers seem to have been rather evenly divided.[21]

How great a proportion of the professional people were

Conclusion

Tory is difficult to say, but Moses Coit Tyler believed that a "clear majority" were so inclined.[22] Lorenzo Sabine held that a majority of colonial lawyers were Whig, but that the "giants of the law" were generally loyal.[23] The latter point is somewhat borne out by the preceding thirteen chapters.

The Loyalists recruited heavily from the poor people, particularly in New York and Connecticut and to a lesser extent in Pennsylvania; in the South and also in Massachusetts the Loyalists were drawn much more from the rich.

Wealth of Claimants (A)

Colony	% Claimed £500 or Less	% Claimed £5,000 or More	% Claimed £10,000 or More
New Hampshire	28.0	16.0	4.0
Massachusetts	21.2	22.2	9.2
Rhode Island	21.8	9.3	3.1
Connecticut	49.0	10.6	5.3
New York	64.0	6.9	3.7
New Jersey	26.0	9.9	3.5
Pennsylvania	35.0	13.0	6.0
Delaware	22.2	11.1	0.0
Maryland	12.5	28.0	17.0
Virginia	9.7	28.4	16.0
North Carolina	21.0	19.6	14.6
South Carolina	24.0	21.8	11.8
Georgia	16.5	36.5	19.0

Colony	% Claimed £500 or Less in Descending Order
New York	64.0
Connecticut	49.0
Pennsylvania	35.0
New Hampshire	28.0

The King's Friends

New Jersey	26.0
South Carolina	24.0
Delaware	22.2
Rhode Island	21.8
Massachusetts	21.2
North Carolina	21.0
Georgia	16.5
Maryland	12.5
Virginia	9.7

Colony	% Claimed £5,000 or More in Descending Order
Georgia	36.5
Virginia	28.4
Maryland	28.0
Massachusetts	22.2
South Carolina	21.8
North Carolina	19.6
New Hampshire	16.0
Pennsylvania	13.0
Delaware	11.1
Connecticut	10.6
New Jersey	9.9
Rhode Island	9.3
New York	6.9

Colony	% Claimed £10,000 or More in Descending Order
Georgia	19.0
Maryland	17.0
Virginia	16.0
North Carolina	14.6
South Carolina	11.8
Massachusetts	9.2
Pennsylvania	6.0
Connecticut	5.3
New Hampshire	4.0
New York	3.7
New Jersey	3.5

| Rhode Island | 3.1 |
| Delaware | 0.0 |

Wealth of Claimants (B)

Claims	Percentage
£ 500 or less	41.8
£ 501–£ 1,000	13.2
£ 1,001–£ 2,000	15.9
£ 2,001–£ 5,000	14.9
£ 5,001–£ 10,000	6.9
£ Over 10,000	7.3

Fifty-five per cent of the claimants asked for £ 1,000 or less. Thus the bulk can be described as of modest means. However, bearing in mind that only a small part of the total population was worth £ 5,000 and over, the more than 14 per cent who so claimed suggests that the wealthy produced proportionately more Loyalists than the lower economic groups.

This is as far as the statistics take us in considering the structure of Loyalism. But a word remains to be said on religion. Religion was not usually the key to Loyalism, with the exception of Anglicanism in certain colonies. It was a serious factor in Massachusetts, Rhode Island, New York (par excellence), and New Jersey. There was an Anglican tinge to Loyalism in New Hampshire, Connecticut, and Maryland. The doctrines and outlook of the Church of England and its fashionable appeal to the wealthy made this church supply a higher proportion of Loyalists than any other. It seems unlikely that a majority of Anglicans were Loyalists, however. It must be remembered that the Anglican church claimed more signers of the Declaration of Independence than any other, and generally it produced a large share of the leading Whigs, especially in the South.[24] Conversely the Presbyterian church produced hardly a Loyalist, with the very unusual exceptions of William Smith of New York and Chief Justice William Allen of Pennsylvania, and was more solidly Whig. [25] The Calvinist churches were normally patriotic, but always there were exceptions.

The Quakers, often at the time, and sometimes since, have been called Loyalists. Clearly one reason for this was the refusal of most Friends to fight. However, a contemporary, Brissot de Warville, wrote that the Quakers "were treated by both sides with confidence. The spies, encouraged by this, at length habited themselves as Quakers and several were actually hung in that costume." [26] The fact that very few Quakers appeared before the claims commissioners supports the view of a fairly recent authority that the Friends were generally neutral, not Tory.[27] This seems also to have been true of the other pacifist sects.

To describe the structure of the Loyalist movement is a fairly straightforward task. To ascribe motives and reasons for Loyalism is a more subtle and complex one. Enough has already been said about the not surprising loyalty of the royal officials, British Seven Years War veterans, recent immigrants, some merchants with strong British economic interests, many Anglicans, and certain individual cases in each colony. Also, of course, the Loyalists, being a minority everywhere, required a British military presence to flush them from their nests; hence the obvious connection between the British occupation and Loyalist strength in Georgia, South Carolina, and New York. But this rather begs the question—the problem is, *why* did some people then decide to show themselves as Tories? Most Loyalists would have said simply that they were opposed to the "temper of the times." And why were they opposed? Because they were conservative, because they were satisfied with things as they were, or at least feared revolution more than they feared British encroachments.

Crèvecoeur put it quite simply: "I am conscious that I was happy before this unfortunate Revolution. I feel that I am no longer so; therefore I regret the change." [28]

Fear of change could take a thousand forms, but everpresent with most well-to-do Loyalists was the dread of social change as foreshadowed by the rise of mobs after the Stamp Act crisis. In 1780 Samuel Curwen complained that "those who five years ago were the *'meaner people'* are now by strange revolution, become almost the only men of power, riches and influence . . . The Cabots of Beverly, who you know, had but five years ago a very moderate share of property, are now said to be by far the most wealthy in New England." [29] A few Loyalists even had plans to establish a nobility in America after the Revolution had been crushed. [30]

Immigrants from the British Isles were much more likely to be loyal than native-born Americans. This was recognized by both sides. Jacob Ellegood of Virginia was taken prisoner and "from his being a Native of the Country he met much harsher Treatment than Officers of his Majesty's British forces." [31] The claims commissioners praised the American-born claimant over the immigrant [32] and also the long-time resident over the recent arrival. Thus they pronounced on a New York claimant, "This Gentleman tho' not an American had been so long in America before the troubles that he may be Supposed to have entertained all the prejudices of a native American. He has therefore the greater merit in his Loyalty . . ."[33] About 60 per cent of the immigrant claimants had arrived in America after 1763, but it must be noted that Richard Montgomery, Horatio Gates, and Thomas Paine were leading Patriots and also recent immigrants.[34]

Frequent examples are found of Americans educated in England who became Loyalists. But contact with England through education has not always resulted in leaders devoted to continuing colonial status, as the recent history of India and British Africa shows. The four South Carolina signers of the Declaration of Independence were educated in England.[35]

Roughly half the claimants were immigrants and their loyalty is not surprising. The other half, the American-born (very few of whom were educated in England), are more intriguing. They were not generally wealthy, as might be expected. In New Hampshire, Massachusetts, Rhode Island, Delaware, Maryland, Virginia, and Georgia this tendency is found, but these seven colonies contained a substantial minority of the native claimants.

The American-born Tories (and some of the foreign-born) were every bit as American as their Whig brethren. They feared social change and any increase in the power of the democratic element in society, but one looks in vain for Loyalists who were opposed to liberty or the rights of Englishmen. The great majority did not even favor the "new" English legislation after the Seven Years War. The quarrel was over the *mode* of opposition; the Loyalists would not admit violence and believed the future of their country would be ruined by revolution and independence. It was not a case of colonial rights or "passive obedience," but rather whether the colonies' future well-being could be best assured within the empire or without. The Loyalists had a fundamental trust in Britain, the Whigs a fundamental distrust.

Nothing stands out so strongly and so poignantly in Loyalist writings as the authors' affection for their native land, an affection often sharpened by galling English superciliousness. One exile called England "the land of liberty and pride." [36] Edward Oxnard wrote in his journal, June 30, 1777: "This day I completed my thirtieth year of age. May Heaven grant me the happy sight of my native land before the return of another birthday." [37] In February, 1779, a visitor to Governor Wentworth of New Hampshire recorded, "I have found him very much dejected and pining for his native country." [38] In January, 1780, Samuel Curwen wrote, "For my native country I feel a filial fondness; her follies I lament, her misfortunes I pity; her good I ardently wish, and to be restored to her embraces is the warmest of my desires." [39]

Typically of expatriates it was sometimes the little things that told. In 1783 Edward Chandler wrote, "Mrs. Chandler is of this opinion that the *Hams* in England are by no means equal in quality to those in America, particularly those made in the Jerseys . . ." [40]

What made it worse for the exiles was the high cost of living in London and the sheer discomfort, mental and physical, of England. Dr. John Jeffries of Boston, while exiled in London, mainly attended his fellow countrymen, who, as he said, "from difference of climate, chagrin, and various circumstances, are very frequently disordered." [41]

Several exiles, such as Curwen, returned home after the war, and many more would have liked to if they had been allowed. Thus Thomas Robinson petitioned the governor of Delaware in September, 1786, correctly pointing out that although his politics had differed from theirs, he had helped his captured fellow countrymen, had collected and preserved the New Castle County records, and was now "desirous to spend the Evening of his Life among the Friends of his Earlier Years in his Native Country . . ."[42] As late as 1793 Count Rumford informed a friend, "I think it very probable that both you and I shall end our days" in America; "Great Britain is not a place for you, nor for me . . ."[43]

There are several contemporary accounts (mainly by Whigs) describing the motivation of the Loyalists. Dr. Benjamin Rush divided American society into six classes: First, "*A rank tory.* This class are advocates for unconditional submission to Great Britain." Second, "*Moderate men*" who wished to return to the situation of 1763, had "no relish for independence," were influenced by connection with office-holders, the "pomp, and hiarchy of the church of England," or a liking for English luxuries such as sugar, tea, and coffee, and whose characteristic it was to "hate all true whigs, and to love all rank tories." Third, "*timid Whigs*" who were frightened of Britain's power. Fourth, "*furious whigs*," a cowardly lot who were too violent and unprincipled. Fifth, "*Staunch whigs*" who were "friends of liberty from principle." Sixth, "Neither Whigs nor Tories" who had "no principles of any kind."[44]

John Eardly-Wilmot, one of the claims commissioners, wrote that some were Loyalists

from their native attachment; and what they thought their duty to their Sovereign; others from their official situations; many from policy, the dread of Civil War, and of its issue; and many more, perhaps, from an opinion that Great Britain would soon relax from the rigour of her demands, or at least would never abuse the power she claimed; but on the contrary, confine it within such limits, and subject it to such restrictions, as would remove all just cause of dissatisfaction, and prevent all possibility of future abuse and oppression. This was the case in the years 1773 and 1774, prior to the declaration of the American Congress, setting forth "the causes of their taking up arms," and previously to their Declaration of Independence in July, 1776. But when these measures were adopted by the Congress, and by the Colonies at large, and when Great Britain had, in 1776 shewn a fixed determination to support her Authority by force of arms, accompanied with conciliatory propositions, and a disposition "to revise the Laws by which the Americans might think themselves aggrieved;" the friends of Great Britain, who now came to be all denominated Loyalists, encreased in number, and were joined, not only by many men of property and abilities who had hitherto taken no part, but also by many who had been adverse to her at the first, and even by some of the Members of the Congress itself.[45]

The Philadelphia Committee of Secret Correspondence wrote to Silas Deane in Paris, October 1, 1776, stating a fear of the number of Tories throughout America, and continued that they were "of various kinds and various principles. Some are so from real attachment to *Britain*, some from interested view, many, very many, from fear of the *British* force; some because they are disatisfied with the general measures of Congress, more because they disapprove of the men in power and the measures in their respective States . . . if America falls, it will be owing to such divisions more than the force of our enemies." [46]

Thomas McKean believed that the Loyalists "consisted chiefly of the Friends or Quakers, the Menonists, the Protestant Episcopalians—whose clergy received salaries from the Society for Propagating the Gospel in Foreign Parts—and from the officers of the Crown and proprietors of provinces, with their connections,—adding the timid and those who believed the colonies would be conquered, and that, of course, they would be safe in their persons and property from such conduct, and also have a probability of obtaining office and distinction,—and also the discontented and capricious of all grades." [47]

As far as they go there is little to quarrel with in these statements (except McKean's view on the pacifist sects). Benjamin Franklin was rather more partial when he wrote to Francis Maseres, June 26, 1785, that the war against America was "begun by a general act of Parliament declaring all our estates confiscated; and probably one great motive to the loyalty of the royalists was the hope of sharing in these confiscations. They have played a deep game, staking their estates against ours; and they have been unsuccessful." [48]

John Adams was not impartial either, but is always worth listening to. He wrote to Dr. Jedidiah Morse, December 22, 1815, "In 1765 the colonies were more unanimous than they ever have been since, either as colonies or States. No party was formed against their country. The few who voted against the general sentiment, were but a handful." But after that

Hopes and fears, promises and threatenings, avarice and ambition, were excited; promotion, advancement, honor, glory, wealth, and power were promised; disgrace, ruin, poverty, contempt, torture, and death were threatened; and this pious moral system was pursued with steady and invariable perserverance for ten years, that is, from 1765 to 1775. And what was their success? Blot it out, my tears! . . . In the course of these ten years, they formed and organized and drilled and disciplined

Conclusion

a party in favor of Great Britain, and they seduced and deluded nearly one third of the people of the colonies.[49]

Adams then gave examples from Massachusetts of Loyalists motivated by personal gain and concluded very interestingly that he could give examples in other states, "but I give you notice, that not one of your friends, the federalists, through the continent will thank you for your curiosity."[50]

Benjamin West's painting of the Loyalists being welcomed to England in 1783 by Britannia includes an emancipated Negro family and an Indian chief.[51] These two groups, the Negroes and the Indians, although highly unusual and outside the main story, deserve brief mention.

At the time of the Revolution, of course, Negroes as individuals were outside political society. Crèvecoeur in one of his sketches has one of his characters address a Negro thus: "They say you are a good fellow, only a little Toryfied like most of your colour."[52] There was a widespread fear among the Whigs that the Negroes were going to be a serious threat, especially as Dunmore, Clinton, and Cornwallis offered the Patriots' slaves their freedom in return for military service. Actually, both sides used the black man in any way which aided their cause, and Negroes fought in both Whig and Tory ranks. It is clear that the Negro who was active during the Revolution joined one side or the other for reasons of advancement and freedom rather than for any political philosophy. A Virginian, John Twine, one of about forty Negro claimants, told the commissioners that he was a wagoner with the Americans but "was kept very bare in Cloaths and little Money and therefore he ran away from home when he heard there was more Money and better Usage in the British Army."[53]

[275]

A Georgia Negro, William Prince, appeared in London asking for Temporary Support. He said that he had been born free but cheated into slavery. When the British troops appeared in Georgia, he deserted his master and served for six years under General Prevost. He claimed the loss of two cows, two horses, and some pigs. The commissioners gave him short shrift, declaring him to be "a greater gainer by the troubles in America for being in a situation in which he could loose [*sic*] nothing he has gained everything, for he has gained his Liberty and he comes in our Opinion with a very bad grace to plead sufferings . . ." [54] These words sum up the position of the Negro Loyalist—he had indeed nothing to lose and everything to gain. The hope of freedom was presumably the only reason the Negroes were, in the words of one Stuart, a witness, "strongly attached to the British," adding that "these poor creatures [Negroes] are esteemed no better than cattle by those virtuous Sons of Liberty." [55] Not that the Loyalists quarreled with the institution of slavery; many were able to carry their slaves away with them to St. Augustine, or the West Indies, and others put slaves on board privateers in order to collect prize money. [56]

There were many "Tory" Negroes, but there were also many "Whigs." Thomas Harper, a loyal Charleston jeweller, told the commissioners that his Negro ran away and joined the Americans, and this was doubtless not an unusual case. [57] There was never any question of the British freeing the Loyalists' slaves except that after Somersett's case any exile's slave who reached the British Isles was automatically free.

Like the Negroes the Indians are a very special kind of Loyalist. Whigs and Tories alike treated the Indians gingerly, and several claimants admitted having borne arms against the aborigines, an act they considered entirely different from fighting the British. Indians as allies have always tended to be a two-edged sword. Thomas Anburey related that a young Loyalist lady, engaged to a provincial officer, was making her way towards the British troops when she met Indian scouts who agreed to take her to the British camp. However, two of the Indians argued over whose prisoner she was, whereupon one of them tomahawked the unfortunate girl for fear of losing the reward money.[58]

The British used Indians on the southern frontier and in upstate New York where Joseph Brant (whose half-caste family were the only Indians to submit claims) led the remnants of the Six Nations. Loyal Indians were simply following self-interest. Their supplies and trade came from the British government; they were used to dealing with its representatives, like Sir John Johnson, whose power they respected; further they had no enthusiasm for the westward-pushing, uncontrollable colonial settler and believed that the British rather than the Americans would be likely to exercise control.

A letter to Sir Guy Carleton from the Associated Loyalists bound for Port Roseway, Nova Scotia, invoked their devotion to the king and "that constitution, under which we had been particularly blest." [59] Jacob Rundell of Cortlandts Manor, New York, wrote that in joining the British he fled "from Usurpation to the best of Constitutions." [60] Beverly Robinson, Sr., of New York, was a Loyalist, he said, "not only to recover my Estate, but [to] have the happiness of contributing in restoring my Country to a Just mild and happy Constitution." A Loyalist poem of 1776 began, "Happy were the days, When *Laws* were in force,"

The King's Friends

and ended, "Still we sing, Bless the King, And again our banish'd Laws restore!" [61] Statements like these are common. And one did not need to have been particularly familiar with the subtleties of the British constitution to feel this way. Anthony Mosengeil, a German copper-mining expert resident in New Jersey, asserted simply that he joined the Loyalists, "being accustomed to regular and established Governments." [62] An Alsatian Loyalist characterized the Americans as "deluded" and their ways as "Licentiousness" compared with the "true Liberty" of Britain. [63]

No one who studies the Loyalists for any length of time can doubt that among the educated a genuine, often touching, zeal for the British constitution flourished. This very rarely meant approval of the unpopular parliamentary legislation since 1763; but it did mean trust in the basic system and in peaceful methods of redress. Also, such Loyalists pointed to the amazing growth and prosperity of the colonies within the empire and to the great freedom already enjoyed; how much more could a reasonable man want, they asked, and many argued that if anything the power of the masses should be diminished.

But comparatively few Loyalists took a reasoned position. Most colonists, like most people anywhere, followed their leaders. Thus the quality and type of leaders, Whig and Tory, is important. This helps to explain why Loyalism barely existed in Virginia and was strong in South Carolina, why it was stronger in New York than in Massachusetts.

Self-interest and greed are obviously important factors in all human affairs and Loyalism is no exception. Many examples in various colonies have been given of merchants who traded with the British during the war, a fact which probably induced loyalty. James Simpson reported to the claims commissioners: "Such were the incidents of the war, that the profits upon a single voyage sometimes enabled the Adventurers, not only to emerge from Indigence and obscurity, but to rise to a great degree of opulence . . ."[64] However, the Whig side was often economically more attractive. Schlesinger has suggested that although the merchants did not usually favor independence, "the line of least resistance" was to accept it, especially if their wealth was not removable, and their business and customers could not be transferred to the British lines.[65] Also, although many lawyers were Loyalists, many others, like certain merchants, were sham Whigs. William Franklin reported that Isaac Ogden, a New Jersey lawyer who was a member of the provincial congress, went in "as many of his Profession did, with a view of promoting his popularity and preventing others from running away with his business."[66] Hard money was often a temptation over paper continentals. When the British troops returned to Charleston, Joshua Lockwood, a substantial mechanic, changed from Whiggery to Toryism in order to collect his debts in specie.[67]

Whether it was true or not, several Tories (especially in Boston) from split families were suspected of opportunism, of deliberately splitting so that the family would retain the property whichever side won. Benjamin Pickman fled from Salem, Massachusetts, in 1775, but left his wife behind to look after their property, to which he returned ten years later. The Dulanys of Maryland were charged with a similar subterfuge.[68]

Similarly, quite apart from the consideration of their oaths, royal and proprietary officials would lose their jobs by rebellion. But even if they never guessed that they would lose them, many office-holders were able people who

The King's Friends

could have had, and indeed frequently were offered, attractive appointments with the Whig regimes. Thus, loyalty was certainly not always a simple case of self-interest, a conclusion reinforced by the number of merchant-partners who chose opposite sides (assuming the economic interest was clear).

Thomas McKean's identification of the Loyalists with the "timid" has sometimes been taken up by historians, and other contemporaries agreed with the Pennsylvania statesman. Ambrose Serle, who as secretary to Lord Howe in New York became disillusioned with the Loyalists, in December, 1776, quoted his master as observing "to me this morning, that almost all the People of Parts and Spirit were in the Rebellion." [69] A few days later Serle himself complained of the Loyalists, "alas, they all prate and profess much; but when You call upon them, they will *do* nothing." [70] Lord Cornwallis also designated the Loyalists as "timid," [71] and while praising their fortitude condemned their "indecision." [72]

Perhaps most men of "parts" were Patriots; the Loyalist leadership could not remotely match the Whigs in talent. Some Loyalists were undoubtedly timid. (This was especially the case in South Carolina.) They were afraid of the turbulence and change of the Revolution—Crèvecoeur was held back by the "respect I feel for the ancient connection, and the fear of innovations, with the consequences of which I am not well acquainted" [73]—and convinced that the British army, the representative, after all, of the greatest empire the world had yet seen, must triumph. They shared Samuel Curwen's strong conviction of the almost physical impossibility of the colonies' "waging a successful war" with Great Britain.[74]

Conclusion

But timidity was not always, or perhaps even usually, the rule. Some Loyalists were never daunted, such as Philip Skene, of Skenesborough, New York, who, Governor Franklin related, even when jailed at Hartford, Connecticut, would "still harangue the people from the prison windows." [75] Joshua North of Delaware was so anxious to join the British army in 1779 in Carolina that he rode the 1,100 miles, 400 of which were under snow, and often slept in "a Temporary Hut of Saplins." [76]

It took great courage to express a violently unpopular minority view, to undergo social ostracism, economic ruin, and even physical torture and death, which many suffered with great fortitude. Admittedly these were not normally the results that had been expected, but many Loyalists stuck to their position even when it was clear they were on the losing side. The claims commission testimony is replete with examples of Loyalists who refused tempting offers of official positions with the rebels. Further, many Loyalists were so in spite of the lack of British encouragement and even in the face of British harassment, complaints of which are a common feature of the claims commission testimony and of Loyalist writings.

Other keys to Loyalism than timidity have been offered. William H. Nelson has suggested that the various Loyalist groups were usually "cultural minorities" in need of British help or protection and fearful of an increase in the power of the majority. [77]

This view is echoed by William W. Sweet who rightly points out that the number of Anglican Loyalists is in inverse proportion to the strength of the church; thus in New England they were loyal almost to a man, in Virginia most Anglicans were Whig. [78]

This theory of "cultural minorities" is undoubtedly valuable. As Nelson points out, the Dutch and Germans were Tory mainly where they had not been Anglicized, and New Rochelle, the only place where the French Calvinists still spoke French, seems to have been the one area of substantial Huguenot Loyalism.[79] One can add such examples as the small farmers of New York who had rebelled under Pendergast against their Whig landlords, the Highland Catholic tenants of Sir John Johnson, the Baptists of Ashfield, Massachusetts, who were struggling against the established Congregational church; the conferentie minority of the Dutch Reformed church who feared the majority coetus group in the Hackensack Valley, New Jersey; the back-country farmers of the Carolinas who were restless under the dominating Whiggish seaboard; Indians and Negroes who were social outcasts; and Scottish merchants and creditors in the South who had little in common with their indebted American planter-customers.

Most Loyalists had, or thought they had, something material or spiritual to lose from the break with Britain. This fear was the great unifying factor. Officials had their jobs to lose, lawyers their fees, merchants their trade, landowners their proprietorships, Anglicans their dream of a bishop, king-worshippers and aristocrats their idol, Anglophiles their membership in the empire, some Regulators and Massachusetts Baptists their hope of royal help, Negroes their freedom, Indians the British alliance against the frontiersman. Conservatives and the better off in general had most to lose in a revolutionary upheaval; the timid became Loyalists in areas occupied by British troops; some officeholders, and perhaps the Highlanders were loath to break their oaths of allegiance.

John Eardly-Wilmot, one of the claims commissioners,

Conclusion

began his enquiry with no particular liking for the Loyalists, but long familiarity with their misfortunes produced in him considerable admiration, so that his account of the claims commission proceedings, published in 1815, was prefaced, rather appropriately, with the following lines from Milton:

Their Loyalty they kept, their love, their zeal,
Nor number, nor example with them wrought
To swerve from truth, or change their constant mind.

APPENDIX: STATISTICAL TABLES

A NOTE ON THE TABLES

THE TABLES which follow have been compiled from the records of the British government claims commission. Apart from the help of the local military commanders in America during the war (the surviving records of which are of no use for this study) two kinds of aid were given to the Loyalists: temporary pensions to exiles in Great Britain during the war known as "Temporary Support"; and, after the peace treaty, permanent pensions and lump sums of money for losses caused by loyalty during the Revolution. The comparatively brief "Temporary Support" records have been used because some Loyalists appear there and not in the records for permanent compensation. But these latter records are the more important and account for the bulk of the tables.

To obtain permanent compensation a Loyalist had to appear before the specially appointed commissioners who were stationed in London and in Canada, submit a written memorial recounting his loyal actions and indicating his losses, show affidavits and supporting letters, produce witnesses, and undergo oral examination. Considerable detail was expected and given; full lists of all lost property, real and personal, were submitted, and, whenever possible, proof (such as certified deeds and copies of American confiscation acts). If written proofs were not available the commissioners questioned witnesses who had first-hand knowledge, either orally or by letter. In examining a claimant there was no prepared form, simply as thorough an examination as possible.

The procedure for examining the earlier claims for Temporary Support was similar, only briefer and less exhaustive. Where a Loyalist is found successfully claiming Temporary Support and later permanent compensation, the latter record generally confirms the earlier claim. Only in the comparatively few cases where a Loyalist has not been found in the permanent compensation record has the Temporary Support evidence been relied upon.

The commissioners also collected evidence on general conditions in each colony and were very thorough in their examinations, so thorough that many Loyalists compared the commission to the Inquisition. (Technical accounts of the work of the claims commissioners can be found in many places. See in particular, Eardly-Wilmot, *Historical View*, for a description by one of the commissioners; also Egerton [ed.], *American Loyalists*, pp. xiii–lii; Flick, *Loyalism in New York*, pp. 204–211; Van Tyne, *The Loyalists*, pp. 300–304.) Undetected frauds were probably extremely rare and the information found in the tables is therefore normally very accurate. (Claimants would be tempted to give only two kinds of false information: the amount of losses and actions proving loyalty, and in each case the commissioners would be likely to find them out.)

In constructing the tables evidence which the commissioners rejected and claims by any fraudulent Loyalists have not been used. If the commissioners merely discounted *part* of the evidence but accepted the claimant as a Loyalist, only the fraudulent element has been omitted. A few people with American property gained compensation although they had never lived in America or had left long before the troubles began. These claimants are not included in the tables. Almost all claimants sought compensation for virtually their entire property. However, a few (and the commissioners always established this point) had managed to save something, for which, of course, they could expect no compensation. In these cases the claimant's entire wealth (usually given in evidence and confirmed by witnesses) has been used in the relevant tables. Figures given in local currencies have been converted to sterling using the scale established by the commissioners.

The question arises: how typical a sample of the Loyalists as a whole were the claimants? They are certainly not *all* the Loyalists in each colony, but probably represent most of the very active, and a substantial segment of those exiled. Multiplication by five or six will add each claimant's presumed family. It may be that the very humble Loyalists are underrepresented because they had lost little and therefore might not bother to submit a claim. However, the large number of claims by poor people, and even Negroes, suggests that this is not necessarily true. It is certain that the Loyalist claimants are the only accessible large sample (for all the colonies) of the undoubted Loyalists about whom enough information is known to make a general analysis.

The number of claims analyzed for each colony is as follows:

New Hampshire	42
Massachusetts	313
Rhode Island	54
Connecticut	150
New York	1,106
New Jersey	239
Pennsylvania	206
Delaware	10
Maryland	82
Virginia	130
North Carolina	153
South Carolina	320
Georgia	103
Total	2,908

New Hampshire

In the following tables forty-two claims are analyzed. Twenty-seven were filed in London, fifteen in Nova Scotia. One London claimant lived in Nova Scotia, and one returned to New Hampshire. (Apart from claimants from each colony who made special journeys from the United States or the West Indies, most seemed to have lived either in London [a very few gave a provincial address, usually Bristol where living costs were lower], or in the area which became the Canadian Maritime Provinces [and sometimes more westerly parts of Canada]. The geographical distribution of the claimants in Britain and Canada is beyond the scope of this work.)

National Origin (25 known)

Country of Birth	Nova Scotia Claimants	London Claimants	Combined	% of Known
England	0	1	1 ⎤	4.0 ⎤
Scotland	0	2	2 ⎬ 6	8.0 ⎬ 24.0
Ireland	0	3	3 ⎦	12.0 ⎦
America	8	11	19	76.0
Unknown	7	10	17	
Total	15	27	42	100.00

Date of Immigrants' Arrival in America (6 known)

	Nova Scotia	London	Combined
1763 and earlier	0	4	4
1764 and later	0	2	2
Unknown	0	0	0
Total	0	6	6

Tables—New Hampshire

Occupations (41 known)

	Nova Scotia	London	Combined	% of Known
Farmers and Landowners	7	4	11	26.8
Commerce				
(a) Artisans and craftsmen	1[a]	2[b]	3 ⎫	7.3 ⎫
(b) Merchants	2	3	5 ⎬ 10	12.2 ⎬ 24.3
(c) Ship's captain	0	2	2 ⎭	⎭
Professions				
(a) Lawyers	1	2	3 ⎫ 5	⎫ 12.2
(b) Doctors	1	1	2 ⎭	⎭
Office-Holders	2[c]	13[d]	15	36.6
Unknown	1	0	1	
Total	15	27	42	100.0

[a] A weaver.

[b] Two printers.

[c] One governor and one commander of Fort William and Mary.

[d] Five customs officers, one postmaster, one surveyor-general, one receiver of quit rents, one governor's secretary, one judge of probate court, one deputy surveyor of H.M. woods, one clerk of Common Pleas, one deputy register to probate court.

Amount of Claims (25 known)

	Nova Scotia	London	Combined	% of Known
£500 or less	5	2	7	28.0
£501–£1,000	1	1	2	8.0
£1,001–£2,000	3	1	4	16.0
£2,001–£5,000	1	7	8	32.0
£5,001–£10,000	2	1	3	12.0
Over £10,000	1	0	1	4.0
Unknown	2	11	13	
Claim for salary or income only	0	4	4	
Total	15	27	42	100.00

Tables—New Hampshire

Service to the British
(London and Nova Scotia Claimants Combined)[a]

Served in the armed forces including the militia

Probably in the ranks[b]	7
Officers	4
Probably officers	2
Status unknown	5
Total	18 or 43.0%
Served in some other official way[c]	3 or 7.6%
Total who served in some way	21 or 50.0%
Claimants killed or wounded	0
Claimants captured or imprisoned	6 or 14.0%

---

[a] In this category the number shown is always the total number of claims analyzed.

[b] I have used my judgment in assigning claimants to the two categories, "Probably in the ranks," and "Probably officers." Normally a claimant would emphasize that he was an officer in order to prove his loyalty, but very occasionally a claimant's social position or type of service would indicate he was an officer although the fact is not specifically stated. More often a claimant's low social position, failure to mention a commission, and other internal evidence would indicate a position probably in the ranks.

[c] For the colonies as a whole this category includes service with British departments such as the commissary, engineer's, quartermaster's, forage, and armorer's, such activities as prisoner supervisor, pilot, privateer, and contracted blacksmith and baker, and also various offices held during the military occupation.

Geographic Distribution (38 known)

Cheshire County		8
Keene	3	
Alstead	1	
Richmond	1	
Packersfield	1	
Charlestown	1	
Claremont	1	
Hillsborough County		7
Merrimack	1	

Hollis	1	
Amherst	1	
Dunbarton	2	
Litchfield	1	
Hillsborough County	1	
Rockingham County		22
Portsmouth	20	
Londonderry	1	
Pembroke	1	
Strafford County		1
Wolfeboro	1	
Unknown		4
Total		42

MASSACHUSETTS

In the following tables 313 claims are analyzed. Two hundred and twenty-two were filed in London, ninety-one in Nova Scotia. Twenty-three London claimants returned to the United States, fifteen lived in Canada, one in the Bahamas, and one in Flanders. Ten of the Nova Scotia claimants returned to the United States.

National Origin (268 known)

Country of Birth	Nova Scotia Claimants	London Claimants	Combined		% of Known	
Great Britain (country unknown)	2	7	9		3.4	
England	4	19	23		8.0	
Scotland	9	5	14		5.2	
Ireland	5	8	13	65	4.9	27.0
Wales	0	2	2			
Germany	0	2	2			
Switzerland	1	0	1			
Sweden	0	1	1			
America	59	144	203		73.0	
Unknown	11	34	45			
Total	91	222	313		100.00[a]	

[a] In this and some other tables the percentages of very small numbers have not been calculated; hence the full 100 per cent is not always shown in the column above.

Date of Immigrants' Arrival in America (49 known)

	Nova Scotia	London	Combined
1763 and earlier	5	23	28
1764 and later	11	10	21
Unknown	4	12	16
Total	20	45	65

Occupations (302 known)

	Nova Scotia	London	Combined	% of Known
Farmers and Landowners	20	17	37	11.5
Commerce				
(a) Artisans and craftsmen	12[a]	15[b]	27	9.1
(b) Merchants and shopkeepers	39	67	106	35.0
(c) Seamen and pilots	2	8	10	
(d) Innkeepers	2	1	3	
(e) Shipbuilders	1	1	2	
(f) Auctioneer	0	1	1	

Commerce combined: 149 — 50.0 %

	Nova Scotia	London	Combined	% of Known
Professions				
(a) Anglican ministers	1	8	9	
Congregational minister	0	1	1	
(b) Lawyers	4	13	17	
(c) Schoolmasters	1	1	2	
(d) Doctors	1	16[c]	17	
(e) Surgeon's mate	0	1	1	
(f) Dentist	0	1	1	
(g) Musician and organist	0	1	1	
(h) Limner and painter	0	1	1	
(i) Fencing master	1	0	1	

Professions combined: 51 — 17.0 %

	Nova Scotia	London	Combined	% of Known
Office-Holders	6[d]	58[e]	64	21.5
Unknown	1	11	12	
Total	91	222	313	100.00

[a] One carpenter, one weaver, one tailor, one painter and glazier, two bakers, two mastmakers, two blacksmiths, one coppersmith, and one master builder.

Tables—Massachusetts

Amount of Claims (238 known)

	Nova Scotia	London	Combined	% of Known
£500 or less	24	27	51	21.2
£501–£1,000	17	17	34	14.5
£1,001–£2,000	14	30	44	18.6
£2,001–£5,000	12	44	56	23.5
£5,001–£10,000	9	22	31	13.0
Over £10,000	6	15	21	9.2
Unknown	7	51	58	
Claim for salary or income only	2	16	18	
Total	91	222	313	100.00

Service to the British
(London and Nova Scotia Claimants Combined)

Served in the armed forces including the militia

In the ranks	3
Probably in the ranks	14
Officers	64
Probably officers	5
Status unknown	45
Total	131 or 42.0%
Served in some other official way	22 or 7.0%
Total who served in some way	153 or 49.0%
Claimants killed or wounded	16 or 4.8%
Claimants captured or imprisoned	59 or 19.0%

ᵇ Two master builders, one painter, two printers, one barber, three tailors, one watchmaker, one silversmith, one farrier, one shoemaker, one tin-plate maker and one ropemaker.

ᶜ Includes one doctor's apprentice.

ᵈ Four customs officers, one clerk of Common Pleas, and one surveyor of the king's woods.

ᵉ Thirty-nine customs officers, four judges of Common Pleas, one paymaster of British troops in North America, two deputy surveyors of the king's woods, one register of court of admiralty, one attorney-general, one advocate-general, one chief justice, three vice-admiralty court judges, one treasurer of Bahamas, one lieutenant-governor, one secretary of Massachusetts, one treasurer, and one deputy treasurer. (Fourteen of these also merchants, one a doctor, and six lawyers.)

Tables—Massachusetts

Geographic Distribution (299 known)

Berkshire County		9
New Ashford	5	
Lanesboro	1	
Pittsfield	1	
Stockbridge	1	
Gt. Barrington	1	
Bristol County		8
Taunton	6	
Freetown	1	
Berkley	1	
Cumberland County		14
Falmouth	14	
Essex County		24
Salem	12	
Marblehead	6	
Newbury	4	
Haverhill	1	
Ipswich	1	
Hampshire County		1
Deerfield	1	
Lincoln County		22
Penobscot and environs	15	
Deer Island nr. Penobscot	3	
Machias	2	
Pownal	1	
Woolwich	1	
Middlesex County		22
Cambridge	7	
Charlestown	5	
Groton	3	
Townsend	2	
Littleton	1	
Marlboro	1	
Medford	1	
Stow	1	
Middlesex County	1	

Nantucket County		2
Nantasket	1	
Nantucket County	1	
Plymouth County		6
Middleboro	2	
Bridgewater	1	
Halifax	1	
Marshfield	1	
Plymouth County	1	
Suffolk County		167
Boston	157	
Brookline	2	
Dorchester	2	
Roxbury	2	
Braintree	1	
Dedham	1	
Milton	1	
Wrentham	1	
Worcester County		24
Worcester	9	
Hardwick	3	
Lancaster	3	
Brookfield	2	
Rutland	2	
Oakham	1	
Petersham	1	
Princeton	1	
Shrewsbury	1	
Worcester County	1	
Unknown		14
Total		313

In the following tables fifty-four claims are analyzed. Forty-five were filed in London, nine in Nova Scotia. Two London claimants lived in Canada.

National Origin (33 known)

Country of Birth	Nova Scotia Claimants	London Claimants	Combined		% of Known	
Great Britain (country unknown)	0	3	3 }		9.1 }	
England	0	7	7 } 12		21.3 } 36.4	
Scotland	0	1	1 }		3.0 }	
Germany	0	1	1 }		3.0 }	
America	8	13	21		63.6	
Unknown	1	20	21			
Total	9	45	54		100.00	

Date of Immigrants' Arrival in America (12 known)

	Nova Scotia	London	Combined
1763 and earlier	0	6	6
1764 and later	0	6	6
Unknown	0	0	0
Total	0	12	12

Occupations (45 known)

	Nova Scotia	London	Combined		% of Known	
Farmers and Landowners	4	5	9		20.0	
Commerce						
(a) Artisans and craftsmen	1[a]	0	1 }		2.2 }	
(b) Merchants and shopkeepers	4	16	20 } 26		44.0 } 58.0	
(c) Seamen and pilots	0	5	5 }		}	

[299]

Professions

(a) Lawyers	0	1	1	
(b) Doctors	0	2	2	
(c) Anglican minister	0	1	1	5 11.0
(d) Royal naval officer	0	1	1	
Office-Holders	0	5[b]	5	11.0
Unknown	0	14	14	
Total	9	45	54	100.00

[a] One tanner.

[b] Four customs officers, and one attorney-general and judge of vice-admiralty.

Amount of Claims (32 known)

	Nova Scotia	London	Combined	% of Known
£500 or less	2	5	7	21.8
£501–£1,000	2	4	6	18.8
£1,001–£2,000	2	1	3	9.4
£2,001–£5,000	2	11	13	40.6
£5,001–£10,000	0	2	2	6.2
Over £10,000	0	1	1	3.1
Unknown	1	8	9	
Claim for salary or income only	0	12	12	
Total	9	45	54	100.00

Service to the British
(London and Nova Scotia Claimants Combined)

Served in the armed forces including the militia

In the ranks	1
Officers	12
Status unknown	4
Total	17 or 32%

Tables—Rhode Island

Served in some other official way	8 or 15%	
Total who served in some way	25 or 47%	
Claimants killed or wounded	0	
Claimants captured or imprisoned	16 or 30%	

Geographic Distribution (49 known)

Kings County		5
North Kingstown	3	
Richmond	1	
Kings County	1	
Newport County		44
Newport	44	
Unknown		5
Total		54

CONNECTICUT

In the following tables 150 claims are analyzed. Seventy-nine were filed in London, seventy-one in Nova Scotia. Fifteen London claimants lived in Canada and one in Connecticut. One Nova Scotia claimant indicated that he intended to return to New York.

National Origin (90 known)

Country of Birth	Nova Scotia Claimants	London Claimants	Combined		% of Known	
Great Britain (country unknown)	0	2	2 ⎫		2.2 ⎫	
England	0	3	3 ⎬ 15		3.3 ⎬ 16.5	
Scotland	0	4	4 ⎮		4.4 ⎮	
Ireland	2	4	6 ⎭		6.6 ⎭	
America	52	23	75		84.5	
Unknown	17	43	60		———	
Total	71	79	150		100.00	

Date of Immigrants' Arrival in America (15 known)

	Nova Scotia	London	Combined
1763 and earlier	1	4	5
1764 and later	1	8	9
Unknown	0	1	1
Total	2	13	15

Occupations (138 known)

	Nova Scotia	London	Combined		% of Known	
Farmers and Landowners	31	28	59		42.8	
Commerce						
(a) Artisans and craftsmen	11[a]	9[b]	20 ⎫		14.5 ⎫	
(b) Merchants and shopkeepers	18	17	35 ⎬ 60		25.3 ⎬ 43.4	
(c) Seamen and pilots	2[c]	2	4 ⎮		⎮	
(d) Innkeeper	1	0	1 ⎭		⎭	

Tables—Connecticut

Professions					
(a) Anglican ministers	1	1	2		
Dissenting minister	0	1	1		
(b) Lawyers	1	2	3	11	8.0
(c) Schoolmaster	1	0	1		
(d) Military officer	0	1	1		
(e) Doctors	3	0	3		
Office-Holders	1[d]	7[e]	8		5.8
Unknown	1	11	12		
Total	71	79	150		100.00

[a] One tanner, one weaver, one breeches-maker, two carpenters, two hatters, two millers, and two shoemakers.

[b] One cooper, one breeches-maker, one carpenter, one tanner, one silversmith and jeweler, one printer, one silversmith, one leatherer and skinner, one blacksmith.

[c] Including one fisherman. The two London claimants were one captain and one master of navigation.

[d] One gauger and deputy postmaster.

[e] All customs officers.

Amount of Claims (129 known)

	Nova Scotia	London	Combined	% of Known
£ 500 or less	39	25	64	49.0
£ 501–£ 1,000	16	11	27	20.0
£ 1,001–£ 2,000	11	9	20	15.0
£ 2,001–£ 5,000	2	4	6	5.3
£ 5,001–£ 10,000	2	4	6	5.3
Over £ 10,000	0	6	6	5.3
Unknown	2	16	18	
Claim for salary or income only	0	3	3	
Total	72	78	150	100.00

Tables—Connecticut

Service to the British
(London and Nova Scotia Claimants Combined)

Served in the armed forces including the militia

In the ranks	8
Probably in the ranks	13
Officers	34
Probably officers	1
Status unknown	18
Total	74 or 49.3%
Served in some other official way	20 or 13.3%
Total who served in some way	94 or 62.6%
Claimants killed or wounded	9 or 6.0%
Claimants captured or imprisoned	52 or 33.0%

Geographic Distribution (146 known)

Fairfield County		80
Norwalk	25	
Stamford	18	
Fairfield	12	
Stratford	4	
Danbury	5	
Redding	4	
Ridgefield	3	
Greenwich	4	
Fairfield County	5	
Hartford County		14
Middletown	6	
Hartford	3	
Glastonbury	2	
Farmington	1	
Simsbury	1	
Suffield	1	
Litchfield County		15
Woodbury	6	
New Milford	4	
Torrington	1	

Litchfield	1	
Litchfield County	3	
New Haven County		22
New Haven	16	
Derby	1	
Waterbury	2	
Branford	2	
Wallingford	1	
New London County		13
New London	6	
Norwich	6	
Stonington	1	
Windham County		2
Plainfield	1	
Voluntown	1	
Unknown		4
Total		150

NEW YORK

In the following tables (which include Vermont) 1,106 claims are analyzed. Two hundred and twenty-five were filed in London, 881 in Nova Scotia. Ten London claimants returned to the United States, twenty-six were resident in Canada, one in the West Indies, and one in the East Indies. Eight Nova Scotia claimants returned to the United States.

National Origin (974 known)

Country of Birth	Nova Scotia Claimants	London Claimants	Combined		% of Known	
Great Britain (country unknown)	4	15	19		1.92	
England	43	38	81		8.3	
Scotland	191	23	214		21.5	
Ireland	65	32	97		10.0	
Wales	2	2	4	489		50.0
Germany	64	5	69		7.1	
Holland	1	2	3			
Minorca	0	1	1			
Alsace	1	0	1			
America	405	80	485		50.0	
Unknown	105	27	132			
Total	881	225	1,106		100.00	

Date of Immigrants' Arrival in America (438 known)

	Nova Scotia	London	Combined
1763 and earlier	111	87	198
1764 and later	209	31	240
Unknown	51	0	51
Total	371	118	489

Tables—New York

Occupations (1,071 known)

	Nova Scotia	London	Combined		% of Known	
Farmers and Landowners	742	58	800		74.7	
Commerce						
(a) Artisans and craftsmen	65[a]	29[b]	94		8.9	
(b) Merchants and shopkeepers	27	50	77		7.3	
(c) Seamen	1	8[c]	9	190		17.7
(d) Innkeepers	4	4	8			
(e) Boarding-house keepers	0	2	2			
Professions						
(a) Anglican ministers	0	9	9			
German Reformed	1	0	1			
Roman Catholic	0	1	1			
(b) Doctors	6	7	13			
(c) Lawyers	3	5	8	39		3.7
(d) Surveyors	0	2	2			
(e) Schoolmasters	0	2	2			
(f) King's College professors	0	2	2			
(g) Broker and vendue master	1	0	1			
Office-Holders	5[d]	37[e]	42		3.9	
Unknown	26	9	35			
Total	881	225	1,106		100.00	

[a] Nineteen blacksmiths, seven shoemakers, five tanners, five carpenters, four each: weavers, coopers, three millers, three tailors, two tinmen (one also a japanner), one each: silversmith, cordwainer, armorer, gardener, woodcutter, bricklayer, joiner, carter, ferryman, gunsmith, cutler, hatter, and millwright.

[307]

Tables—New York

Amount of Claims (1,025 known)

	Nova Scotia	London	Combined	% of Known
£500 or less	630	30	660	64.0
£501–£1,000	110	23	133	13.5
£1,001–£2,000	58	29	87	8.5
£2,001–£5,000	40	33	73	7.1
£5,001–£10,000	9	24	33	3.2
Over £10,000	2	37	39	3.7
Unknown	31	38	69	
Claim for salary or income only	1	11	12	
Total	881	225	1,106	100.00

Service to the British
(London and Nova Scotia Claimants Combined)

Served in the armed forces including the militia

In the ranks	113
Probably in the ranks	70
Officers	160
Status unknown	390
Total	733 or 67.0%
Served in some other official way	87 or 8.0%
Total who served in some way	820 or 75.0%

ᵇ Four watchmakers, three shoemakers, two each: tanner, hairdresser, one each: livery-stable keeper, saddler, cooper, silversmith, last-maker, brewer, carpenter and herring smoker, potash works and nailery, milk-man, carter, baker, blacksmith, "labourer," butcher, housekeeper, flax-dresser, waiter at a tavern, pavior.

ᶜ Five masters of vessels and three mariners.

ᵈ Three sheriffs, one deputy commissary, one deputy surveyor-general.

ᵉ Six customs officials, four in Indian Department, three judges of Common Pleas, three sheriffs, two clerks of peace, two supreme court judges, one each: governor, chief justice, commander of sloop on Lake Champlain, deputy secretary of New York, mayor of New York, barrack-master, attorney-general, governor of Oswego, judge of admiralty, sur-veyor-general, secretary to Tryon, lieutenant-governor of Crown Point and Ticonderoga, chief engineer in America, master carpenter, land office, mayor and coroner of Albany, agent to Governor Skene.

Claimants killed or wounded	36 or	3.3%
Claimants captured or imprisoned	313 or	28.5%

Geographic Distribution (1,068 known)

Albany County		259
Albany and environs	32	
Arlington	10	
Balls Town	5	
Bennington	5	
Cambridge	12	
Hosack	8	
Manor of Livingston	3	
Manor of Rensselaer	7	
Pittstown	11	
Rensselaerwick	2	
Saratoga	43	
Schoharie	12	
Stillwater	10	
Albany County	99	
Charlotte County		143
Crown Point	11	
Fort Edward	10	
Kingsbury	20	
Skenesborough	13	
Ticonderoga	5	
Charlotte County	84	
Cumberland County		9
Rockingham	1	
Wethersfield	1	
Windsor	1	
Cumberland County	6	
Dutchess County		64
Fredericksburg	4	
Nine Partners	6	
Poughkeepsie	4	
Dutchess County	50	

Gloucester County		4
Mooretown	1	
Gloucester County	3	
Long Island—Kings County		3
Brookline	2	
Kings County	1	
Long Island—Queens County		16
Buskwick	1	
Flushing	2	
Hampstead	2	
Jamaica	1	
Jericho	1	
Newtown	1	
Queens County	8	
Long Island—Suffolk County		5
Brookhaven	1	
Suffolk County	4	
Long Island—county unknown		1
New York County		138
New York City	138	
Orange County		17
Goshen	5	
Haverstraw District	1	
Orange County	11	
Richmond County—Staten Island		4
Staten Island	4	
Tryon County		262
Canajoharie	6	
Cherry Valley	7	
German Flats	4	
Johnstown	58	
Sir John Johnson's land	36	
Sir Wm. Johnson's land	11	
Johnson's Bush	18	
Albany Bush	2	

Kingsborough	14	
Scotch Bush	4	
Stone Arabia	5	
Tryon County	97	
Ulster County		26
On Delaware River	9	
Newburgh	3	
Ulster County	14	
Westchester County		117
Bedford	4	
Crumpond	3	
Cortlandt Manor	22	
East Chester	7	
Frog's Neck	3	
Morrisania	2	
New Rochelle	5	
North Castle	15	
Philipsburg	16	
Westchester	2	
White Plains	10	
Westchester County	28	
Unknown		38
Total		1,106

NEW JERSEY

In the following tables 239 claims are analyzed. One hundred and two were filed in London, 137 in Nova Scotia. Eight London claimants returned to the United States, thirteen lived in Canada, two in the West Indies, and one in Germany. Twelve Nova Scotia claimants returned to the United States, and one lived in the West Indies.

National Origin (209 known)

Country of Birth	Nova Scotia Claimants	London Claimants	Combined		% of Known	
England	6	19	25		12.0	
Scotland	2	5	7		3.4	
Ireland	4	10	14	49	6.75	23.0
Germany	1	1	2			
France	1	0	1			
America	102	58	160		77.0	
Unknown	20	10	30			
Total	137	102	239		100.00	

Date of Immigrants' Arrival in America (42 known)

	Nova Scotia	London	Combined
1763 and earlier	6	10	16
1764 and later	5	21	26
Unknown	3	4	7
Total	14	35	49

Occupations (228 known)

	Nova Scotia	London	Combined	% of Known
Farmers and Landowners	87	28	115	50.1

Tables—New Jersey

Commerce						
(a) Artisans and craftsmen	12[a]	13[b]	25		11.0	
(b) Merchants and shopkeepers	14	18	32		14.0	
(c) Seamen and pilots	1[c]	1[d]	2	63		28.0
(d) Innkeepers	1	1	2			
(e) Ferry keeper	1	0	1			
(f) Fisherman	0	1	1			
Professions						
(a) Anglican ministers	3	2	5			
Dutch Reformed clergy	0	1	1			
(b) Lawyers	2	4	6			
(c) Schoolmaster	1	0	1	26		11.5
(d) Army officer	0	1	1			
(e) Studying law	0	1	1			
(f) Doctors	5	5	10			
(g) Studying medicine	0	1	1			
Office-Holders	6[e]	18[f]	24			10.4
Unknown	3	7	10			
Total	136	102	239			100.00

[a] Four carpenters, one each: groom, tailor, tanner, stonecutter, shoemaker, butcher, baker, and blacksmith.

[b] Three carpenters, two managers of iron works, one each: blacksmith, tailor, copper smelter, baker, cooper, shoemaker, soap boiler, and brewer.

[c] A mariner.

[d] A master of a ship.

[e] Three sheriffs, one deputy surveyor, one clerk of courts and keeper of records, Bergen County, one surveyor-general.

[f] Two sheriffs, two judges of Common Pleas, one each: sergeant of supreme court, chief justice, treasurer of N.J., governor, attorney-general, justice of supreme court, in general surrogate office, three customs officials, two masters in chancery to N.J., two service of Gov. Franklin.

Amount of Claims (226 known)

	Nova Scotia	London	Combined	% of Known
£ 500 or less	45	14	59	26.2
£ 501–£ 1,000	36	10	46	20.2
£ 1,001–£ 2,000	36	23	59	26.2
£ 2,001–£ 5,000	16	24	40	17.5
£ 5,001–£ 10,000	2	12	14	6.4
Over £ 10,000	0	8	8	3.5
Unknown	1	8	9	
Claim for salary or income only	1	3	4	
Total	137	102	239	100.00

Service to the British
(London and Nova Scotia Claimants Combined)

Served in the armed forces including the militia

In the ranks	5
Probably in the ranks	14
Officers	84
Probably officers	1
Status unknown	27
Total	131 or 54.0%
Served in some other official way	34 or 14.0%
Total who served in some way	165 or 68.0%
Claimants killed or wounded	19 or 8.0%
Claimants captured or imprisoned	72 or 30.0%

Geographic Distribution (232 known)

Bergen County		29
Hackensack	13	
English Neighborhood	3	
New Bridge	1	
Pavonia	1	
Ramapo	1	
Bergen County	10	

Burlington County   7
   Burlington   2
   Mansfield   1
   Nottingham   1
   Crosswicks   2
   Bordentown   1

Cumberland County   3
   Stow Creek   1
   Roadstown   1
   Cumberland County   1

Essex County   31
   Elizabeth   11
   Newark   15
   Rahway   3
   Horseneck   1
   Acquackanonk   1

Gloucester County   7
   Woolwich   1
   Coopers Ferry   1
   Gloucester   2
   Gloucester County   3

Hunterdon County   15
   Trenton   8
   Kingwood   3
   Alexandria   1
   Hunterdon County   3

Middlesex County   63
   Perth Amboy   20
   Woodbridge nr. Amboy   15
   Raritan Landing   1
   New Brunswick   10
   Piscataway   6
   Blazing Star   1
   Princeton   6
   Spotswood   1
   Middlesex County   3

Monmouth County   36
   "Monmouth Township"   1
   Dover Township   2
   Freehold   10
   Middletown   5
   Shrewsbury   10
   Sandy Hook   1
   Scotch Meeting House   2
   Monmouth County   5
Morris County   11
   Hanover   4
   Morristown   3
   Morris County   4
Salem County   3
   Salem   1
   Pittsgrove Township   1
   Salem County   1
Somerset County   9
   Bernards Township   1
   Bound Brook   1
   Rocky Hill   1
   Hillsborough   1
   Middlebrook   1
   Somerset County   4
Sussex County   12
   Hardiston   1
   Newton   1
   Wantage   1
   Knowlton   1
   Greenwich   1
   Sussex County   7
Unknown   13
Total   239

PENNSYLVANIA

In the following tables 206 claims are analyzed. One hundred and twenty-eight were filed in London, seventy-eight in Nova Scotia. Six London claimants returned to the United States, five lived in Canada, three lived in the West Indies, and one in Switzerland. One Nova Scotia claimant lived in the West Indies.

National Origin (186 known)

Country of Birth	Nova Scotia Claimants	London Claimants	Combined		% of Known	
Great Britain (country unknown)	2	9	11		5.9	
England	4	31	35		18.8	
Scotland	4	10	14		7.5	
Ireland	9	19	28	103	15.0	55.0
Germany	9	3	12		6.5	
Switzerland	0	1	1		0.52	
Holland	2	0	2		1.04	
America	42	41	83		45.0	
Unknown	6	14	20			
Total	78	128	206		100.00	

Date of Immigrants' Arrival in America (84 known)

	Nova Scotia	London	Combined
1763 and earlier	8	21	29
1764 and later	12	43	55
Unknown	10	9	19
Total	30	73	103

Tables—Pennsylvania

Occupations (200 known)

	Nova Scotia	London	Combined	% of Known
Farmers and Landowners	48	19	67	33.5
Commerce				
(a) Artisans and craftsmen	12[a]	29[b]	41 ⎫	20.5 ⎫
(b) Merchants and shopkeepers	13	20	33 ⎪	16.5 ⎪
(c) Seamen and pilots	0	3	3 ⎬ 84	⎬ 42.0
(d) Innkeepers	0	6	6 ⎪	⎪
(e) Shipbuilder	0	1	1 ⎭	⎭
Professions				
(a) Anglican ministers	0	7	7 ⎫	⎫
(b) Lawyers	0	4	4 ⎪	⎪
(c) Schoolmaster	0	1	1 ⎪	⎪
(d) Doctors	0	7	7 ⎬ 23	⎬ 11.5
(e) Newspaper printers	0	2	2 ⎪	⎪
(f) Broker	0	1	1 ⎪	⎪
(g) Clerk to mayor of Philadelphia	0	1	1 ⎭	⎭
Office-Holders	4[c]	22[d]	26	13.0
Unknown	1	5	6	
Total	78	128	206	100.00

[a] Five carpenters, two each: blacksmiths, millers, one each: millwright, leather-breeches maker, and whitesmith.

[b] Three blacksmiths, three tanners, two each: masons, weavers, whitesmiths, coachmakers, brewers, and carpenters, one each: snuff maker, silversmith, soap boiler, laborer, tailor, baker, watchmaker, millwright, livery stable, jeweler, and miller.

[c] One each: deputy surveyor of Pennsylvania, customs official, Indian Department, and judge of Common Pleas.

[d] Ten customs officers, four judges of Common Pleas, one each: high constable of Philadelphia, judge of King's Bench, mayor of Philadelphia, attorney-general, clerk to the master of the rolls, military officer, lieutenant-governor, and marshal of admiralty court.

Tables—Pennsylvania

Amount of Claims (168 known)

	Nova Scotia	London	Combined	% of Known
£500 or less	35	23	58	35.0
£501–£1,000	14	16	30	18.0
£1,001–£2,000	15	19	34	20.0
£2,001–£5,000	5	19	24	14.0
£5,001–£10,000	3	9	12	7.0
Over £10,000	0	10	10	6.0
Unknown	2	24	26	
Claim for salary or income only	4	8	12	
Total	78	128	206	100.00

Service to the British
(London and Nova Scotia Claimants Combined)

Served in the armed forces including the militia

In the ranks	7
Probably in the ranks	28
Officers	29
Probably officers	1
Status unknown	10
Total	75 or 36.0%
Served in some other official way	50 or 24.0%
Total who served in some way	125 or 60.0%
Claimants killed or wounded	10 or 4.9%
Claimants captured or imprisoned	59 or 28.0%

Geographic Distribution (190 known)

Bedford County	1
Berks County	2
Reading	2
Bucks County	12
Hill Town	1
Attleborough	1
Middletown	1
Burton	1

New Britain	1	
Bucks County	7	
Cumberland County		3
Chester County		8
Moorehall	1	
Goshen	1	
West Bradford	1	
Providence	1	
Chester County	4	
Lancaster County		6
Middleton	1	
Lancaster	1	
Lancaster County	4	
Montgomery County		1
Lower Merion	1	
Northampton County		4
Penn Township	2	
Allentown	1	
Northampton County	1	
Northumberland County		26
At Susquehanna River	19	
Chambertown	2	
Northumberland County	5	
Philadelphia County		111
Philadelphia	104	
Germantown	2	
Abingdon	2	
Graham Park	1	
Bristol	1	
Philadelphia County	1	
Westmoreland County		8
Pittsburgh	4	
Westmoreland County	4	

Wyoming		1
York County		7
York	3	
Abbottstown	1	
Newberry	1	
Huntingdon	1	
York County	1	
Unknown		16
Total		206

DELAWARE

In the following tables ten claims are analyzed. Seven were filed in London and three in Nova Scotia.

National Origin (10 known)

Country of Birth	Nova Scotia Claimants	London Claimants	Combined		% of Known	
Great Britain (country unknown)	0	1	1	⎱	10.0	⎱
Scotland	0	1	1	} 4	10.0	} 40.0
Ireland	0	2	2	⎰	20.0	⎰
America	3	3	6		60.0	
Unknown	0	0	0			
Total	3	7	10		100.00	

Date of Immigrants' Arrival in America (3 known)

	Nova Scotia	London	Combined
1763 and earlier	0	1	1
1764 and later	0	2	2
Unknown	0	1	1
Total	0	4	4

Occupations (10 known)

	Nova Scotia	London	Combined		% of Known	
Farmers and Landowners	2	1	3		30.0	
Commerce						
(a) Merchants and shopkeepers	0	2	2	⎱	20.0	⎱
(b) Innkeeper	0	1	1	} 4		} 40.0
(c) Fisherman	1	0	1	⎰		⎰

Professions
(a) Anglican
minister	0	1	1 } 2	} 20.0
(b) Doctor	0	1	1 }	}
Office-Holders	0	1ª	1	10.0
Unknown	0	0	0	
Total	3	7	10	100.00

ª A customs official.

Amount of Claims (10 known)

	Nova Scotia	London	Combined	% of Known
£500 or less	1	1	2	22.2
£501–£1,000	1	1	2	22.2
£1,001–£2,000	0	2	2	22.2
£2,001–£5,000	0	2	2	22.2
£5,001–£10,000	1	0	1	11.1
Unknown	0	0	0	
Claim for salary or income only	0	1	1	
Total	3	7	10	100.00

Service to the British
(London and Nova Scotia Claimants Combined)

Served in the armed forces including the militia
Probably in the ranks	1
Officers	2
Status unknown	2
Total	5 or 50.0%
Served in some other official way	1 or 10.0%
Total who served in some way	6 or 60.0%
Claimants killed or wounded	1 or 10.0%
Claimants captured or imprisoned	3 or 30.0%

Tables—Delaware

Geographic Distribution (10 known)

Kent County		3
Dover	1	
Kent County	2	
Sussex County		2
New Castle County		5
New Castle	3	
Brandywine Hundred	1	
New Castle County	1	
Unknown		0
Total		10

MARYLAND

In the following tables eighty-two claims are analyzed. Seventy-nine claimed in London, three in Nova Scotia. Six London claimants returned to the United States, four lived in Canada. One Nova Scotia claimant lived in the West Indies.

National Origin (76 known)

Country of Birth	Nova Scotia Claimants	London Claimants	Combined		% of Known	
Great Britain (country unknown)	0	9	9		12.0	
England	0	16	16		21.0	
Scotland	1	12	13	56	17.0	73.5
Ireland	1	12	13		17.0	
Wales	0	1	1			
Germany	0	4	4		5.2	
America	1	19	20			26.5
Unknown	0	6	6			
Total	3	79	82		100.00	

Date of Immigrants' Arrival in America (56 known)

	Nova Scotia	London	Combined
1763 and earlier	0	20	20
1764 and later	2	29	31
Unknown	0	5	5
Total	2	54	56

Tables—Maryland

Occupations (78 known)

	Nova Scotia	London	Combined		% of Known	
Farmers and Landowners	1	10	11		14.2	
Commerce						
(a) Artisans and craftsmen	1[a]	9[b]	10		13.0	
(b) Merchants and shopkeepers	1	15	16	33	20.5	42.0
(c) Seamen and pilots	0	5	5			
(d) Innkeepers	0	2	2			
Professions						
(a) Anglican ministers	0	9	9			
(b) Lawyers	0	4	4	19		24.5
(c) Schoolmaster	0	1	1			
(d) Doctors	0	5	5			
Office-Holders	0	15[c]	15		19.3	
Unknown	0	4	4			
Total	3	79	82		100.00	

[a] A manufacturer of linen goods.

[b] Two carpenters, one each: brewer, shoemaker, laborer, distiller, gunsmith, stuccoworker, and staymaker.

[c] Five customs officials, two sheriffs, two judges of land office, one each: proctor of vice-admiralty court, clerk of Hartford and Baltimore Counties, postmaster of Baltimore, governor, judge of vice-admiralty court, and clerk of upper house of Assembly.

Tables—Maryland

Amount of Claims (64 known)

	Nova Scotia	London	Combined	% of Known
£500 or less	1	7	8	12.5
£501–£1,000	0	6	6	9.5
£1,001–£2,000	2	13	15	23.5
£2,001–£5,000	0	17	17	26.5
£5,001–£10,000	0	7	7	11.0
Over £10,000	0	11	11	17.0
Unknown	0	5	5	
Claim for salary or income only	0	13	13	
Total	3	79	82	100.00

Service to the British
(London and Nova Scotia Claimants Combined)

Served in the armed forces including the militia

In the ranks	4
Probably in the ranks	3
Officers	16
Status unknown	1
Total	24 or 29.5%
Served in some other official way	7 or 8.5%
Total who served in some way	31 or 38.0%
Claimants killed or wounded	5 or 6.1%
Claimants captured or imprisoned	15 or 18.4%

Tables—Maryland

Geographic Distribution (70 known)

Anne Arundel County		17
Annapolis	17	
Baltimore County		26
Baltimore and environs	25	
St. Thomas's Parish	1	
Charles County		2
Eastern Shore—county unknown		1
Frederick County		12
Frederick	6	
George Town	2	
Hagerstown	1	
Frederick County	3	
Kent County		3
Chester Parish	2	
Shrewsbury Parish	1	
Prince Georges County		4
Queen Anne's Parish	1	
North Potomac	1	
Bladensburg	1	
Prince Georges County	1	
Somerset County		1
St. Marys County		1
Worcester County		1
Pt. Pocomoke	1	
Unknown		12
Total		82

VIRGINIA

In the following tables 130 claims are analyzed. One hundred and nine were filed in London, twenty-one in Nova Scotia. Eight London claimants lived in Canada, one in Jamaica, and one probably returned to Hesse Cassel. One Nova Scotia claimant resided in Bermuda. In addition, of the total claimants three were resident in Virginia and two apparently returned there.

National Origin (112 known)

Country of Birth	Nova Scotia Claimants	London Claimants	Combined		% of Known	
Great Britain (country unknown)	1	9	10		9.0	
England	4	21	25		22.5	
Scotland	8	39	47	88	42.0	78.5
Ireland	0	3	3			
France	1	0	1			
Germany	0	2	2			
America	4	20	24		21.5	
Unknown	3	15	18			
Total	21	109	130		100.00	

Date of Immigrants' Arrival in America (81 known)

	Nova Scotia	London	Combined
1763 and earlier	6	33	39
1764 and later	7	35	42
Unknown	1	6	7
Total	14	74	88

Occupations (125 known)

	Nova Scotia	London	Combined		% of Known	
Farmers and Landowners	2[a]	14	16		12.8	
Commerce						
(a) Artisans and craftsmen	2[b]	6[c]	8 ⎫		6.4 ⎫	
(b) Merchants and shopkeepers	15[d]	50[e]	65 ⎬ 80		52.0 ⎬ 64.0	
(c) Seamen and pilots	0	6	6 ⎪		4.8 ⎪	
(d) Innkeeper	0	1	1 ⎭		⎭	
Professions						
(a) Anglican ministers	1	8	9 ⎫		7.2 ⎫	
(b) Lawyers	1[f]	2	3		2.4	
(c) Schoolmaster	0	1	1			
(d) Military officers	0	2	2 ⎬ 20		⎬ 16.0	
(e) Doctors	0	4	4			
(f) Studying medicine	0	1	1 ⎭		⎭	
Office-Holders	0	9[g]	9		7.2	
Unknown	0	5	5			
Total	21	109	130		100.00	

---

[a] One also a ship's carpenter.
[b] One baker, and one carpenter.
[c] Two cabinetmakers, one each: shoemaker, salt manufacturer, tallow chandler and soap boiler, and shipwright.
[d] One a former doctor.
[e] Including one clerk to a merchant.
[f] But was employed as a schoolmaster.
[g] Four customs officers, one each: governor, judge of admiralty, superintendent of the auditor's office, lieutenant-governor of S.C., keeper of the military magazine.

Tables—Virginia

Amount of Claims (113 known)

	Nova Scotia	London	Combined	% of Known
£500 or less	3	8	11	9.7
£501–£1,000	1	11	12	10.6
£1,001–£2,000	9	19	28	24.8
£2,001–£5,000	5	25	30	26.5
£5,001–£10,000	2	12	14	12.4
Over £10,000	1	17	18	16.0
Unknown	0	11	11	
Claim for salary or income only	0	6	6	
Total	21	109	130	100.00

Service to the British
(*London and Nova Scotia Claimants Combined*)

Served in the armed forces including the militia

In the ranks	5
Probably in the ranks	2
Officers	28
Probably officers	2
Status unknown	19
Total	56 or 43.0%
Served in some other official way	13 or 10.0%
Total who served in some way	69 or 53.0%
Claimants killed or wounded	7 or 5.3%
Claimants captured or imprisoned	43 or 33.0%

Geographic Distribution (114 known)[a]

Accomac County	1
Augusta County	1
Bedford County	1
Charles City County	2
Dinwiddie County	3
Petersburg	3

[331]

Tables—Virginia

Elizabeth City County		3
Essex County		2
Gloucester County		6
Hanover County		1
Isle of Wight County		4
James City County		14
Williamsburg	14	
Middlesex County		1
Nansemond County		11
Suffolk	3	
Nansemond County	8	
Norfolk County		49
Norfolk	34	
Portsmouth	12	
Gosport	2	
Norfolk County	1	
Northampton County		1
Princess Anne County		3
Richmond County		1
Rockingham County		1
Spotsylvania County		7
Fredericksburg	5	
Spotsylvania County	2	
Kaskaskia, Kentucky		1
Fort Pitt		1
Unknown		16
Total		130

[a] All claimants lived in the tidewater area except the four in Bedford County, Rockingham County, Kaskaskia, and Fort Pitt. Fort Pitt was in dispute between Virginia and Pennsylvania. The claimant listed here owned land at Fort Pitt, but was active in Virginia. Other Fort Pitt claimants are considered in the section on Pennsylvania.

NORTH CAROLINA

In the following tables 153 claims are analyzed. One hundred and twenty-five were filed in London, twenty-eight in Nova Scotia. Fourteen of the London claimants lived in Canada, six in the West Indies. Two of the Nova Scotia claimants lived in the West Indies.

National Origin (138 known)

Country of Birth	Nova Scotia Claimants	London Claimants	Combined		% of Known	
Great Britain (country unknown)	0	5	5 ⎫		3.6 ⎫	
England	2	15	17 ⎪	110	12.4 ⎪	79.7
Scotland	9	66	75 ⎪		54.3 ⎪	
Ireland	2	11	13 ⎭		9.4 ⎭	
America	13	15	28		20.3	
Unknown	2	13	15			
Total	28	125	153		100.00	

Date of Immigrants' Arrival in America (91 known)

	Nova Scotia	London	Combined
1763 and earlier	2	20	22
1764 and later	6	63	69
Unknown	5	14	19
Total	13	97	110

Tables—North Carolina

Occupations (142 known)

	Nova Scotia	London	Combined	% of Known
Farmers and Landowners	17	49	66	46.5
Commerce				
(a) Artisans and craftsmen	1[a]	8[b]	9	6.3
(b) Merchants and shopkeepers	7	35	42	29.5
(c) Seamen and pilots	0	2	2	
(d) Fisherman	1	0	1	
(e) Innkeeper	0	1	1	
			55	39.0
Professions				
(a) Anglican minister	0	1	1	
(b) Schoolmaster	0	1	1	
(c) Doctors	1	2	3	
			5	3.5
Office-Holders	0	16[c]	16	11.0
Unknown	1	10	11	
Total	28	125	153	100.00

[a] One miller.

[b] Two tailors, two coopers, and one each: saddler, baker, salt works owner, miller and blacksmith.

[c] Five were also lawyers, two were also merchants. Three customs officials, one each: lieutenant at Fort Johnston, crown lawyer, deputy auditor and deputy naval officer, chief justice, surveyor-general, receiver of quit rents, governor, attorney-general, surveyor of king's lands, judge of vice-admiralty court, secretary of Proprietary Department, receiver-general of quit rents, and deputy surveyor.

Tables—North Carolina

Amount of Claims (130 known)

	Nova Scotia	London	Combined	% of Known
£500 or less	7	20	27	21.0
£501–£1,000	6	19	25	19.0
£1,001–£2,000	9	24	33	25.5
£2,001–£5,000	3	17	20	15.0
£5,001–£10,000	1	6	7	5.0
Over £10,000	0	18	18	14.6
Unknown	2	17	19	
Claim for salary or income only	0	4	4	
Total	28	25	153	100.00

Service to the British
(London and Nova Scotia Claimants Combined)

Served in the armed forces including the militia
In the ranks	2
Probably in the ranks	11
Officers	79
Status unknown	12
Total	104 or 68.0%
Served in some other official way	8 or 5.0%
Total who served in some way	112 or 73.0%
Claimants killed or wounded	16 or 10.4%
Claimants captured or imprisoned	75 or 49.0%

Geographic Distribution (121 known)

Anson County		18
Bertie County		1
Windsor	1	
Bladen County		10
Moores Creek	1	
Bladen County	9	
Brunswick County		7
Cape Fear	4	

[335]

Brunswick	2	
Ft. Johnston	1	
Carteret County		1
Ocracoke	1	
Chowan County		1
Edenton	1	
Craven County		6
New Bern	6	
Cumberland County		35
Cross Creek	13	
Cumberland County	22	
Dobbs County		1
Edgecomb County		1
Tarboro	1	
Granville County		1
Halifax County		7
Halifax	6	
Halifax County	1	
Mecklenberg County		3
Montgomery County		1
New Hanover County		14
Wilmington	13	
New Hanover County	1	
Orange County		2
Hillsboro	2	
Pasquotank County		2
Rowan County		5
Salisbury	4	
Rowan County	1	
Tryon County		2
Wake County		1
County Unascertained		2
Pee Dee River	1	
Tarr River	1	
Unknown		32
Total		153

In the following tables 320 claims are analyzed. Two hundred and forty-four were filed in London, seventy-six in Nova Scotia. Two of the London claimants returned to the United States, nine lived in the West Indies. Five of the Nova Scotia claimants lived in the West Indies.

National Origin (285 known)

Country of Birth	Nova Scotia Claimants	London Claimants	Combined		% of Known	
Great Britain (country unknown)	0	22	22		8.0	
England	1	46	47		16.5	
Scotland	3	53	56	223	19.6	78.4
Ireland	21	51	72		25.0	
Wales	0	3	3		1.1	
Germany	19	4	23		8.2	
America	24	38	62		21.6	
Unknown	8	27	35			
Total	76	244	320		100.00	

Date of Immigrants' Arrival in America (205 known)

	Nova Scotia	London	Combined
1763 and earlier	10	57	67
1764 and later	25	113	138
Unknown	9	9	18
Total	44	179	223

Occupations (317 known)

	Nova Scotia	London	Combined		% of Known	
Farmers and Landowners	67	77[a]	144		45.5	
Commerce						
(a) Artisans and craftsmen	1[b]	29[c]	30 ⎫		9.3 ⎫	
(b) Merchants and shopkeepers	3	62	65 ⎪		20.5 ⎪	
(c) Seamen and pilots	0	2[d]	2 ⎬ 101		⎬ 31.5	
(d) Innkeepers	1	2	3 ⎪		⎪	
(e) Ferry keeper	0	1	1 ⎭		⎭	
Professions						
(a) Anglican ministers	0	6	6 ⎫		⎫	
Presbyterian minister	0	1	1 ⎪		⎪	
(b) Lawyers	0	4	4 ⎪		⎪	
(c) Doctors	1	10	11 ⎪		⎪	
(d) Midwife	0	1	1 ⎬ 36		⎬ 11.5	
(e) Schoolmasters	2	7	9 ⎪		⎪	
(f) Artist	0	1	1 ⎪		⎪	
(g) Organist	0	1	1 ⎪		⎪	
(h) Fencing master	0	1	1 ⎪		⎪	
(i) Surveyor	0	1	1 ⎭		⎭	
Office-Holders	0	36[e]	36		11.5	
Unknown	1	2	3			
Total	76	244	320		100.00	

[a] Includes three overseers.
[b] One blacksmith.
[c] Four carpenters, three shoemakers, two each: millers, bakers, and blacksmiths, one each: tin-plate worker, jeweler, butcher, leather dresser, drayer, carter, weaver, tailor, gunsmith, distiller, saddler, coachmaker, shipwright, mantuamaker, upholsterer, and bricklayer.
[d] One master and one pilot.

Tables—South Carolina

Amount of Claims (293 known)

	Nova Scotia	London	Combined	% of Known
£500 or less	48	23	71	24.0
£501–£1,000	11	38	49	16.5
£1,001–£2,000	10	40	50	17.2
£2,001–£5,000	3	57	60	20.5
£5,001–£10,000	2	27	29	10.0
Over £10,000	1	33	34	11.8
Unknown	1	15	16	
Claim for salary or income only	0	11	11	
Total	76	244	320	100.00

Service to the British
(London and Nova Scotia Claimants Combined)

Served in the armed forces including the militia

In the ranks	7
Probably in the ranks	57
Officers	82
Probably officers	3
Status unknown	12
Total	161 or 50.0%
Served in some other official way	24 or 7.5%
Total who served in some way	185 or 57.5%
Claimants killed or wounded	27 or 8.5%
Claimants captured or imprisoned	95 or 30.0%

° Ten customs officials, four in Indian Department, two receiver-generals of quit rents, one each: deputy to surveyor-general of woods, deputy surveyor-general, governor of Fort Johnson, treasurer, lieut.-governor, gunner at the fort, coxswain at the fort, judge of vice-admiralty, marshal of vice-admiralty court, chief justice, clerk of crown, deputy secretary of S.C., deputy register, clerk of council's office, harbor master of Charleston, sheriff, chief clerk of Common Pleas, secretary of S.C., and two attorney-generals.

Geographic Distribution (309 known)

Beaufort District		8
Beaufort	4	
Beaufort District	4	
Camden District		36
Charleston District		155
Charleston	136	
Charleston District	19	
Cheraw District		1
Georgetown District		10
Georgetown	5	
Georgetown District	5	
Ninety-Six District		93
Orangeburg District		6
Unknown		11
Total		320

In the following tables 103 claims are analyzed. Ninety-one were filed in London, twelve in Nova Scotia. One London claimant returned to the United States, two lived in Nova Scotia, thirteen in the West Indies. Three of the Nova Scotia claimants lived in the West Indies.

National Origin (69 known)

Country of Birth	Nova Scotia Claimants	London Claimants	Combined		% of Known	
Great Britain (country unknown)	0	3	3		4.2	
England	0	10	10		14.5	
Scotland	4	18	22	54	32.0	78.0
Ireland	2	14	16		23.0	
Germany	1	1	2		2.9	
Portugal	0	1	1		1.4	
America	3	12	15		22.0	
Unknown	2	32	34			
Total	12	91	103		100.00	

Date of Immigrants' Arrival in America (54 known)

	Nova Scotia	London	Combined
1763 and earlier	2	18	20
1764 and later	5	29	34
Unknown	0	0	0
Total	7	47	54

Tables—Georgia

Occupations (91 known)

	Nova Scotia	London	Combined	% of Known
Farmers and Landowners	8	22	30	33.0
Commerce				
(a) Artisans and craftsmen	1ᵃ	5ᵇ	6 ⎫	6.5 ⎫
(b) Merchants and shopkeepers	1	18	19 ⎬ 28	20.0 ⎬ 30.0
(c) Seamen	0	2	2 ⎪	⎪
(d) Tavern keeper	0	1	1 ⎭	⎭
Professions				
(a) Anglican ministers	0	4ᶜ	4 ⎫	⎫
Lutheran minister	0	1	1 ⎪	⎪
(b) Lawyers	0	2	2 ⎬ 11	⎬ 12.0
(c) Doctors	0	3ᵈ	3 ⎪	⎪
(d) Soldier	0	1	1 ⎭	⎭
Office-Holders	0	22ᵉ	22	24.0
Unknown	2	10	12	
Total	12	91	103	100.00

ᵃ One tinworker (also a farmer).

ᵇ One each: silversmith, cooper, carpenter, cabinetmaker, and ship's carpenter.

ᶜ One also a planter.

ᵈ One also a schoolmaster.

ᵉ One each: comptroller, register and clerk of council, lieutenant-governor, secretary of the province, naval officer, collector of customs at Sunbury, attorney-general, commander of scout boat, advocate-general, chief justice of Georgia, clerk in prothonotary's office, customs officer, governor, clerk of council, treasurer, Indian Department, three each: commissary-generals, admiralty judges.

Tables—Georgia

Amount of Claims (81 known)

	Nova Scotia	London	Combined	% of Known
£500 or less	5	8	13	16.5
£501–£1,000	3	9	12	15.0
£1,001–£2,000	2	13	15	18.5
£2,001–£5,000	1	10	11	13.5
£5,001–£10,000	1	13	14	17.5
Over £10,000	0	16	16	19.0
Unknown	0	11	11	
Claim for salary or income only	0	11	11	
Total	12	91	103	100.00

Service to the British
(London and Nova Scotia Claimants Combined)

Served in the armed forces including the militia

In the ranks	2		
Probably in the ranks	6		
Officers	31		
Probably officers	4		
Total	43	or	43.5%
Served in some other official way	5	or	5.5%
Total who served in some way	48	or	49.0%
Claimants killed or wounded	6	or	6.0%
Claimants captured or imprisoned	16	or	16.0%

Geographic Distribution (75 known)

Christchurch Parish		47
Savannah	45	
Tybee Island	1	
Hutchinsons Island	1	
St. John's Parish		4
Sunbury	4	

St. George's Parish		5
St. George	5	
St. Matthew's Parish		2
Ebenezer	2	
St. Paul's Parish		5
Augusta	3	
St. Paul	2	
St. Philip's Parish		2
St. Philip	2	
Parish Unknown		10
Skittuiry Province	1	
Crackner's Neck	1	
"Ceded Lands"	2	
Queensborough	2	
Bryar Creek	2	
St. Marys River	1	
St. John's River (plantation)	1	
Unknown		28
Total		103

NOTES

PREFACE

1. I mean the school of historiography associated with such great writers as Macaulay and G. M. Trevelyan who, like Chatham, have tended to glorify the American colonists as the first to oppose the so-called despotic, unconstitutional encroachments of George III.
2. Charles F. Adams (ed.), *The Works of John Adams* (Boston, 1856), X, 196.
3. Claude H. Van Tyne, *The Loyalists in the American Revolution* (New York, 1902).
4. William H. Nelson, *The American Tory* (Oxford, 1962); Paul H. Smith, *Loyalists and Redcoats* (Chapel Hill, 1964), a good book, appeared after this work was written, and effectively shows British shortcomings in utilizing the Loyalists militarily.
5. See *infra*, pp. 288–289.

I. NEW HAMPSHIRE

1. Nathaniel Bouton (ed.), *Documents and Records Relating to the State of New Hampshire During the Period of the American Revolution, from 1776 to 1783* (Concord, 1874), VIII, 810–812.
2. *Ibid.*, VIII, 813–814.
3. New Hampshire Loyalists: Transcripts from the Records of the Commission for Enquiring into the Losses and Services of American Loyalists, 1783–1790, preserved in the Public Record Office, London, England (5 vols. in the New Hampshire State Library, Concord), III, 1048. Henceforth cited as N.H.L.
4. Peter Force (ed.), *American Archives* (4th Ser., 6 vols.; Washington, 1837–1846), III, 1252.
5. For the New Hampshire statistical tables see the Appendix, pp. 290–293.
6. Evarts B. Green and Virginia Harrington, *American Population before the Federal Census of 1790* (New York, 1932), p. 78.
7. Richard F. Upton, in *Revolutionary New Hampshire* (Hanover, 1936), p. 53, calculated that there were 100 royal officials including minor ones such as county officials and militia officers. Of these, forty-one were Loyalists, fifty-six Whigs, and three doubtful. But he admits that nearly all the major office-holders were loyal.
8. A 1770 tax list for Portsmouth shows that the four highest taxpayers later became Tories. *Ibid.*, p. 58.
9. Otis G. Hammond, *Tories of New Hampshire in the War of the Revolution* (Concord, 1917), pp. 29–30.

10. See *infra*, p. 253.
11. U.S. Department of Commerce, *Historical Statistics, Colonial Times to 1957* (Washington, 1960), p. 756. Figures are given for 1770 and 1780. The population for 1776 is obtained by adding six-tenths of the decade's increase to the 1770 figure (0.06 can be multiplied by five to include the claimants' families).
12. Hammond, *Tories of New Hampshire*, p. 12.
13. N.H.L., II, 749, 735.
14. Bouton (ed.), *Documents and Records*, VIII, 468.
15. Hammond, *Tories of New Hampshire*, p. 52.
16. Kenneth Scott, "New Hampshire Tory Counterfeiters Operating from New York City," New York Historical Society, *Quarterly*, XXXIV (January, 1950), 47.
17. American Loyalists: Transcripts of the Manuscript Books and Papers of the Commission of Enquiry into the Losses and Services of the American Loyalists (60 vols.; New York Public Library), XIV, 550. Henceforth cited as Loyalist Transcripts. Scott, "New Hampshire Counterfeiters," p. 57.
18. Merrill Jensen, *The New Nation* (New York, 1950), p. 268.
19. Hugh E. Egerton (ed.), *The Royal Commission on the Losses and Services of American Loyalists* (Oxford, 1915), p. 30.
20. Arthur M. Schlesinger, *The Colonial Merchants and the American Revolution, 1763–1776* (New York, 1918), p. 442.
21. Loyalist Transcripts, VIII, 434.
22. Hammond, *Tories of New Hampshire*, pp. 38–39.
23. *Ibid.*, pp. 41, 43–45.
24. *Ibid.*, pp. 26–29.
25. *Ibid.*, p. 25; W. H. Siebert, *The Loyalist Refugees of New Hampshire* (Columbus, 1916), p. 29.
26. Albert Smith, *History of the Town of Peterborough* (Boston, 1876), pp. 273–274.
27. Loyalist Transcripts, VII, 429; Lawrence S. Mayo, *John Wentworth, Governor of New Hampshire, 1767–1775* (Cambridge, 1921), p. 79n.; Nathaniel Adams, *Annals of Portsmouth* (Portsmouth, 1825), p. 246.
28. See Kenneth Scott, "Tory Associations of Portsmouth," *William and Mary Quarterly*, 3d Ser., XVII (October, 1960), 507–510.
29. Mayo, *John Wentworth*, pp. 141–143, 145, 149–156.
30. See *supra*, p. 7.
31. See Scott, "New Hampshire Counterfeiters," pp. 31–57. Just how notable is a moot point because of the lack of similar studies for other colonies.

32. Quoted *ibid.*, p. 37.
33. Langdon to Lord North, February 7, 1777, Public Record Office, Colonial Office Papers, 5/115. Colonial Office Papers henceforth cited as CO.
34. Loyalist Transcripts, XIV, 589, 595.
35. Scott, "New Hampshire Counterfeiters," p. 35.
36. CO 5/115.
37. Egerton (ed.), *Royal Commission*, p. 194.
38. Quoted in Hammond, *Tories of New Hampshire*, p. 26.
39. N.H.L., II, 736, 688.

II. MASSACHUSETTS

1. The Reverend William Walter, rector of Trinity Church, was presumably exaggerating when he said that he was the only clergyman in Boston who condemned "the mob's violence against Andrew Oliver, the Stamp Distributor." (Edward A. Jones, *The Loyalists of Massachusetts, Their Memorials, Petitions and Claims* [London, 1930], p. 288). Carl Bridenbaugh, in his *Mitre and Sceptre* (New York, 1962), states that the American Anglican clergy opposed the resistance to the Stamp Act "almost without exception" (p. 255).
2. Adams, *Works*, X, 192; Jones, *Loyalists of Massachusetts*, p. 234; Loyalist Transcripts, XIII, 201; Jones, *Loyalists of Massachusetts*, p. 186; Loyalist Transcripts, XIII, 343; Jones, *Loyalists of Massachusetts*, p. 25; Loyalist Transcripts, III, 265; XIV, 209; Jones, *Loyalists of Massachusetts*, pp. 254, 251; Loyalist Transcripts, XIII, 320.
3. Henry Hulton to Robert Nicholson, August 3, 1771, Shepherd MSS, Vol. XVIII, Manchester College, Oxford.
4. Jones, *Loyalists of Massachusetts*, pp. 58, 69, 139, 128.
5. *Ibid.*, p. 14; Loyalist Transcripts, XIII, 195; Jones, *Loyalists of Massachusetts*, p. 116; Loyalist Transcripts, XIII, 243; Jones, *Loyalists of Massachusetts*, pp. 25, 180; Loyalist Transcripts, IV, 688; Jones, *Loyalists of Massachusetts*, p. 260.
6. *Ibid.*, p. 170; Loyalist Transcripts, III, 140; the addresses are printed in James H. Stark, *The Loyalists of Massachusetts* (Boston, 1910), pp. 123–133.
7. See Appendix, pp. 294–298.
8. Jones, *Loyalists of Massachusetts*, p. 206.
9. Benjamin W. Labaree, *Patriots and Partisans, The Merchants of Newburyport, 1764–1815* (Cambridge, 1962), p. 42, notes that Newburyport contained scarcely a Loyalist and that merchants

were solidly Whig. The reasons he ascribes are the sheer distance from Boston and the lack of business ties with that city and the fact that "Government privilege rarely reached as far as the Merrimack."

10. Artisans, of course, did not always share the same interests as merchants who traded overseas. On the other hand, both groups bought and sold in the same home economy and often their fortunes were closely linked. The claims testimony does not usually indicate if a merchant was engaged in overseas trade.

11. Schlesinger, *Colonial Merchants, passim.*

12. Ann Hulton, *Letters of a Loyalist Lady* (Cambridge, 1927), p. 26.

13. Robert A. East, *Business Enterprise in the American Revolutionary Era* (New York, 1938), p. 219 and n.; Samuel E. Morison, "The Commerce of Boston on the Eve of the Revolution," *American Antiquarian Society Proceedings,* XXXII (April, 1922), 51n., shows that a minority of the 147 merchants who formed the Society for Encouraging Trade and Commerce in 1763 became Loyalists.

14. *Gazetteer and New Daily Advertiser* (London), December 24, 1777, British Museum.

15. Jones, *Loyalists of Massachusetts,* p. xv; Lee N. Newcomer, *The Embattled Farmers, A Massachusetts Countryside in the American Revolution* (New York, 1953), p. 60.

16. Charles E. Allen, "Loyalists of the Kennebec," *New England Magazine,* XXXVII (1907–1908), 624.

17. Jones, *Loyalists of Massachusetts,* p. 93.

18. Hutchinson died in 1780 so there is no claim from him, but there is from his sons.

19. "List of Graduates at Harvard University of Anti-Revolutionary or Loyalist Principles," *The American Quarterly Register,* XIII (May, 1841), 407, 403–417; XIV (November, 1841), 167–172; "The Harvard Loyalists," *The Harvard Graduate Magazine,* XIV (December, 1905), 358–360. Lists of all Harvard graduates for the appropriate years are found in *Quinquennial Catalogue of the Officers and Graduates of Harvard University, 1636–1900* (Cambridge, 1900).

20. Loyalist Transcripts, XIV, 200; Jones, *Loyalists of Massachusetts,* p. 218.

21. Loyalist Transcripts, XIII, 213; Massachusetts Historical Society, *Proceedings,* 2d Ser., XII (February, 1898), 153.

22. See Hulton, *Letters,* p. 13; Arthur L. Cross, *The Anglican Episcopate and the American Colonies* (Cambridge, 1902), *passim;* Bridenbaugh, *Mitre and Sceptre, passim.*

23. Jones, *Loyalists of Massachusetts*, pp. 77, 289, 288; Egerton (ed.), *Royal Commisison*, p. 154; Jones, *Loyalists of Massachusetts*, pp. 218, 292, 303, 67, 78, 303.

24. Loyalist Transcripts, III, 264; XIII, 201, 202; XIV, 477; III, 106; Jones, *Loyalists of Massachusetts*, pp. 116, 180; Stark, *Loyalists of Massachusetts*, p. 125.

25. Jones, *Loyalists of Massachusetts*, pp. 224, 252; Loyalist Transcripts, II, 436; XIII, 357; Stark, *Loyalists of Massachusetts*, p. 321; Jones, *Loyalists of Massachusetts*, p. 48; Newcomer, *Embattled Farmers*, pp. 140–142; Robert Taylor, *Western Massachusetts in the American Revolution* (Providence, 1954), pp. 68–69.

26. Jones, *Loyalists of Massachusetts*, p. 301; Harry H. Edes, "The Places of Worship of the Sandemanians in Boston," Colonial Society of Massachusetts, *Publications*, VI (March, 1899), 120 and n.; Oscar Zeichner, *Connecticut's Years of Controversy, 1750–1776* (Chapel Hill, 1949), p. 230; Newcomer, *Embattled Farmers*, p. 59. Newcomer does not elaborate his point about the Baptists, nor do his footnotes. Ezra Stiles, *The Literary Diary of Ezra Stiles D.D., L.L.D.*, ed. Franklin B. Dexter (3 vols.; New York, 1901), II, 51, 23.

27. Loyalist Transcripts, I, 202; VI, 448. For more see Frank W. C. Hersey, "The Misfortunes of Dorcas Griffiths," Colonial Society of Massachusetts, *Publications*, XXXIV (1937–1942), 13–25.

28. Jones, *Loyalists of Massachusetts*, p. 155; Loyalist Transcripts, III, 124–125; Jones, *Loyalists of Massachusetts*, pp. 121–122; Stark, *Loyalists of Massachusetts*, p. 405; Jones, *Loyalists of Massachusetts*, p. 170.

29. Jonathan Smith, "Toryism in Worcester County during the War for Independence," Massachusetts Historical Society, *Proceedings*, XLVIII (October, 1914), 31–33.

30. Newcomer, *Embattled Farmers*, pp. 78, 59.

31. Henry Hulton to Robert Nicholson, August 3, 1771, Shepherd MSS.

32. A recent article concludes that confiscation of Loyalist estates in Suffolk County had little social or fiscal result. Richard D. Brown, "The Confiscation and Disposition of Loyalists' Estates in Suffolk County, Massachusetts," *William and Mary Quarterly*, 3d Ser., XXI (October, 1964), 534–550.

33. I have been aided in making out this list by Jones, *Loyalists of Massachusetts*, pp. ix–xviii.

34. Actually, Copley was really a neutralist who left in 1773 before the crisis became acute. See Brooke Hindle, "American Culture and the Migrations of the Revolutionary Era," in *"John and*

Mary's College," *The Boyd Lee Spahr Lectures in Americana* (Carlisle, 1956), p. 111. Copley's pupil and half-brother Henry Pelham was a claimant.

35. Jones, *Loyalists of Massachusetts*, p. ix; Moses C. Tyler, "The Party of the Loyalists in the American Revolution," *American Historical Review*, I (October, 1895), 31.

36. The social and other effects of the flight of the Loyalists is beyond the scope of this work. It is certainly true that some social change occurred in Boston where several leading families were replaced by such out-of-towners as the Cabots and Lowells.

37. *Historical Statistics*, p. 756.

38. Richard Lechmere, "Letters of Richard Lechmere," Massachusetts Historical Society, *Proceedings*, 2d Ser., XVI (1902), 289; Hulton, *Letters*, p. 73; Jones, *Loyalists of Massachusetts*, p. 24.

39. Franklin B. Dexter, *Biographical Sketches of the Graduates of Yale* (2 vols.; New Haven, 1885), II, 699; Loyalist Transcripts, III, 277; Hulton, *Letters*, p. 70.

40. Loyalist Transcripts, III, 352; Jones, *Loyalists of Massachusetts*, pp. 124, 139; Loyalist Transcripts, XIV, 209; Hulton, *Letters*, p. 85.

41. For details see Van Tyne, *Loyalists*, pp. 133, 135, 194, 201, 220, 237–240, and the appendixes.

42. Jensen, *New Nation*, pp. 269–270.

43. Ward Chipman, "Diary," ed. J. B. Berry, Essex Institute, *Historical Collections*, LXXXVII (July, 1951), 231.

44. Samuel Curwen, *Journal and Letters, 1775-1784*, ed. G. A. Ward (New York, 1842), p. 393.

45. Lechmere, "Letters," p. 285; Lorenzo Sabine, *Biographical Sketches of Loyalists of the American Revolution* (2 vols.; Boston, 1864), I, 25; Carl Bridenbaugh, *Cities in Revolt* (New York, 1955), p. 216.

46. John Gallison to the Town of Marblehead, January 5, 1775, in a box marked "Loyalists," New York Public Library, MSS Division.

47. Jones, *Loyalists of Massachusetts*, p. 57; Loyalist Transcripts, XIII, 241; Jones, *Loyalists of Massachusetts*, p. 297; Loyalist Transcripts, XIV, 414.

48. Hulton, *Letters*, p. 74.

49. See, for example, his letter to James Murray of March 3, 1779, in James Murray, *Letters of James Murray*, ed. Nina M. Tiffany and Susan I. Lesley (Boston, 1901), p. 257.

50. See Douglas Adair and John A. Schutz (eds.), *Peter Oliver's*

Origin and Progress of the American Rebellion (San Marino, 1961).

51. Arthur W. H. Eaton, *The Famous Mather Byles* (Boston, 1914), p. 145; James R. Gilmore, "Nathaniel Emmons and Mather Byles," *New England Magazine* (August, 1897), p. 735.

52. For this last point see Taylor, *Western Massachusetts in the American Revolution*, pp. 43-44.

53. Adams, *Works*, X, 192-196.

54. Newcomer, *Embattled Farmers*, p. 61.

55. George Inman, "George Inman's Narrative of the American Revolution," *Pennsylvania Magazine of History and Biography*, VII (1883), 237; Loyalist Transcripts, V, 70; Jones, *Loyalists of Massachusetts*, pp. 180, 201; Stark, *Loyalists of Massachusetts*, p. 274.

56. Loyalist Transcripts, XIII, 493; Adams, *Works*, X, 231.

57. Of course, many well-read Americans were led directly to Whiggism by their understanding of history. Alexander Hamilton was a staunch admirer of the British constitution.

58. Jones, *Loyalists of Massachusetts*, pp. 134-135.

59. Quoted in Stark, *Loyalists of Massachusetts*, p. 424.

60. Charles F. Adams (ed.), *Letters of John Adams Addressed to his Wife* (2 vols.; Boston, 1841), I, 96.

61. Jones, *Loyalists of Massachusetts*, p. 111.

62. Jessica Hill [Bridenbaugh], "Catherine and Mary Byles," (1931), typescript in the possession of Carl Bridenbaugh; "Unreconstructed Loyalists," *Atlantic Monthly*, LXVII (April, 1891), 571.

III. RHODE ISLAND

1. Frank Moore, *Diary of the American Revolution* (2 vols.; New York, 1860), I, 362-363.

2. Quoted in David S. Lovejoy, *Rhode Island Politics and the American Revolution, 1760-1776* (Providence, 1958), p. 188.

3. Samuel G. Arnold, *History of the State of Rhode Island* (2 vols.; New York, 1860), II, 380.

4. Thomas Vernon, *The Diary of Thomas Vernon* ("Rhode Island Historical Tracts," No. 13 [Providence, 1881]), pp. 34n., 44, 65.

5. Moore, *Diary*, I, 183.

6. Jarvis M. Morse, "The Wanton Family and Rhode Island Loyalism," Rhode Island Historical Society, *Collections*, XXXI (April, 1938), 50.

7. Bridenbaugh, *Cities in Revolt*, pp. 216-217; an account of Newport and the British invasion can be found in Edmund S.

Morgan, *The Gentle Puritan, A Life of Ezra Stiles, 1727–1795* (New Haven and London, 1962), chap. xviii.
8. Rhode Island Historical Society, *Proceedings* (1874–1875), pp. 48–50.
9. Egerton (ed.), *Royal Commission*, p. 307.
10. Loyalist Transcripts, V, 409–413.
11. *Historical Statistics*, p. 743. For Rhode Island tables see Appendix, pp. 299–301.
12. Loyalist Transcripts, V, 409–413; VII, 383; Egerton (ed.), *Royal Commission*, pp. 267, 307–308; Loyalist Transcripts, XXVII, 265, 270.
13. Lovejoy, *Rhode Island Politics*, p. 155.
14. Public Record Office, Audit Office Papers, 13/68, Pt. 2. Audit Office Papers henceforth cited as AO.
15. Morse, "The Wanton Family," p. 43; Frank G. Bates, *Rhode Island and the Formation of the Union* (New York, 1898–1899), p. 61; Jensen, *New Nation*, p. 268.
16. Quoted in Sabine, *Biographical Sketches*, I, 26.
17. Vernon, *Diary*, p. 9.
18. Lovejoy, *Rhode Island Politics*, pp. 181, 192–193.
19. See Vernon, *Diary*, Introduction, p. vi.
20. Lovejoy, *Rhode Island Politics*, p. 177; Egerton (ed.), *Royal Commission*, p. 3n.; Loyalist Transcripts, V, 64.
21. Arnold, *History of Rhode Island*, II, 412 and n.
22. Loyalist Transcripts, XLVI, 402.
23. *Ibid.*, XXVII, 277; Egerton (ed.), *Royal Commission*, p. 262; Lovejoy, *Rhode Island Politics*, p. 188.
24. Schlesinger, *Colonial Merchants*, pp. 153, 195, 486.
25. Loyalist Transcripts, VIII, 428–429; Vernon, *Diary*, p. 2n.
26. Morse, "The Wanton Family," pp. 34, 37.
27. Loyalist Transcripts, VI, 175, 173.
28. See Carl Bridenbaugh, *Peter Harrison, First American Architect* (Chapel Hill, 1949), pp. 124–126. Harrison and his brother Joseph, at New Haven, were connected with the Junto.
29. Bridenbaugh, *Cities in Revolt*, p. 309; Morse, "The Wanton Family," p. 34; Alexander Fraser (ed.), *Second Report of the Bureau of Archives for the Province of Ontario, 1904* (Toronto, 1905), p. 1191; Lovejoy, *Rhode Island Politics*, p. 155; Vernon, *Diary*, p. 30n.
30. Bates, *Rhode Island and the Formation of the Union*, p. 115; Arnold, *History of Rhode Island*, II, 447; Loyalist Transcripts, V, 366–369; VI, 56–57.

31. Lovejoy, *Rhode Island Politics*, pp. 179–184. In his able book Lovejoy is not entirely consistent. On page 178 he says no significant political figure in Rhode Island was a Tory; yet on page 184 he claims that the Wanton-Hopkins regime collapsed because the front rank "was shot through with Toryism."

32. It is possible that they were representatives of the famous "Narragansett Planters," those uniquely rich New England farmers who traded overseas to the West Indies, and had close ties with Newport merchants. See William Davis Miller, "The Narragansett Planters," *American Antiquarian Society Proceedings*, XLIII (April, 1933), 49–115.

33. Howard is discussed in the section on North Carolina.

IV. CONNECTICUT

1. See Appendix, pp. 302–305.

2. *Historical Statistics*, p. 756. Historians generally accept R. R. Hinman's estimate of 2,000 male Tories in Connecticut in 1774; the latest historian of the colony during the Revolutionary period puts the figure at between 2,000 and 2,500. Royal R. Hinman (ed.), *A Historical Collection . . . of the Part Sustained by Connecticut during the War of the Revolution* (Hartford, 1842), p. 12; Zeichner, *Connecticut's Years of Controversy*, pp. 232–233. If the average family were five, the total number of Loyalists would be 10,000 or about 5 per cent of the population. Of the 2,000 males "scanty evidence" suggests that 1,000 remained in Connecticut and an equal number went into exile. Oscar Zeichner, "The Rehabilitation of the Loyalists in Connecticut," *New England Quarterly*, XI (June, 1938), 309; W. H. Siebert, "The Refugee Loyalists of Connecticut," Royal Society of Canada, *Transactions*, 3d Ser., X (1916), 92.

3. AO 13/41.

4. Loyalist Transcripts, XLI, 453.

5. *Ibid.*, I, 264, 266.

6. Hulton, *Letters*, p. 105.

7. Siebert, "Refugee Loyalists of Connecticut," pp. 75–76; Loyalist Transcripts, I, II, III, IV, V, VI, VII, VIII, XII, *passim*.

8. American Loyalists, Royal Institution Transcripts (8 MS vols.; New York Public Library), VI, 17.

9. Loyalist Transcripts, XII, 414; AO 13/41; Loyalist Transcripts, XII, 633; VI, 10.

10. Stinson Jarvis (ed.), "Reminiscences of a Loyalist," *Canadian Magazine*, XXVI (1905–6), 227–233.

11. G. A. Gilbert, "The Connecticut Loyalists," *American Historical Review*, IV (January, 1899), 273, 276.

12. Samuel Peters, *General History of Connecticut* (New York, 1877), p. 247.

13. American Loyalists, Royal Institution Transcripts, VI, 16.

14. Epaphroditus Peck, *The Loyalists of Connecticut* (New Haven, 1934), p. 11.

15. AO 13/42; Loyalist Transcripts, VII, 506.

16. Zeichner, *Connecticut's Years of Controversy*, p. 355.

17. Zeichner, "Rehabilitation of the Loyalists in Connecticut," p. 310.

18. Frequently claimants did not give the dates of their sufferings.

19. Loyalist Transcripts, XII, 480.

20. *Ibid.*, p. 363.

21. *Ibid.*, p. 411.

22. *Ibid.*, II, 503; I, 267; American Loyalists, Royal Institution Transcripts, I, 369.

23. Loyalist Transcripts, XII, 387, 273, 193.

24. *Ibid.*, VII, 562; AO 13/41.

25. *Ibid.*, 13/42; Loyalist Transcripts, XLI, 457–458.

26. Richard H. Phelps, *Newgate of Connecticut* (Hartford, 1892), p. 28; Loyalist Transcripts, XII, 610–611; Peck, *Loyalists of Connecticut*, p. 23.

27. AO 13/41; AO 13/42.

28. Thomas Anburey, *Travels Through the Interior Parts of America, 1776–1781* (2 vols.; Boston, 1923), II, 303.

29. Loyalist Transcripts, XXI, 54.

30. For a general account see Phelps, *Newgate of Connecticut.*

31. See Zeichner, "Rehabilitation of the Loyalists in Connecticut," pp. 308–330.

32. Loyalist Transcripts, V, 23.

33. An exception seems to have been Danbury, because Stephen Jarvis, writing a journal long after the event, referred to persons who helped him there by an initial letter instead of their full names, lest they be incriminated. The reason for bitterness at Danbury was that Governor Tryon of New York in a raid on the town in 1777 had burnt the Whig houses and spared the Tory ones. Jarvis himself had been mobbed when he visited the area in 1783. Jarvis (ed.), "Reminiscences of a Loyalist," pp. 228n., 377.

34. Charles J. Hoadly (ed.), *The Public Records of the State of Connecticut* (Hartford, 1894, 1895), I, 254; II, 279; Gilbert, "Connecticut Loyalists," pp. 289–290.

35. See Zeichner, "Rehabilitation of the Loyalists in Connecticut," pp. 324-325.
36. AO 13/93.
37. Zeichner, "Rehabilitation of the Loyalists in Connecticut," p. 309.
38. Frances P. Church, "Richard Grant White," *Atlantic Monthly*, LXVII (March, 1891), 303-314.
39. Peck, *Loyalists of Connecticut*, p. 13.
40. Loyalist Transcripts, XII, 247; V, 555.
41. *Ibid.*, XVIII, 82.
42. Schlesinger, *Colonial Merchants*, pp. 112, 150, 196, 444-448.
43. Loyalist Transcripts, XII, 236.
44. *Ibid.*, pp. 675-676, 381.
45. AO 13/42.
46. Stiles, *Diary*, III, 151; Gilbert, "Connecticut Loyalists," p. 279n.; Zeichner, *Connecticut's Years of Controversy*, p. 229; AO 13/80.
47. Gilbert, "Connecticut Loyalists," pp. 278, 277n., 279n.; Loyalist Transcripts, XII, 391, 301, 287.
48. The terms "radical" and "conservative" describe attitudes towards British policy.
49. Zeichner, *Connecticut's Years of Controversy*, pp. 221-224, 229, 109, and *passim*.
50. Loyalist Transcripts, I, 266.
51. *Ibid.*, XII, 127.
52. See *supra*, p. 63.
53. Peck, *Loyalists of Connecticut*, p. 16.
54. Hoadly (ed.), *Public Records of the State of Connecticut*, II, 33.
55. Stiles, *Diary*, III, 111-112.
56. Count Rumford (see p. 12) is another, and there were many more with lesser-known names.
57. Loyalist Transcripts, XII, 317.
58. Hoadly (ed.), *Public Records of the State of Connecticut*, II, 279.

V. NEW YORK

1. *Historical Statistics*, p. 756. See the Appendix, pp. 306-311, for the New York tables.
2. E.g. Force (ed.), *American Archives*, 4th Ser., IV, 359.
3. Alexander C. Flick, *Loyalism in New York during the American Revolution* (New York, 1901), p. 113n., lists some of the most

important New York regiments which include most of the above.

4. These are summarized in Van Tyne, *Loyalists*, Appendixes B and C. Van Tyne, *The American Revolution, 1776-1783* (New York, 1905), map facing p. 250, shows New York and South Carolina as having the severest anti-Loyalist legislation.

5. Quoted in Wilbur C. Abbott, *New York in the Revolution* (New York, 1929), p. 174. See also Moore, *Diary*, I, 288.

6. Loyalist Transcripts, XLV, 470.

7. *Ibid.*, pp. 101-102.

8. *Ibid.*, p. 536.

9. *Ibid.*, XLI, 226.

10. Historical Manuscript Commission, *Report on the Manuscripts of Mrs. Stopford-Sackville* (London, 1910), II, 77.

11. American Loyalists, Royal Institution Transcripts, I, 488.

12. *Ibid.*, V, 49-50.

13. E.g. *ibid.*, VI, 21-23, 49-50, 291-293, 351-352.

14. E. Alfred Jones (ed.), "Letter of David Colden, 1783," *American Historical Review*, XXV (October, 1919), 83.

15. E.g. American Loyalists, Royal Institution Transcripts, V, 223-226, 381; VI, 131-133, 135.

16. See *infra*, pp. 82-83.

17. See Jensen, *New Nation*, pp. 271-272. The decision in this case virtually denied the right of Patriots to sue Tories who had occupied their property.

18. Evarts B. Greene, *The Revolutionary Generation, 1763-1790* (New York, 1943), p. 307.

19. Loyalist Transcripts, XLIII, 492.

20. Greene, *Revolutionary Generation*, p. 308.

21. The figures are given in Flick, *Loyalism in New York*, pp. 112-113.

22. *Ibid.*, p. 182.

23. Quoted by Oscar Zeichner, "The Loyalist Problem in New York After the Revolution," *New York History*, XXI (1940), 296.

24. Adams, *Works*, X, 63.

25. Loyalist Transcripts, XLV, 396.

26. E. B. O'Callaghan (ed.), *Documents Relative to the Colonial History of New York* (Albany, 1857), VIII, 663.

27. Stella H. Sutherland, *Population Distribution in Colonial America* (New York, 1936), pp. 69-70. The population figures for Tryon and Charlotte are estimates because neither county had been set up in 1771. The Albany population has been calculated by subtracting the estimate for Tryon (Tryon was included with

Albany in the 1771 census). County figures for 1776 are not available, but the comparative proportions would presumably be the same.

28. Flick, *Loyalism in New York*, pp. 163–164. New York is the only colony where in certain areas the distribution of clamaints may not be an accurate reflection of over-all Loyalist strength.
29. Loyalist Transcripts, XVIII, 260.
30. American Loyalists, Royal Institution Transcripts, III, 39, 21–22.
31. Bridenbaugh, *Cities in Revolt*, p. 216.
32. Flick, *Loyalism in New York*, p. 181.
33. Bridenbaugh, *Cities in Revolt*, p. 216.
34. Loyalist Transcripts, XLII, 281.
35. *Ibid.*, IV, 18.
36. *Ibid.*, XLI, 289.
37. *Ibid.*, II, 293; Irving Mark, *Agrarian Conflicts in Colonial New York, 1711–1775* (New York, 1940), p. 199, agrees that Vermont was largely "Whiggish."
38. Loyalist Transcripts, XLV, 407.
39. Egerton (ed.), *Royal Commission*, p. 134n.
40. Peter Force (ed.), *American Archives* (5th Ser., 3 vols.; Washington, D.C., 1848–1853), II, 182.
41. Loyalist Transcripts, XLII, 281.
42. Alexander C. Flick, "The Loyalists," in Alexander C. Flick (ed.), *History of the State of New York* (10 vols.; New York, 1933–1937), III, 346.
43. Loyalist Transcripts, XLIII, 582.
44. *Ibid.*, XLIV, 139; Justin Winsor, *Narrative and Critical History of America* (8 vols.; Boston, 1884–1889), VIII, 190n., wrote that prejudice against New England gave rise to Loyalism in New York, but he offered no details.
45. Frederick Smyth to Charles Blagden, December 5, 1781. Blagden Collection, Royal Society, London, England.
46. Thomas Jones, *History of New York* (2 vols.; New York, 1879), II, chap. v.
47. Quoted in W. O. Raymond, "Loyalists in Arms," *Collections of the New Brunswick Historical Society*, No. 5 (St. John, N.B., 1904), p. 189.
48. American Loyalists, Royal Institution Transcripts, III, 297.
49. *Ibid.*, IV, 573–574; Loyalist Transcripts, XLV, 330.
50. American Loyalists, Royal Institution Transcripts, III, 78–79.
51. Flick, *Loyalism in New York*, pp. 14–15, 33.

52. See Alice M. Keys, *Cadwallader Colden* (New York, 1906).
53. Egerton (ed.), *Royal Commission*, p. 326.
54. Loyalist Transcripts, XLII, 124.
55. Quoted in Hilda Neatby, "Chief Justice William Smith: An Eighteenth Century Whig," *Canadian Historical Review*, XXVIII (March, 1947), 44; William H. W. Sabine (ed.), *Historical Memoirs of William Smith* (New York, 1956), p. 247.
56. Henry Cruger Van Schaack, *Memoirs of the Life of Henry Van Schaack* (Chicago, 1892), p. 63.
57. Mabel G. Walker, "Sir John Johnson, Loyalist," *Mississippi Valley Historical Review*, III (December, 1916), 318.
58. Flick, *Loyalism in New York*, p. 11.
59. Henry C. Van Schaack, *Peter Van Schaack* (New York, 1842), pp. 54–58, 71–76, 61; see also Allen Johnson (ed.), *Dictionary of American Biography* (20 vols.; New York, 1928–1937), XIX, 213–214. Henceforth cited as *D.A.B.*
60. Carl Becker, *Everyman His Own Historian* (New York, 1935), pp. 284–298.
61. *Travels*, II, 279.
62. Flick, *Loyalism in New York*, p. 36.
63. Loyalist Transcripts, XLI, 225.
64. Flick, *Loyalism in New York*, p. 20.
65. Van Tyne, *Loyalists*, pp. 109, 26.
66. Loyalist Transcripts, VIII, 56.
67. Flick, *Loyalism in New York*, pp. 15–25.
68. The bulk (fourteen) of the nineteen legislators were natives of America.
69. Loyalist Transcripts, XLI, 290–291.
70. See Schlesinger, *Colonial Merchants*, *passim*.
71. Virginia D. Harrington, *The New York Merchants on the Eve of the Revolution* (New York, 1935), p. 348.
72. Schlesinger, *Colonial Merchants*, p. 186.
73. Harrington, *New York Merchants*, p. 349.
74. East, *Business Enterprise*, p. 221.
75. Harrington, *New York Merchants*, pp. 349–351.
76. Loyalist Transcripts, XLIII, 72.
77. *Ibid.*, XLV, 115.
78. *Ibid.*, XLIII, 77.
79. *Ibid.*, XLII, 361–364.
80. Flick, *Loyalism in New York*, pp. 33–34.
81. Loyalist Transcripts, XLIII, 681.
82. Van Schaack, *Memoirs of Henry Van Schaack*, p. 64.

83. Loyalist Transcripts, XXI, 35.
84. New York Historical Society, *Collections*, X (New York, 1877), 223.
85. E.g. Force (ed.), *American Archives*, 4th Ser., I, 301.
86. Loyalist Transcripts, XLII, 551.
87. Flick, *Loyalism in New York*, p. 36n.
88. Douglas Brymner (ed.), *Report on Canadian Archives, 1894* (Ottawa, 1895), p. 407.
89. Flick, *Loyalism in New York*, p. 36.
90. Loyalist Transcripts, XLII, 544, 560–561. An extract of the sermon is given, pp. 559ff.
91. The proportion, one in eight, is calculated on the basis of the twenty-three alumni claimants and the 179 graduates up to 1776, but some of these may have died before the Revolution began. They are listed in *Columbia University Alumni Register, 1754–1931* (New York, 1932), p. 989. John H. Amringe, "King's College and Columbia College," in *A History of Columbia University, 1754–1904* (New York, 1904), p. 47, claims that very few alumni were Tory—a definite exaggeration. George L. Rives (ed.), *Correspondence of Thomas Barclay* (New York, 1814), p. 14, says (without footnotes) that more graduates of King's College entered the royal army than entered the continental forces.
92. Loyalist Transcripts, XLII, 541–548.
93. *Ibid.*, XLI, 559.
94. *Ibid.*, pp. 559–561.
95. *Ibid.*, XVII, 51.
96. Jensen, *New Nation*, pp. 270–271; Mark, *Agrarian Conflicts*, p. 201; George Dangerfield, *Chancellor Robert R. Livingston of New York, 1746–1813* (New York, 1960), p. 20.
97. Quoted in Staughton Lynd, "Who Should Rule at Home? Dutchess County, New York, in the American Revolution," *William and Mary Quarterly*, 3d Ser., XVIII (July, 1961), 355.
98. Richard B. Morris, "Class Struggle and the American Revolution," *ibid.*, XIX (January, 1962), 12–13.
99. Mark, *Agrarian Conflicts*, pp. 200–201 and n.
100. American Loyalists, Royal Institution Transcripts, III, 27, 32.
101. *Ibid.*, pp. 56–57.
102. See Flick, *Loyalism in New York*, p. 33 and n.
103. Loyalist Transcripts, XLI, 602.
104. *Ibid.*, XLIII, 215.
105. *Ibid.*, XLII, 475.

106. Walker, "Sir John Johnson," p. 320; John P. McLean, *An Historical Account of the Settlements of Scotch Highlanders in America prior to the Peace of 1783: together with Notices of Highland Regiments and Biographical Sketches* (Cleveland, 1900), p. 197.

107. Force (ed.), *American Archives*, 4th Ser., VI, 647.

108. Loyalist Transcripts, XLV, 395–405.

109. *Ibid.*, V, 149.

110. *Ibid.*, XLII, 429.

111. Flick, *Loyalism in New York*, p. 34; Schlesinger, *Colonial Merchants*, p. 332.

112. For obvious reasons the Indians are not found as claimants —apart from members of the Brant family.

113. The picture is the frontispiece of Egerton (ed.), *Royal Commission*.

114. Walker, "Sir John Johnson," p. 320; Wilbur H. Siebert, "The Loyalists and Six Nation Indians in the Niagara Peninsula," Royal Society of Canada, *Transactions*, 3d Ser., IX (1915), 79.

115. Loyalist Transcripts, XLIII, 646–647.

VI. NEW JERSEY

1. Amandus Johnson (ed. and trans.), *The Journal and Biography of Nicholas Collin, 1746–1831* (Philadelphia, 1936), p. 27.

2. For the New Jersey statistical tables see Appendix, pp. 312–316.

3. *Historical Statistics*, p. 756.

4. A. Van Doren Honeyman, "Concerning the New Jersey Loyalists in the Revolution," New Jersey Historical Society, *Proceedings*, LI (April, 1933), 126.

5. John C. Fitzpatrick (ed.), *The Writings of George Washington . . . 1745–1799* (39 vols.; Washington, D.C., 1931–1944), VI, 397–398.

6. Charles Stedman, *The History of the Origin, Progress, and Termination of the American War* (2 vols.; London, 1794), I, 242.

7. Anburey, *Travels*, II, 160.

8. Loyalist Transcripts, XXXVIII, 296–297.

9. Stedman, *History*, I, 242.

10. Loyalist Transcripts, XV, 157.

11. *Ibid.*, XXXIX, 73–74.

12. Balch Papers, New York Public Library, MSS Division.

13. Loyalist Transcripts, XVI, 398; Adrian C. Leiby, *The Revolutionary War in the Hackensack Valley, The Jersey Dutch and*

the Neutral Ground, 1775-1783 (New Brunswick, 1962), p. 83n., believes that the Hackensack Valley, mainly Bergen and Essex Counties (certainly an area strong in claimants), contained at most between one-third and one-half Tories or "Tory-minded neutrals."

14. Van Tyne, *American Revolution*, p. 132, calls the defeat the "final lesson" as Loyalist uprisings had already been put down in Maryland, Delaware, and North Carolina.

15. Schlesinger, *Colonial Merchants*, p. 455 and n.

16. Loyalist Transcripts, XV, 409.

17. *Ibid.*, XXXVIII, 413.

18. Quoted in Egerton (ed.), *Royal Commission*, p. 280.

19. Leonard Lundin, *Cockpit of the Revolution: The War for Independence in New Jersey* (Princeton, 1940), pp. 76-81.

20. Thomas J. Wertenbaker, *Princeton, 1746-1896* (Princeton, 1946), pp. 55-57.

21. This analysis is based on a check of all the graduating classes from 1748 to 1776 in Samuel D. Alexander, *Princeton College During the Eighteenth Century* (New York, 1872), pp. 1-199.

22. James Allen, "Diary," *Pennsylvania Magazine of History*, IX (1885-1886), 280.

23. Richard P. McCormick, *Experiment in Independence: New Jersey in the Critical Period, 1781-1789* (New Brunswick, 1950), pp. 31-39; Ruth M. Keesey, "New Jersey Legislation Concerning Loyalists," New Jersey Historical Society, *Proceedings*, LXXXIX (April, 1961), 75.

24. Loyalist Transcripts, XXXIX, 146; XVI, 44, 175.

25. Sabine, *Biographical Sketches*, I, 403.

26. Collin, *Journal*, pp. 250-251.

27. Loyalist Transcripts, XL, 190; VIII, 480; II, 209; XV, 576, 579.

28. *Ibid.*, VII, 540; II, 213.

29. Collin, *Journal*, p. 249; see Leiby, *The Revolutionary War in the Hackensack Valley*, pp. 83n., 125 and *passim*. After the war the Hackensack Valley was the one part of New Jersey where the Whigs could not forgive and forget (see p. 305).

30. McCormick, *Experiment in Independence*, p. 39.

31. E. Alfred Jones (ed.), *The Loyalists of New Jersey, Their Memorials, Petitions, Claims, etc. from English Records* (Newark, 1927), p. 112; American Loyalists, Royal Institution Transcripts, VI, 123; Loyalist Transcripts, XVI, 479.

32. McCormick, *Experiment in Independence*, pp. 28-29.

33. Fitzpatrick (ed.), *Writings of George Washington*, V, 226, 220, 225.
34. Jones (ed.), *Loyalists of New Jersey*, p. 102.
35. *Ibid.*, p. 41.
36. Moses C. Tyler, *Literary History of the American Revolution, 1763-1783* (2 vols.; New York and London, 1897), II, 98, 99.
37. See *supra*, pp. 114, 111; James Moody, another distinguished Loyalist, is discussed *infra*, pp. 123-124.
38. Frederick W. Ricord and William Nelson (eds.), *New Jersey Archives* (Newark, 1886), X, 595.
39. See Jones (ed.), *Loyalists of New Jersey*, p. 7.
40. Richard S. Field, *Provincial Courts of New Jersey* (New York, 1849), p. 181.
41. For Odell and Chandler see *supra*, pp. 119-120.
42. Lundin, *Cockpit of the Revolution*, p. 103.
43. Jones (ed.), *Loyalists of New Jersey*, p. 42.
44. Isaac Ogden to Joseph Galloway, November 22, 1778, Balch Papers.
45. Ruth M. Keesey, "Loyalism in Bergen County, New Jersey," *William and Mary Quarterly*, 3d Ser., XVIII (October, 1961), 569.
46. Honeyman, "Concerning the New Jersey Loyalists," p. 131, thought so, but was at a loss for an explanation.
47. *Historical Statistics*, p. 756.
48. Loyalist Transcripts, XXXIV, 171.
49. American Loyalists, Royal Institution Transcripts, IV, 505; Lundin, *Cockpit of the Revolution*, p. 100, says that the Dutch Reformed ministers were usually Whig.
50. Leiby, *The Revolutionary War in the Hackensack Valley*, pp. 19-23, 114. In general Americans affected by the Great Awakening seem to have been Whig.
51. *Ibid.*, p. 17.
52. Loyalist Transcripts, XV, 119.
53. Keesey, "Loyalism in Bergen County," p. 570.
54. Keesey, in *ibid.*, is very weak on the motives of the Loyalists, ascribing them to the "usual forces of conservatism." But, it seems to me, these apply equally well to the Patriots.
55. James Moody, *Narrative of the Exertions and Sufferings of Lieut. James Moody, in the Cause of Government since the Year 1776* (New York, 1865), pp. 10-11, 13-14; Loyalist Transcripts, IV, 15.
56. Collin, *Journal*, p. 245.
57. Jones (ed.), *Loyalists of New Jersey*, p. 76.

58. *Ibid.*, pp. 198, 157–159, 15, 234, 153.
59. *Ibid.*, p. 87.
60. Loyalist Transcripts, XL, 185, 293.
61. Keesey, "Loyalism in Bergen County," pp. 560, 570; Loyalist Transcripts, XVI, 265–266; XV, 563; XVI, 389.
62. Collin, *Journal*, pp. 244–245.

VII. PENNSYLVANIA

1. *Historical Statistics*, p. 756.
2. See *infra*, pp. 148–149.
3. Robert Proud, "Letters of Robert Proud," *Pennsylvania Magazine of History and Biography*, XXXIV (January, 1910), 64.
4. *Ibid.*, p. 63.
5. Loyalist Transcripts, XLIX, 265.
6. Samuel Shoemaker, "A Pennsylvania Loyalist's Interview with George III," *Pennsylvania Magazine of History and Biography*, II (1878), 35–36; Sabine, *Biographical Sketches*, II, 301.
7. Loyalist Transcripts, L, 410.
8. *Ibid.*, V, 615.
9. *Ibid.*, III, 401.
10. *Ibid.*, L, 443.
11. Sabine, *Biographical Sketches*, I, 157.
12. Egerton (ed.), *Royal Commission*, pp. 310, 333.
13. Loyalist Transcripts, XLIX, 373, 375.
14. For further examples of equivocal behavior see the discussions of the Penns and Duché, *infra*, pp. 148 and 144.
15. Allen, "Diary," p. 193.
16. See Van Tyne, *Loyalists*, Appendixes B and C; Van Tyne, *American Revolution*, map facing p. 250.
17. Loyalist Transcripts, LI, 115; Sabine, *Biographical Sketches*, II, 86.
18. American Loyalists, Royal Institution Transcripts, I, 467.
19. Loyalist Transcripts, L, 227; LI, 165; Grace Growden Galloway, "Diary of Grace Growden Galloway," ed. Raymond C. Werner, *Pennsylvania Magazine of History and Biography*, LV (1931), 48n.
20. Loyalist Transcripts, XXV, 305.
21. *Ibid.*, pp. 296, 17; VIII, 472.
22. *Ibid.*, V, 244; III, 425; LI, 21; XLIX, 263; XXXV, 197.
23. *Ibid.*, XLIX, 420–423; Sabine, *Biographical Sketches*, I, 597; Moore, *Diary*, I, 148.

24. Allen, "Diary," p. 287.
25. Loyalist Transcripts, XLIX, 254–255.
26. Jensen, *New Nation*, pp. 273–274.
27. Van Tyne, *American Revolution*, p. 74.
28. Galloway, "Diary," p. 64.
29. Potts to Galloway, December 17, 1778, Balch Papers.
30. Anburey, *Travels*, II, 173–174.
31. E.g. Loyalist Transcripts, V, 615; L, 412, 263–264.
32. *Ibid.*, LI, 524.
33. *Ibid.*, III, 405, 407.
34. *Ibid.*, L, 537.
35. Galloway, "Diary," LVIII (1934), 160.
36. For the Pennsylvania tables see Appendix, pp. 317–321.
37. This is partly surmise because eleven of the twenty-six give their residences simply as on the Susquehanna River, but the evidence suggests that they in fact lived in Northumberland County.
38. Wilbur H. Siebert, *The Loyalists of Pennsylvania* (Columbus, 1920), p. 58.
39. Nicholas Cresswell, *Journal of Nicholas Cresswell, 1774–1777* (London, 1925), p. 101.
40. Loyalist Transcripts, XXV, 444–464, 436–443; Sabine, *Biographical Sketches*, I, 474; Walter R. Hoberg, "History of Colonel Alexander McKee," *Pennsylvania Magazine of History and Biography* (January, 1934), pp. 26–36.
41. Quoted in Theodore Thayer, *Pennsylvania Politics and the Growth of Democracy, 1740–1776* (Harrisburg, 1953), p. 36. This may be an exaggeration, but as Frank R. Diffenderffer, *The German Immigration into Pennsylvania* (Lancaster, 1900), p. 105, points out, there is considerable unanimity that in the eighteenth century Germans made up about one-third of the population.
42. Loyalist Transcripts, XLIX, 452.
43. Thayer, *Pennsylvania Politics*, pp. 170–171.
44. Proud, "Letters," p. 64.
45. Loyalist Transcripts, VII, 555.
46. Quoted by William W. Sweet, "The Role of the Anglicans in the American Revolution," *Huntington Library Quarterly*, XI (November, 1947), 60.
47. Loyalist Transcripts, XLIX, 244; Egerton (ed.), *Royal Commission*, p. 200.
48. Loyalist Transcripts, L, 6.
49. Sweet, "Role of Anglicans," pp. 59–60.
50. Henry P. Thompson, *Into All Lands: The History of the*

Society for the Propagation of the Gospel in Foreign Parts, 1701–1950 (London, 1951), p. 94.

51. Egerton (ed.), *Royal Commission*, p. 201.
52. Loyalist Transcripts, L, 370–371.
53. *Ibid.*, pp. 12, 157.
54. *Ibid.*, p. 138.
55. *Ibid.*, III, 425.
56. *Ibid.*, L, 7.
57. Jones, *Loyalists of Massachusetts*, p. 106.
58. John R. Alden, *The American Revolution, 1775–1783* (New York, 1954), p. 201.
59. Sabine, *Biographical Sketches*, I, 25.
60. This is based on the population figures of 1776 after the British occupation. Boston dropped from 16,000 to 3,500, Philadelphia from 40,000 to 21,767; Bridenbaugh, *Cities in Revolt*, p. 216. It must be noted, somewhat in opposition to the argument of the above paragraph, that proportionately far fewer Philadelphians fled at the British invasion than did Bostonians, Philadelphia's population halving while Boston's dropped nearly 80 per cent. If the 1775 populations are used, a very slightly higher proportion left Philadelphia.
61. Benjamin F. Stevens (ed.), *Facsimiles of Manuscripts in European Archives Relating to America, 1773–1783* (25 vols.; London, 1889–1898), No. 1109.
62. Edward H. Tatum (ed.), *The American Journal of Ambrose Serle, 1776–1778* (San Marino, 1940), p. 296.
63. East, *Business Enterprise*, p. 220.
64. *Ibid.*, p. 220.
65. Loyalist Transcripts, XLIX, 293.
66. Sabine, *Biographical Sketches*, II, 164.
67. *D.A.B.*, XIV, 430–432; Loyalist Transcripts, LI, 492–500, 501–503.
68. *Ibid.*, L, 477; XXV, 15; Fraser (ed.), *Ontario Archives*, p. 498; Loyalist Transcripts, L, 57, XLIX, 163–164.
69. Egerton (ed.), *Royal Commission*, p. 200.
70. Loyalist Transcripts, XLIX, 224.
71. Washington, *Writings*, IX, 382n.
72. Loyalist Transcripts, III, 445.
73. Shoemaker, "Interview," p. 39.
74. Allen, "Diary," pp. 179, 185, 186, 187.
75. Moore, *Diary*, I, 369.
76. Loyalist Transcripts, III, 401.

77. Marquis de Chastellux, *Travels in North America* (New York, 1828), p. 270n. This charge is not repeated by the Girtys' biographer, Consul W. Butterfield, *History of the Girtys* (Cincinnati, 1890).

VIII. DELAWARE

1. *Historical Statistics*, p. 756. For Delaware tables see Appendix, pp. 322–324.
2. Loyalist Transcripts, XXXVII, 428–429.
3. See Harold B. Hancock, *The Delaware Loyalists* (Wilmington, 1940), pp. 1–2.
4. *Ibid.*, p. 57.
5. Loyalist Transcripts, XXXVII, 390–391, 409.
6. Hancock, *Delaware Loyalists*, p. 34.
7. *Ibid.*, pp. 1, 57, quoted.
8. See Christopher L. Ward, *The Delaware Continentals, 1776–1783* (Wilmington, 1941), *passim*.
9. Quoted in John A. Munroe, *Federalist Delaware, 1775–1815* (New Brunswick, 1954), p. 88. Munroe notes that in 1813 McKean expressed an opinion entirely opposite to that of John Adams.
10. See Schlesinger, *Colonial Merchants*, pp. 149–150, 196, 357–358, 460, 502–503, 574.
11. Loyalist Transcripts, XXXVII, 375; Fraser (ed.), *Ontario Archives*, pp. 519–520. The laws passed affecting the Loyalists were considered among the lightest of all the states. See Van Tyne, *American Revolution*, map facing p. 250; *Loyalists*, appendixes.
12. Stevens, *Facsimiles*, XXIV, 2068.
13. See Hancock, *Delaware Loyalists*, pp. 1, 56–57.
14. *Ibid.*, p. 55.
15. Loyalist Transcripts, XXXVII, 390, 400.
16. Hancock, *Delaware Loyalists*, p. 52.
17. Loyalist Transcripts, XXXVII, 426, 428.
18. Hancock, *Delaware Loyalists*, p. 61.
19. Loyalist Transcripts, XIII, 20.
20. Hancock, *Delaware Loyalists*, pp. 3, 44–45; Munroe, *Federalist Delaware*, pp. 46–47. On p. 43 Munroe says that the Presbyterians were second in numbers to the Anglicans.
21. Hancock, *Delaware Loyalists*, pp. 45–47.
22. Loyalist Transcripts, XXXVII, 411.
23. See Harold Hancock, "The New Castle County Loyalists,"

Delaware History, IV (September, 1951), 316.
24. Munroe, *Federalist Delaware*, pp. 44-46.
25. Hancock, *Delaware Loyalists*, p. 49.
26. Munroe, *Federalist Delaware*, pp. 53-57.
27. Hancock, *Delaware Loyalists*, pp. 51-52.
28. *Ibid.*, pp. 55-56.
29. Potts to Galloway, December 17, 1778, Balch Papers.
30. Listed, but not analyzed, by Hancock in *Delaware Loyalists*, pp. 62-64.

IX. MARYLAND

1. For Maryland tables see Appendix, pp. 325-328.
2. Bridenbaugh, *Cities in Revolt*, p. 217; Greene and Harrington, *American Population*, p. 133.
3. See *infra*, p. 253.
4. Loyalist Transcripts, XXXV, 411.
5. William Eddis, *Letters from America, Historical and Descriptive, 1769-77* (London, 1792), pp. 24, 49.
6. Loyalist Transcripts, XXXV, 6, 268.
7. *Historical Statistics*, p. 756.
8. Schlesinger, *Colonial Merchants, passim*.
9. Loyalist Transcripts, XXXV, 7-9, 37.
10. *Ibid.*, p. 17.
11. *Ibid.*, p. 268.
12. Eddis, *Letters from America*, p. 271.
13. See Philip A. Crowl, *Maryland during and after the Revolution* (Baltimore, 1943), *passim*.
14. Loyalist Transcripts, XXXV, 272.
15. Van Tyne, *American Revolution*, map facing p. 250; for details see Van Tyne, *Loyalists*, appendixes, and Crowl, *Maryland during the Revolution*, pp. 41-63.
16. Loyalist Transcripts, XXXV, 382; Greene, *Revolutionary Generation*, p. 307.
17. Loyalist Transcripts, II, 186-187.
18. *Ibid.*, XXVI, 17-18; XIII, 159; American Loyalists, Royal Institution Transcripts, III, 274-275; see Dorothy M. Quynn, "The Loyalist Plot in Frederick," *Maryland Historical Magazine*, XL (September, 1945), 201-210, for further details; also Loyalist Transcripts, VI, 160.
19. Van Tyne, *Loyalists*, p. 160n.; Loyalist Transcripts, XIII, 158-159.

20. See Charles A. Barker, *The Background of the Revolution in Maryland* (New Haven, 1940), *passim.*

21. Loyalist Transcripts, XXXV, 13.

22. Rosamond R. Beirne, "Governor Robert Eden," *Maryland Historical Magazine*, XLV (September and December, 1950), 168, 298.

23. See Grace A. Cockroft, *The Public Life of George Chalmers* (New York, 1939).

24. Loyalist Transcripts, XXXV, 14.

25. Eddis, *Letters from America*, p. 257.

26. Beirne, "Governor Robert Eden," p. 300. See the whole article for a very good general account of the governor.

27. Eddis, *Letters from America*, p. 151; *D.A.B.*, VI, 6; Cockroft, *George Chalmers*, p. 36.

28. Loyalist Transcripts, XXXVI, 169–170.

29. The whole letter is in Janet B. Johnson, *Robert Alexander, Maryland Loyalist* (New York, 1942), p. 108.

30. Charles A. Barker, "Maryland Before the Revolution," *American Historical Review*, XLVI (October, 1940), 10; see also Aubrey C. Land, *The Dulanys of Maryland* (Baltimore, 1955).

31. Loyalist Transcripts, XXXV, 303–334.

32. One other interesting Maryland Loyalist should be mentioned—John Ferdinand Dalziel Smyth, a colorful, mendacious Scotsman who wrote about his travels in America. Smyth, however, did not add any strength to the Loyalist cause.

33. Barker, "Maryland Before the Revolution," p. 2.

34. Thompson, *Into All Lands*, p. 94; William H. Wroton, Jr., "The Protestant Episcopal Church in Dorchester County, 1692–1860," *Maryland Historical Magazine*, XLV (June, 1950), 118.

35. Jonathan Boucher, "Letters of Rev. Jonathan Boucher," *Maryland Historical Magazine*, VIII (1913), 243; IX (1914), 333.

36. Eddis, *Letters from America*, p. 46.

37. Boucher, "Letters," VIII, 242–243.

38. *Ibid.*, p. 240.

39. Eddis, *Letters from America*, p. 217.

40. Cockroft, *George Chalmers*, p. 37; Loyalist Transcripts, XXXV, 371. There are some claims from British and Scottish houses, but none of the claimants were ever resident in America, and therefore they do not figure in this study.

41. *Ibid.*, XXXVII, 77–78, 81.

42. *Ibid.*, p. 47.

43. *Ibid.*, XXXV, 371.

44. *Ibid.*, p. 356; VI, 289.
45. *Ibid.*, XXXV, 303.
46. *Ibid.*, XXXVI, 247.
47. American Loyalists, Royal Institution Transcripts, IV, 201; see also Land, *Dulanys of Maryland*, p. 330.

X. VIRGINIA

1. Carl Bridenbaugh, *Myths and Realities* (New York, 1963), p. 53.
2. Loyalist Transcripts, LIX, 506. For tables see Appendix, pp. 329–332.
3. See Schlesinger, *Colonial Merchants*, pp. 35–37, 509–511, 513, 516–517, and *passim*.
4. *Journal of the House of Delegates*, May, 1777; quoted in Isaac S. Harrell, *Loyalism in Virginia* (Philadelphia, 1926), p. 76.
5. *Ibid.*, p. 63.
6. Loyalist Transcripts, LIX, 191.
7. This in spite of the assertion that the western parts were strongly loyal, Harrell, *Loyalism in Virginia*, p. 33; Keith B. Berwick, "Loyalties in Crisis: A Study of the Attitudes of Virginians in the Revolution" (unpubl. Ph.D. diss., University of Chicago, 1959), p. 51. Charles Stedman wrote that western Virginia together with the western areas of the other Southern colonies "were strongly attached to the British government," Charles Stedman, *History*, I, 149, but for the Old Dominion there seems to be no real evidence to support this statement.
8. *Historical Statistics*, p. 756.
9. Charles R. Lingley, *The Transition in Virginia from Colony to Commonwealth* (New York, 1910), p. 119; Loyalist Transcripts, LVIII, 113.
10. Harrell, *Loyalism in Virginia*, p. 62; Lingley, *Transition in Virginia*, pp. 115–118; Force (ed.), *American Archives*, 4th Ser., III, 1669; Loyalist Transcripts, V, 18.
11. Public Record Office, Foreign Office Papers, 4/1. Foreign Office Papers henceforth cited as FO.
12. Loyalist Transcripts, LVIII, 84; Harrell, *Loyalism in Virginia*, p. 59.
13. Loyalist Transcripts, LIX, 354, 589; VI, 640; LVIII, 129–130.
14. *Ibid.*, p. 270; II, 52; LVIII, 119.
15. *Ibid.*, V, 61.
16. *Ibid.*, LIX, 235.

[371]

17. John R. Alden, *The South in the Revolution, 1763-1789* (Baton Rouge, 1957), p. 323.
18. Loyalist Transcripts, VII, 455.
19. Schlesinger, *Colonial Merchants*, pp. 134, 197-199, 236, 364, 509-510, and *passim*, shows how the traders of Virginia, and indeed the rest of the plantation provinces, were not adversely affected by British policy after 1763 and were dragged along unwillingly by the planter aristocracy into the various forms of colonial opposition in the years preceding the Revolution.
20. Loyalist Transcripts, XXVII, 583; LVIII, 303; LIX, 443; XXVII, 473; Harrell, *Loyalism in Virginia*, p. 48.
21. Loyalist Transcripts, LVIII, 296-297, 28.
22. *Ibid.*, VII, 95; LVIII, 11, 587-588.
23. Thompson, *Into All Lands*, p. 94.
24. See Cross, *The Anglican Episcopate*, chap. x.
25. Egerton (ed.), *Royal Commission*, p. 343n.; Loyalist Transcripts, LVIII, 378-379; Egerton (ed.), *Royal Commission*, p. 268.
26. Loyalist Transcripts, LVIII, 31.
27. See Daniel J. Boorstin, *The Americans, The Colonial Experience* (New York, 1958), pp. 123-131, for a summary of the Anglican church in Virginia. William H. Seiler, "The Church of England as the Established Church in Seventeenth Century Virginia," *Journal of Southern History*, XV (November, 1949), 478-508, describes the origins of the self-governing vestry.
28. Harrell, *Loyalism in Virginia*, pp. 63, 34, 63n.
29. *Ibid.*, p. 28n.
30. *The History of the College of William and Mary* (Richmond, 1874), p. 47.
31. Loyalist Transcripts, V, 110.
32. Quoted in Berwick, "Loyalties in Crisis," p. 40.
33. However, Emory G. Evans, "Planter Indebtedness and the Coming of the Revolution in Virginia," *William and Mary Quarterly*, 3d Ser., XIX (October, 1962), 511-533, concludes that indebtedness was of little importance in the coming of the Revolution in Virginia.
34. Harrell, *Loyalism in Virginia*, pp. 39-40, 54; Berwick, "Loyalties in Crisis," p. 49.
35. Chastellux, *Travels*, p. 277.
36. *Ibid.*, p. 286.
37. I am much indebted in the preceding six paragraphs to Thad W. Tate, "The Coming of the Revolution in Virginia: Brittain's Challenge to Virginia's Ruling Class, 1763-1776," *William and Mary Quarterly*, 3d Ser., XIX (July, 1962), 323-343; Lingley,

Transition in Virginia, p. 121; Berwick, "Loyalties in Crisis," *passim;* Harrell, *Loyalism in Virginia, passim.*

XI. NORTH CAROLINA

1. Robert O. DeMond, *The Loyalists in North Carolina during the Revolution* (Durham, 1940), p. vii. However, an earlier writer, Isaac S. Harrell, "North Carolina Loyalists," *North Carolina Historical Review,* III (October, 1926), 590, was skeptical about the supposed large number of active Loyalists.
2. William L. Saunders (ed.), *The Colonial Records of North Carolina* (10 vols.; Raleigh, 1880–1890), IX, 1084.
3. *Ibid.,* p. 1167.
4. Alden, *South in the Revolution,* pp. 197–198.
5. Moore, *Diary,* I, 210.
6. Loyalist Transcripts, XLVII, 552.
7. Alden, *South in the Revolution,* p. 256.
8. *Historical Statistics,* p. 756.
9. Van Tyne, *American Revolution,* map facing p. 250. The laws are summarized in Van Tyne, *Loyalists,* Appendix C.
10. Alden, *South in the Revolution,* p. 326.
11. Loyalist Transcripts, XLVIII, 649–652.
12. Van Tyne, *Loyalists,* pp. 218–219.
13. Alden, *South in the Revolution,* p. 325.
14. Stedman, *History,* II, 107–108.
15. See DeMond, *Loyalists in North Carolina,* pp. 118–123.
16. See Appendix, pp. 333–336.
17. Loyalist Transcripts, XLVIII, 193–198.
18. Quoted by Sabine, *Biographical Sketches,* I, 511.
19. Egerton (ed.), *Royal Commission,* p. 217n.
20. *Historical Statistics,* p. 756.
21. DeMond, *Loyalists in North Carolina,* p. 55, thinks differently.
22. Loyalist Transcripts, XLVIII, 701.
23. DeMond, *Loyalists in North Carolina,* p. 58.
24. Loyalist Transcripts, XLVII, 324.
25. Only one example of a family split over the question of Loyalism was revealed to the claims commissioners, a fact which further suggests Whig unanimity.
26. Adams, *Works,* VII, 284.
27. Saunders (ed.), *Colonial Records of North Carolina,* IX, 1228.
28. *Ibid.,* X, xiv.
29. Loyalist Transcripts, XLVII, 680.

30. Fraser (ed.), *Ontario Archives*, p. 42; Loyalist Transcripts, XLVII, 680; Egerton (ed.), *Royal Commission*, p. 99.

31. *Ibid.*, p. 361.

32. Loyalist Transcripts, XLVII, 468–469.

33. *Ibid.*, p. 444; XLVIII, 13.

34. Hulton, *Letters*, pp. 70–71. It should be noted that most of the future Revolutionary leaders in North Carolina marched against the Regulators.

35. Hugh T. Lefler and Albert Ray Newsome, *The History of a Southern State, North Carolina* (Chapel Hill, 1954), p. 178. See also Elisha P. Douglass, *Rebels and Democrats* (Chapel Hill, 1955), p. 353. The view that most Regulators became Tories was first put forward by John S. Bassett, "The Regulators of North Carolina (1765–1771)," American Historical Association, *Annual Report, 1894* (Washington, 1895), p. 209.

36. Douglass, *Rebels and Democrats*, pp. 111–112; Alden, *American Revolution*, p. 91 and n.

37. Saunders (ed.), *Colonial Records of North Carolina*, X, 125.

38. Thompson, *Into All Lands*, p. 93.

39. William K. Boyd (ed.), *Some Eighteenth Century Tracts Concerning North Carolina* (Raleigh, 1927), pp. 397–412.

40. Saunders (ed.), *Colonial Records of North Carolina*, IX, 1086.

41. Loyalist Transcripts, XLVIII, 20–27.

42. Thompson, *Into All Lands*, p. 93.

43. Boyd (ed), *Some Eighteenth Century Tracts*, pp. 395–396.

44. Loyalist Transcripts, II, 30.

45. See Duane Meyer, *The Highland Scots of North Carolina* (Chapel Hill, 1957), pp. 147–156.

46. Ian C. C. Graham, *Colonists from Scotland: Emigration to North America, 1707–1783* (Ithaca, 1956).

47. Loyalist Transcripts, XLVIII, 156.

48. [Janet Schaw], *Journal of a Lady of Quality*, ed. Evangeline W. and Charles M. Andrews (New Haven, 1939), p. 281.

49. Egerton (ed.), *Royal Commission*, p. 278.

50. Loyalist Transcripts, XLVIII, 407.

51. *Ibid.*, XLV, 72–73.

52. The names are in Walter Clark (ed.), *The State Records of North Carolina* (Goldsboro, 1905), XXIV, 263–264.

53. Schlesinger, *Colonial Merchants*, pp. 148–149, 208–209 and *passim*.

54. DeMond, *Loyalists in North Carolina*, p. 54.

55. Clark (ed.), *State Records of North Carolina*, XXIV, 11.

56. Isaac S. Harrell, "North Carolina Loyalists," p. 590.
57. Loyalist Transcripts, XLVIII, 410.
58. DeMond, *Loyalists in North Carolina,* p. 53.
59. Loyalist Transcripts, XLVII, 290.
60. Egerton (ed.), *Royal Commission,* p. 216.
61. Loyalist Transcripts, XLVII, 445.
62. *Ibid.,* XXVII, 160, 164, 167.
63. *D.A.B.,* VI, 264-265.

XII. SOUTH CAROLINA

1. For South Carolina tables see Appendix, pp. 337-340; *Historical Statistics,* p. 756.
2. The figures are given in Ella P. Levett, "Loyalism in Charleston, 1776-1784," South Carolina Historical Association, *Proceedings* (1936), p. 12n.
3. Van Tyne, *American Revolution,* map facing p. 250. The laws are summarized in Van Tyne, *Loyalists,* Appendixes B and C.
4. Jensen, *New Nation,* pp. 275-277.
5. Wilbur H. Siebert, *Loyalists in East Florida, 1774-1785* (2 vols.; Deland, Fla., 1929), II, 315.
6. Loyalist Transcripts, I, 251; Greene, *Revolutionary Generation,* p. 308.
7. Loyalist Transcripts, LII, 99-100.
8. Alden, *South in the Revolution,* p. 250; Anthony Allaire, "Diary," in Lyman C. Draper, *King's Mountain and Its Heroes* (New York, 1929), p. 511.
9. Loyalist Transcripts, LVI, 169.
10. *Ibid.,* p. 295.
11. David Ramsay, *The History of South Carolina* (2 vols.; Charleston, 1809), I, 259.
12. Loyalist Transcripts, LIV, 6.
13. See *infra,* p. 226.
14. Loyalist Transcripts, LII, 88.
15. Alden, *South in the Revolution,* p. 242.
16. Robert Gray, "Colonel Robert Gray's Observations on the War in Carolina," *South Carolina Historical and Genealogical Magazine,* XI (July, 1910), 140.
17. Hugh E. Egerton, *The Causes and Character of the American Revolution* (Oxford, 1923), p. 168.
18. Loyalist Transcripts, LIII, 44.
19. *Ibid.,* LV, 74.

20. Alan S. Brown (ed.), "James Simpson's Reports on the Carolina Loyalists, 1779–1780," *Journal of Southern History*, XXI (November, 1955), 517–518.
21. Gray, "Observations," p. 141.
22. Ramsay, *History of South Carolina*, I, 251.
23. Loyalist Transcripts, LV, 283.
24. *Ibid.*, LVI, 9.
25. *Ibid.*, LIV, 564.
26. *Ibid.*, LVI, 447.
27. *Ibid.*, p. 342.
28. *Ibid.*, LVII, 194.
29. Gray, "Observations," p. 140.
30. Loyalist Transcripts, LVI, 425.
31. *Ibid.*, p. 448. Charles Singer, *South Carolina in the Confederation* (Philadelphia, 1941), p. 102, says, "The great leaders of the colonial period in South Carolina, almost without exception, supported the colonial cause."
32. Loyalist Transcripts, LVI, 418.
33. For the motives of the Germans see *infra*, p. 226.
34. Ramsay, *History of South Carolina*, I, 253.
35. Gray, "Observations," p. 148.
36. Selected Charleston Loyalists have been analyzed, rather inadequately, by Ralph L. Andreano and Herbert D. Werner, "Charleston Loyalists: A Statistical Note," *South Carolina History*, LX (July, 1959), 164–168. They discover surprisingly few merchants.
37. Graham, *Colonists from Scotland*, p. 173.
38. Loyalist Transcripts, LII, 427, 452.
39. *Ibid.*, LVII, 450.
40. *Ibid.*, LV, 596.
41. *Ibid.*, LVI, 295; IV, 282; LV, 227; VIII, 72; LVII, 189.
42. Egerton (ed.), *Royal Commission*, p. 103.
43. Loyalist Transcripts, VIII, 94.
44. *Ibid.*, LVII, 464.
45. I suggest that the native-born claimants were timid. See *infra*, p. 223.
46. Ramsay, *History of South Carolina*, I, 260.
47. *Ibid.*, p. 256.
48. See Siebert, *Loyalists in East Florida*, I, 314.
49. Loyalist Transcripts, VI, 257; LV, 519.
50. *Ibid.*, LIII, 155.
51. South Carolina Box, New York Public Library, MSS Division.

52. Ramsay, *History of South Carolina*, I, 252-253.
53. Richard J. Hooker (ed.), *The Carolina Backcountry on the Eve of the Revolution* (Chapel Hill, 1953), p. 188.
54. *Ibid.*, pp. 188-189; Ramsay, *History of South Carolina*, I, 253-256.
55. Alden, *South in the Revolution*, p. 152.
56. A conclusion confirmed by a recent monograph, Richard M. Brown, *The South Carolina Regulators* (Cambridge, 1962), which concludes that most Regulators were Whigs.
57. Loyalist Transcripts, XXVI, 58-59.
58. Quoted in Hooker (ed.), *Carolina Backcountry*, p. 189. The proportion of German claimants is 8.1 per cent compared with 5 per cent German-born or descended in the whole population of 1790 (See *Historical Statistics*, p. 756).
59. Ramsay, *History of South Carolina*, I, 259.
60. Loyalist Transcripts, LIV, 531; LVII, 291.
61. *Ibid.*, LVI, 304.
62. Richard Walsh, *Charleston's Sons of Liberty* (Columbia, 1959), pp. 88, 93.
63. Loyalist Transcripts, LV, 246, 540; LVIII, 328.
64. *Ibid.*, LV, 356, 466; V, 500; LIII, 328.
65. Ramsay, *History of South Carolina*, I, 259.
66. Thompson, *Into All Lands*, p. 93.
67. Van Tyne, *Loyalists*, p. 111, says five out of twenty were Loyalists, but six claimants are found.
68. Loyalist Transcripts, LIV, 85.
69. *Ibid.*, LII, 585-586.
70. *Ibid.*, p. 525.
71. Singer, *South Carolina*, p. 102.

XIII. GEORGIA

1. For the Georgia tables see Appendix, pp. 341-344.
2. *Collections of the Georgia Historical Society*, III (Savannah, 1873), 171-175.
3. Wilbur W. Abbot, *The Royal Governors of Georgia, 1754-1775* (Chapel Hill, 1959), pp. 17-18.
4. The true percentage is probably even higher because some of the lost Georgia claimants (only one of the original four books of Georgia claims in London remains; their number and names have, however, survived, and some are found in the Temporary Support records) almost certainly must have been residents of Savannah.

For a complete listing see the notes to the text. Only the major useful works cited in the notes are included here, plus a few uncited but important recent studies.

On the assumption the proportion of Savannah claimants is the same among the lost claimants, the percentage would be 9.6.

5. Elizabeth Johnston, *Recollections of a Georgia Loyalist,* ed. Arthur W. Eaton (New York and London, 1901), p. 45.

6. Abbot, *Royal Governors,* p. 179.

7. Loyalist Transcripts, XXXIV, 656.

8. *Ibid.,* VI, 666–667.

9. *Ibid.,* IV, 630.

10. *Ibid.,* VIII, 80–81; VI, 592–593; IV, 630–631; Reba C. Strickland, *Religion and the State in Georgia in the Eighteenth Century* (New York, 1939), p. 149.

11. Loyalist Transcripts, IV, 630–631.

12. *Ibid.,* XIII, 105–111; XXXIV, 383–399.

13. *Ibid.,* XIII, 55–61.

14. Sabine, *Biographical Sketches,* II, 63.

15. Loyalist Transcripts, VIII, 420–421.

16. *Ibid.,* VII, 140–141, 138–139; IV, 278–279; VII, 466–467, 468–469.

17. See *infra,* pp. 237–238.

18. Loyalist Transcripts, VI, 268–269.

19. *Ibid.,* V, 570–571; VIII, 126–127.

20. *Ibid.,* V, 482–483.

21. *Ibid.,* VIII, 420–421.

22. *Ibid.,* IV, 522.

23. Egerton (ed.), *Royal Commission,* p. 360.

24. E. Merton Coulter, *A Short History of Georgia* (Chapel Hill, 1947), p. 117.

25. Abbot, *Royal Governors,* p. 180.

26. Loyalist Transcripts, XXXIV, 639–646; Egerton (ed.), *Royal Commission,* p. 247.

27. Loyalist Transcripts, XIII, 71–77.

28. *Ibid.,* VIII, 116.

29. Sabine, *Biographical Sketches,* II, 503.

30. Kenneth Coleman, *The American Revolution in Georgia, 1763–1789* (Athens, 1958), p. 174; Strickland, *Religion and the State,* p. 149.

31. Loyalist Transcripts, IV, 394–395; VIII, 268–269; IV, 192–193.

32. Strickland, *Religion and the State,* pp. 148, 156.

33. *Ibid.,* pp. 149–150; Coleman, *American Revolution in Georgia,* p. 45.

34. Strickland, *Religion and the State,* p. 150.

35. Coleman, *American Revolution in Georgia,* p. 71.

36. Loyalist Transcripts, XIII, 29–33.

37. Strickland, *Religion and the State*, p. 150.
38. Loyalist Transcripts, XXXIV, 132.
39. Strickland, *Religion and the State*, p. 150.
40. Coleman, *American Revolution in Georgia*, p. 71.
41. Loyalist Transcripts, XIII, 51.
42. Coleman, *American Revolution in Georgia*, p. 71; Strickland, *Religion and the State*, p. 156.
43. *Ibid.*, p. 148.
44. *Ibid.*, p. 151; Coleman, *American Revolution in Georgia*, p. 176.
45. Loyalist Transcripts, VIII, 82.
46. Coleman, *American Revolution in Georgia*, p. 9; Strickland, *Religion and the State*, p. 150.
47. *Ibid.*, p. 152.
48. *Ibid.*, p. 154.
49. Loyalist Transcripts, V, 396–397.
50. *Ibid.*, VII, 20–21.
51. Strickland, *Religion and the State*, p. 155; Coleman, *American Revolution in Georgia*, p. 71; Leon Hunter, "The Jews of Georgia from the Outbreak of the American Revolution to the Close of the 18th Century," American Jewish Historical Society, *Publications*, No. 17 (1909), p. 89.
52. Loyalist Transcripts, IV, 448–449.
53. *Ibid.*, V, 386.
54. *Ibid.*, I, 11.
55. Egerton (ed.), *Royal Commission*, pp. 340, 341; Loyalist Transcripts, XXXIV, 681; XIII, 60.
56. *Ibid.*, VII, 636.
57. *Ibid.*, XIII, 151.
58. *Ibid.*, V, 386.
59. *Loyalists*, p. 303n.
60. *Historical Statistics*, p. 756, gives the white population of 1776 as 26,244, but I have preferred Abbot's figure of 20,000 (see *Royal Governors*, p. 18).
61. Allen D. Candler (ed.), *The Revolutionary Records of the State of Georgia* (3 vols.; Atlanta, 1908), I, 374–387, 348–356.
62. See Abbot, *Royal Governors*, and Coleman, *American Revolution in Georgia*, *passim*.
63. Loyalist Transcripts, XXIV, 61–62.
64. *Ibid.*, p. 422.
65. E.g. Abbot, *Royal Governors*, p. 182.
66. Loyalist Transcripts, XXXIV, 347.
67. *Ibid.*, pp. 705–706, 709.

68. *Ibid.*, I, 80–81.
69. Marjorie Daniel, "John Joachim Zubly—Georgia Pamphleteer of the Revolution," *Georgia Historical Quarterly*, XIX (1935), 1–16; Sabine, *Biographical Sketches*, II, 466–468.
70. Loyalist Transcripts, XIII, 113–136.
71. *Ibid.*, XXXIV, 505; Abbot, *Royal Governors*, pp. 132, 148.
72. Loyalist Transcripts, XXXIV, 545.
73. *Ibid.*, XIII, 94; Coleman, *American Revolution in Georgia*, p. 65.
74. Loyalist Transcripts, XXXIV, 571–572.
75. *Ibid.*, p. 509.

XIV. CONCLUSION

1. Adams, *Works*, X, 87.
2. Phineas Bond, "Letters of Phineas Bond," American Historical Association, *Annual Report, 1896* (2 vols.; Washington, 1897), I, 648.
3. Robert R. Palmer, *The Age of the Democratic Revolution* (Princeton, 1959), p. 188.
4. Alden, *American Revolution*, p. 87; Greene, *Revolutionary Generation*, p. 229. Alden thinks 8,000 Loyalists is too high an estimate and notes that only 5,415 Loyalists were serving in 1781.
5. Esther Clark Wright, *The Loyalists of New Brunswick* (Fredericton, New Brunswick, 1955), p. 165.
6. Jensen, *New Nation*, p. 268.
7. A. Van Doren Honeyman, "Concerning the New Jersey Loyalists in the Revolution," New Jersey Historical Society, *Proceedings*, LI (April, 1933), 126. It is to be hoped that more studies will appear which will estimate the total number of Loyalists in other states.
8. *Loyalists of New Brunswick*, p. 167.
9. Greene and Harrington, *American Population*, p. 7; the number of claimants used is not that found in my tables (because these also include Temporary Support), but those found in Van Tyne, *Loyalists*, p. 303n.
10. Questions Proposed to Messrs. A B & C, February, 1782, CO 5/8, Pt. 2; The Summary Case of the American Loyalists (London, 1785), FO 4/1.
11. Minutes of the Trial and Examination of Certain Persons in the Province of New York charged with being engaged in a Conspiracy against the Authority of the Congress and the Liberties of America, MSS Division, Library of Congress, Washington, D.C.

This trial which has to do with Washington and an alleged mistress is certainly part forgery, but the farmer's remark rings true.

12. Moore, *Diary*, I, 19; *Newport Mercury*, September 2, 1771, quoted in Bruce I. Granger, *Political Satire in the American Revolution, 1763-1783* (Ithaca, 1960), p. 271.

13. It is probable that New York should head the list because the huge numbers of active Loyalists there resulted in the impossibility of exiling them all. See *supra*, pp. 82-83.

14. For example, evidence beyond the claims supports the view that Georgia, New York, South Carolina, and New Jersey were the Loyalist strongholds: 3,100 whites (15 per cent of the 1776 population) fled from Georgia with the British in 1782; New York probably supplied 23,500 men to the British armed forces—more than half the total from all the colonies; 4,000 white refugees left Charleston in 1782; and Cortlandt Skinner's New Jersey Volunteers was the largest single Loyalist regiment.

15. Chastellux, *Travels*, p. 225n.

16. *The Morning Post and Daily Advertizer* (London), December 27, 1777, British Museum.

17. Force (ed.), *American Archives*, 4th Ser., VIII, 820.

18. Hulton to Robert Nicholson, May 4, 1770, Shepherd MSS.

19. Candler (ed.), *Revolutionary Records of Georgia*, XIX, Pt. II, 163-164.

20. Sabine, *Biographical Sketches*, I, 61.

21. More specific localized studies on these points are needed, but an intelligent guess is that doctors were much inclined to Loyalism, teachers only rarely, and lawyers more evenly split.

22. Tyler, "Loyalists," p. 30.

23. Sabine, *Biographical Sketches*, I, 59-60.

24. Sweet, "Role of Anglicans," p. 52.

25. Leonard J. Trinterud, *The Forming of an American Tradition* (Philadelphia, 1949), pp. 242, 243, 251.

26. Quoted in Adair P. Archer, "The Quakers' Attitude towards the Revolution," *William and Mary Quarterly*, 2d Ser., I (July, 1921), 170.

27. Arthur J. Mekeel, "The Society of Friends (Quakers) and the American Revolution" (Unpubl. Ph.D. diss., Harvard, 1940), p. 380.

28. J. Hector St. John Crèvecoeur, *Letters from an American Farmer*, ed. W. P. Trent (New York, 1904), p. 287.

29. Curwen, *Journal*, p. 233.

30. See Francis Bernard, *Select Letters on the Trade and Govern-*

ment of America (London, 1774), p. 88; Lorenzo Sabine, *The American Loyalists* (Boston, 1847), p. 487.
31. Loyalist Transcripts, LVIII, 73–74.
32. E.g. *ibid.*, VI, 337.
33. *Ibid.*, p. 217.
34. Alden, *American Revolution*, p. 86.
35. Robert Mowat, *Americans in England* (Boston, 1935), p. 42.
36. Joshua Wingate Weeks, "Journal of the Reverend Joshua Wingate Weeks, Loyalist Rector of St. Michael's Church, Marblehead, 1778–1779," Essex Institute of Salem, *Collections* (1916), LII, 203.
37. Edward Oxnard, "Extracts from the Journal of Edward Oxnard," *New England Historical and Genealogical Register*, XXVI (1872), 205.
38. Weeks, "Journal," p. 205.
39. Curwen, *Journal*, p. 231.
40. Chandler to Samuel Thorne, August 6, 1783, in box marked "Loyalists," New York Public Library, MSS Division.
41. Jones (ed.), *Loyalists of Massachusetts*, p. 180.
42. The petition is printed in Harold Hancock, "Thomas Robinson: Delaware's Most Prominent Loyalist," *Delaware History*, IV (March, 1950), 32–33.
43. Rumford to Charles Blagden, July 26, 1793, Blagden Collection.
44. Benjamin Rush, "Historical Notes of Dr. Benjamin Rush, 1777," *Pennsylvania Magazine of History and Biography* (1903), XXVII, 143–145.
45. John Eardly-Wilmot, *Historical View of the Commission for Enquiry into . . . the American Loyalists* (London, 1815), pp. 4–5.
46. Force (ed.), *American Archives*, 5th Ser., II, 820.
47. Adams, *Works*, X, 87.
48. John Bigelow (ed.), *The Complete Works of Benjamin Franklin* (New York and London, 1888), IX, 133.
49. Adams, *Works*, X, 192–193.
50. *Ibid.*, p. 196.
51. See Egerton (ed.), *Royal Commission*, frontispiece.
52. J. Hector St. John Crèvecoeur, *Sketches of Eighteenth Century America*, ed. H. L. Bourdin *et al.* (New Haven, 1925), p. 310.
53. Loyalist Transcripts, LVIII, 236.
54. *Ibid.*, V, 194–195.
55. *Ibid.*, I, 85–87.

56. *Ibid.*, pp. 85, 88.

57. *Ibid.*, LVI, 35; for more on the Negroes, see Wallace Brown, "Negroes and the American Revolution," *History Today*, XIV (August, 1964), 556–563.

58. Anburey, *Travels*, I, 219.

59. American Loyalists, Royal Institution Transcripts, IV, 330.

60. *Ibid.*, V, 329.

61. FO 4/1; Loyalist Rhapsodies, 1775–83, Library of Congress, MSS Division.

62. Loyalist Transcripts, XL, 179.

63. Questions Proposed to Messrs. A B & C, February, 1782, CO 5/8, Pt. 2.

64. Loyalist Transcripts, I, 15.

65. Schlesinger, *Colonial Merchants*, p. 602.

66. Loyalist Transcripts, XXXIX, 447.

67. Walsh, *Charleston's Sons of Liberty*, p. 101.

68. William L. Sachse, *The Colonial American in Great Britain* (Madison, 1956), p. 200.

69. Serle, *Journal*, p. 157.

70. *Ibid.*, p. 164.

71. Sydney G. Fisher, *True History of the American Revolution* (Philadelphia, 1902), p. 156n.

72. Historical Manuscript Commission, *Manuscripts of Mrs. Stopford-Sackville*, II, 183.

73. Crèvecoeur, *Letters*, p. 287.

74. Curwen, *Journal*, p. 172.

75. Loyalist Transcripts, XLV, 222.

76. North's memorial is printed in Hancock, "New Castle Loyalists," p. 330.

77. Nelson, *The American Tory*, p. 89.

78. Sweet, "Role of Anglicans," p. 52.

79. Nelson, *The American Tory*, p. 89.

SELECT BIBLIOGRAPHY

MAJOR SOURCES

The sources for the statistical tables and most of the text are the remaining records of the claims commission set up by the British government to give aid and compensation to the Loyalists. These original Audit Office Papers are in the Public Record Office in London, but in 1900 Benjamin F. Stevens had most of the pertinent information which had escaped flood damage transcribed and placed in the New York Public Library. It is mainly these transcripts (on microfilm) which have been used. They are called American Loyalists: Transcripts of the Manuscript Books and Papers of the Commission of Enquiry into the Losses and Services of the American Loyalists, and consist of sixty MS volumes of evidence, hearings, and decisions. (See Charles M. Andrews, *Guide to the Materials for American History to 1783, in the Public Record Office of Great Britain* [two volumes; Washington, D.C., 1912 and 1914], II, 259–264.)

For Rhode Island and Connecticut it was necessary to supplement the Stevens Transcripts by an examination of the original claims materials in the Public Record Office. For Rhode Island Audit Office Papers, 13/42, 68 Pts. 1 and 2, 80, 82, 83 were used; for Connecticut AO 13/21, 41, 42, 70B Pt. 1, 76, 80, 81, 83, 87, 90, 92, 93, 96 Pt. 2, 97, 107.

The Loyalist Transcripts were also supplemented by: Hugh E. Egerton (ed.), *The Royal Commission on the Losses and Services of American Loyalists* (Oxford, 1915), which consists of the notes of Daniel Parker Coke, one of the claims commissioners in London; Alexander Fraser (ed.), *Second Report of the Bureau of Archives for the Province of Ontario, 1904* (Toronto, 1905), which contains the evidence gathered by Thomas Dundas and Jeremy Pemberton, the commissioners in Canada, and is largely, but not entirely, the same as that found in the New York Loyalist Transcripts; Claims of New Hampshire Loyalists, five volumes of transcripts from the Public Record Office, London, in the New Hampshire State Library (Concord), which includes information on some New Hampshire Tories not found elsewhere; E. Alfred Jones (ed.), *The Loyalists of Massachusetts* (London, 1930) and *The Loyalists of New Jersey* (Newark, 1927), which contain the claims information, drawn from the original English sources, for the Loyalists from the two colonies.

The following manuscripts were very useful for illustrative material:

British Public Record Office, Colonial Office Papers, CO 5/8 Pt. 2, Questions Proposed to Messrs. A B & C, February, 1782, which is a Loyalist questionnaire.

Manchester College, Oxford, Shepherd MSS, Vol. XVIII. Copies of lost letters from Henry Hulton to Robert Nicholson, written between 1760 and 1776. (Xerox copies used.)

New York Public Library, Manuscript Division, American Loyalists, Royal Institution Transcripts, 8 MS volumes which contain Loyalist memorials and petitions to the British military authorities and miscellaneous correspondence (microfilm copies used); Balch Papers, which include various Loyalist letters.

The Royal Society, London, Blagden Collection, which contains many interesting Loyalist letters, especially from Count Rumford.

The following printed Loyalist writings were particularly valuable:

Allen, James. "Diary," *Pennsylvania Magazine of History and Biography*, IX (1885–1886), 176–196, 278–296, 424–441.

Boucher, Jonathan. "Letters of Rev. Jonathan Boucher," *Maryland Historical Magazine*, VIII (1913), 34–50, 168–186, 235–256, 338–352; IX (1914), 54–67, 232–241, 327–336.

Cresswell, Nicholas. *Journal of Nicholas Cresswell, 1774–1777.* London, 1925.

Crèvecoeur, J. Hector St. John. *Sketches of Eighteenth Century America*, ed. H. L. Bourdin *et al.* New Haven, 1925.

Curwen, Samuel. *Journal and Letters, 1775–1784*, ed. G. A. Ward. New York, 1842.

Eddis, William. *Letters from America, Historical and Descriptive, 1769–77.* London, 1792.

Galloway, Grace Growden. "Diary of Grace Growden Gallo-

Bibliography

way," ed. Raymond C. Werner, *Pennsylvania Magazine of History and Biography*, LV (1931), 32–94; LVIII (1934), 152–189.

Gray, Robert. "Colonel Robert Gray's Observations on the War in Carolina," *South Carolina Historical and Genealogical Magazine*, XI (July, 1910), 140–159.

Hulton, Ann. *Letters of a Loyalist Lady*. Cambridge, 1927.

Jones, Thomas. *History of New York*. 2 vols. New York, 1879.

Moody, James. *Narrative of the Exertions and Sufferings of Lieut. James Moody, in the Cause of Government since the Year 1776*. New York, 1865.

Proud, Robert. "Letters of Robert Proud," *Pennsylvania Magazine of History and Biography*, XXXIV (January, 1910), 62–73.

[Schaw, Janet]. *Journal of a Lady of Quality*, ed. Evangeline W. and Charles M. Andrews. New Haven, 1934.

Shoemaker, Samuel. "A Pennsylvania Loyalist's Interview with George III," *Pennsylvania Magazine of History and Biography*, II (1878), 35–39.

Vernon, Thomas. *The Diary of Thomas Vernon*. ("Rhode Island Historical Tracts," No. 13). Providence, 1881.

In addition, the following sources proved most useful:

Adams, John. *The Works of John Adams*, ed. Charles Francis Adams. Vol. X. Boston, 1856.

Anburey, Thomas. *Travels Through the Interior Parts of America, 1776–1781*. 2 vols. Boston, 1923.

Chastellux, Marquis de. *Travels in North America*. New York, 1828.

Collin, Nicholas. *The Journal and Biography of Nicholas Collin, 1746–1831*, ed. and trans. Amandus Johnson. Philadelphia, 1936.

Eardly-Wilmot, John. *Historical View of the Commission for Enquiry into . . . the American Loyalists*. London, 1815.

Force, Peter (ed.). *American Archives*. 4th Ser., 6 vols. Washington, D.C., 1837–1846; 5th Ser., 3 vols. Washington, D.C., 1848–1853.

Hoadly, Charles J. (ed.). *The Public Records of the State of Connecticut*. Vols. I and II. Hartford, 1894, 1895.

Bibliography

Moore, Frank. *Diary of the American Revolution*. 2 vols. New York, 1860.

Ramsay, David. *The History of South Carolina*. 2 vols. Charleston, 1809.

Saunders, William L. (ed.). *The Colonial Records of North Carolina*. Vol. IX. Raleigh, 1890.

Serle, Ambrose. *The American Journal of Ambrose Serle, 1776–1778*, ed. Edward H. Tatum. San Marino, 1940.

Stedman, Charles. *The History of the Origin, Progress, and Termination of the American War*. 2 vols. London, 1794.

Stevens, Benjamin F. (ed.). *Facsimiles of Manuscripts in European Archives Relating to America, 1773–1783*. 25 vols. London, 1889–1898.

Stiles, Ezra. *The Literary Diary of Ezra Stiles, D.D., L.L.D.*, ed. Franklin B. Dexter. 3 vols. New York, 1901.

Washington, George. *The Writings of George Washington … 1745–1799*, ed. John C. Fitzpatrick. 39 vols. Washington, D.C., 1931–1944.

MAJOR SECONDARY WORKS

Abbot, Wilbur W. *The Royal Governors of Georgia, 1754–1775*. Chapel Hill, 1959.

Alden, John R. *The American Revolution, 1775–1783*. New York, 1954.

———. *The South in the Revolution, 1763–1789*. Baton Rouge, 1957.

Bridenbaugh, Carl. *Cities in Revolt*. New York, 1955.

Brown, Richard D. "The Confiscation and Disposition of Loyalists' Estates in Suffolk County, Massachusetts," *William and Mary Quarterly*, 3d Ser., XXI (October, 1964), 534–550.

Brown, Wallace. "The Loyalists and the American Revolution," *History Today*, XII (March, 1962), 149–157.

———. "Negroes and the American Revolution," *History Today*, XIV (August, 1964), 556–563.

Cockroft, Grace A. *The Public Life of George Chalmers*. New York, 1939.

Bibliography

Coleman, Kenneth. *The American Revolution in Georgia, 1763-1789.* Athens, 1958.

Crowl, Philip A. *Maryland during and after the Revolution.* Baltimore, 1943.

DeMond, Robert O. *The Loyalists in North Carolina during the Revolution.* Durham, 1940.

East, Robert A. *Business Enterprise in the American Revolutionary Era.* New York, 1938.

Flick, Alexander C. *Loyalism in New York during the American Revolution.* New York, 1901.

Gilbert, G. A. "The Connecticut Loyalists," *American Historical Review,* IV (January, 1899), 273-291.

Graham, Ian C. C. *Colonists from Scotland: Emigration to North America, 1707-1783.* Ithaca, 1956.

Greene, Evarts B. *The Revolutionary Generation, 1763-1790.* New York, 1943.

Greene, Evarts B., and Virginia D. Harrington. *American Population before the Federal Census of 1790.* New York, 1932.

Hammond, Otis G. *Tories of New Hampshire in the War of the Revolution.* Concord, 1917.

Hancock, Harold B. *The Delaware Loyalists.* Wilmington, 1940.

Harrell, Isaac S. *Loyalism in Virginia.* Philadelphia, 1926.

Harrington, Virginia D. *The New York Merchants on the Eve of the Revolution.* New York, 1935.

Jensen, Merrill. *The New Nation.* New York, 1950.

Johnson, Allen (ed.). *Dictionary of American Biography.* 20 vols. New York, 1928-1937.

Keesey, Ruth M. "Loyalism in Bergen County, New Jersey," *William and Mary Quarterly,* 3d Ser., XVIII (October, 1961), 558-571.

Lambert, Robert S. "The Confiscation of Loyalist Property in Georgia, 1782-1786," *William and Mary Quarterly,* 3d Ser., XX (January, 1963), 80-94.

Leiby, Adrian C. *The Revolutionary War in the Hackensack Valley, The Jersey Dutch and the Neutral Ground, 1775-1783.* New Brunswick, 1962.

[391]

Bibliography

Lovejoy, David S. *Rhode Island Politics and the American Revolution, 1760–1776.* Providence, 1958.

Lundin, Leonard. *Cockpit of the Revolution: The War for Independence in New Jersey.* Princeton, 1940.

McCormick, Richard P. *Experiment in Independence: New Jersey in the Critical Period, 1781–1789.* New Brunswick, 1950.

Mark, Irving. *Agrarian Conflicts in Colonial New York, 1711–1775.* New York, 1940.

Mayo, Lawrence S. *John Wentworth, Governor of New Hampshire, 1767–1775.* Cambridge, 1921.

Meyer, Duane. *The Highland Scots of North Carolina.* Chapel Hill, 1957.

Nelson, William H. *The American Tory.* Oxford, 1962.

Newcomer, Lee N. *The Embattled Farmers, A Massachusetts Countryside in the American Revolution.* New York, 1953.

Peck, Epaphroditus. *The Loyalists of Connecticut.* New Haven, 1934.

Sabine, Lorenzo. *Biographical Sketches of Loyalists of the American Revolution.* 2 vols. Boston, 1864.

Schlesinger, Arthur M. *The Colonial Merchants and the American Revolution, 1763–1776.* New York, 1918.

Smith, Paul H. *Loyalists and Redcoats.* Chapel Hill, 1964.

Stark, James H. *The Loyalists of Massachusetts.* Boston, 1910.

Strickland, Reba C. *Religion and the State in Georgia in the Eighteenth Century.* New York, 1939.

Sutherland, Stella H. *Population Distribution in Colonial America.* New York, 1936.

Sweet, William W. "The Role of the Anglicans in the American Revolution," *Huntington Library Quarterly*, XI (November, 1947), 51–70.

Taylor, Robert. *Western Massachusetts in the American Revolution.* Providence, 1954.

Thayer, Theodore. *Pennsylvania Politics and the Growth of Democracy, 1740–1776.* Harrisburg, 1953.

Thompson, Henry P. *Into All Lands: The History of the Society for the Propagation of the Gospel in Foreign Parts, 1701–1950.* London, 1951.

Bibliography

Tyler, Moses C. "The Party of the Loyalists in the American Revolution," *American Historical Review*, I (October, 1895), 24–46.

————. *Literary History of the American Revolution, 1763–1783.* 2 vols. New York and London, 1897.

U.S. Department of Commerce. *Historical Statistics, Colonial Times to 1957.* Washington, 1960.

Upton, Richard F. *Revolutionary New Hampshire.* Hanover, 1936.

Van Tyne, Claude H. *The American Revolution, 1776–1783.* New York, 1905.

————. *The Loyalists in the American Revolution.* New York, 1902.

Zeichner, Oscar. *Connecticut's Years of Controversy, 1750–1776.* Chapel Hill, 1949.

————. "The Rehabilitation of the Loyalists in Connecticut," *New England Quarterly*, XI (June, 1938), 308–330.

INDEX

Index

Blowers, Sampson Salter, 20, 32.
Board of Associated Loyalists, 116, 120.
Boisseau, James, 224.
Bond, Phineas, 133, 153, 249, 250, 251.
Boston, Mass., 21, 22, 23, 24, 27, 31, 33, 35, 36, 37, 39, 41–42, 146, 256, 257.
"Boston Massacre," 20, 37.
Boucher, Rev. Jonathan, 170, 172, 173.
Bowers, Adam, 226.
Bowes, William, 29.
Bowlby, Edward, 116.
Boyd, Colonel, 197–98.
Boynton family, 94.
Branson, Capt. Eli, 196.
Brant, Joseph, 88, 106, 107, 277.
Brattle, Gen. William, 38.
Bremar, John, 223.
Brenton, Benjamin, 50.
Brenton family, 50, 51, 53.
Brenton, Capt. Jahleel, 50.
Bridenbaugh, Carl, 179.
Brinley, Edward, 35.
British constitution, admiration of, 277–78.
British invincibility, Loyalists' belief in, 88–89.
British occupation, 45–46, 50, 68, 83–84, 87–90, 113, 125–26, 130–31, 137–38, 149–50, 158–59, 169, 190, 195–96, 214, 216–18, 241, 268.
Brooks, James, 167.
Brown, John, 237.
Brown, Mary, 37.
Brown, Prosper, 66.
Brown, Thomas, 245.
Brown, Judge William, 20, 38.
Browne, Rev. Arthur, 9.
Browne, Daniel Isaac, 112, 115, 120.
Browne, Rev. Isaac, 121.
Buchanan, Robert, 174.
Buell, Timothy, 98.

Bull, Gov. William, 218, 223.
Bulman, Rev. John, 227.
Butler, James, 233.
Butler, Col. John, 88, 106, 107, 131, 142.
Byles, Catherine, 41–42.
Byles, Mary, 41–42.
Byles, Rev. Mather, Jr., 28.
Byles, Rev. Mather, Sr., 29, 37–38, 41.
Byrd, William III, 186, 189.

Caldwell, William, 135.
Calef, Dr. John, 20.
Calvinists, 268.
Camden, S.C., 213, 220, 221, 222, 226, 258.
Camm, Rev. John, 189.
Campbell, Colin, 226.
Campbell, Gov. William, 218, 224, 225.
Caner, Rev. Henry, 27, 28.
Carey, Bernard, 187.
Carleton, Sir Guy, 98.
Carlisle, Abraham, 134.
Chalmers, George, 167, 168, 169, 170, 172.
Chalmers, James, 172.
Chaloner, Walter, 50.
Chandler, Edward, 271.
Chandler family, 31, 39.
Chandler, John, 32.
Chandler, Joshua, 62.
Chandler, Rev. Thomas Bradbury, 100, 101, 116, 119, 121, 144.
Charleston, S.C., 213, 214, 216, 218, 220, 221, 222, 225, 226, 227, 228, 256, 257.
Chastellux, Marquis de, 153, 190, 191, 260.
Cherokees, 213, 216, 217.
Chesapeake Bay, 256.
Chew, Benjamin, 136.
Chipman, Ward, 25, 35.
Christie, James, 174.

Index

Index

Cropsey, Jacobus, 90.
Cruden, Rev. Alexander, 187, 188.
Cruger family, 94.
Cruger, John Harris, 94, 103, 107.
"Cultural minorities," 281–82.
Cumming, Janet, 223.
Cunningham, Patrick, 214.
Cunningham, William, 87, 224.
Curry, Rev. Daniel, 160.
Curwen, Samuel, 32, 35, 146, 269, 271, 280.
Cutler, Rev. Ebenezer, 28.
Cutting, Rev. Leonard, 90.
Cuyler, Abraham, 85, 91, 94, 107.
Cuyler family, 103.

Danbury, Conn., 68.
Darnforth, Thomas, 41.
Davies, William, 64.
Davis, Benjamin, 39.
Davis, Richard, 235.
Dawson, John, 97.
Deblois family, 23, 32, 39.
Deblois, George, 19, 28.
Deblois, Gilbert, 20, 28.
Declaration of Independence, 93, 96, 132, 144, 157, 188, 252, 267, 270, 273.
Definitions of Loyalists, 252, 272.
DeLancey family, 94.
Delancey, James, 91, 94, 96, 100, 107.
DeLancey, James, Jr., 84.
DeLancey, Oliver, 94, 103, 107.
DeLancey party, 77, 94, 96, 98, 101.
Delaware, strength of Loyalists, 157; Presbyterians and Anglicans, 160–61; Methodists, 161; economic status, 161; analysis of claimants, 161–62; geographical distribution, 162; see also 256, 258.
DeMond, Robert O., 195.
DePuyster family, 94, 103.
De Rossett, Lewis Henry, 203.

Devereux, James, 84.
Diblee, Filer, 60, 65.
Dickinson, John, 130, 133, 134, 148.
Dissenters, 227–28, 238, see also Baptists, Congregationalists, Quakers.
Divided families, 14, 39, 61–62, 94, 124, 174–75, 209, 223, 235–36, 279.
Divided partners, 39–40, 94, 125, 245–46, 280.
Doctors, 23, 50, 264.
Dongan, Edward Vaughan, 120.
Donnelly, Mary, 79.
Doty, Rev. John, 98.
Douglas, John, 227.
Dowd, Connor, 209.
Draper, Margaret, 30.
Drummond, Robert, 120.
Duché, Rev. Jacob, 134, 136, 143, 144, 150, 153.
Dudley, Charles, 48, 54.
Dulany, Daniel, 171, 172, 174.
Dulany, Daniel III, 170, 175.
Dulany family, 170, 174, 279.
Dulany, Walter, 175.
Dunbar, Daniel, 35.
Dunbar, Moses, 65.
Dunkers, 142.
Dunmore, Lord, Governor of Va., 179, 182, 187, 189, 190, 196, 275.
Dutch, 121–23, 282.
Dutch Reformed church, 122, 263.
Dutchess County, N.Y., 81, 82, 83.

Eardly-Wilmot, John, 272, 282.
Earl, Ralph, 61–62.
East, Robert, 96, 147.
Ebenezer, Ga., 238.
Economic status of Loyalists, N.H., 5; Mass., 24; R.I., 45; Conn., 60–61; N.Y., 86, 87; N.J., 118, Pa., 141, 147; Del., 161; Md., 165; Va., 180; N.C., 198–99; S.C., 219–20; Ga., 231–32.

Index

Index

Gibbs, Dr. Robert, 215.
Gilbert, G.A., 62, 70.
Gilman, Peter, 11.
Gilmore, George, 68.
Girty, Simon, 140, 153.
Gist, William, 222.
Glocester, R.I., 46, 50.
Goldthwaite, Col. Thomas, 32.
Goodgion, William, 240.
Gordon, James, 245.
Gordon, Chief Justice Thomas Knox, 218, 219, 225.
Granger, John, 149.
Graves, Adam, 168.
Graves, George, 168.
Gray, Elizabeth, 48.
Gray, Harrison, 38.
Gray, Col. Robert, 217, 218, 221.
Great Bridge, Va., 179, 190.
Greatrex, Samuel, 183.
Greed of Loyalists, 278–80.
Green, Francis, 32, 33.
Greenleaf, Ann, 30.
Griffiths, Dorcas, 30.
Grymes, John Randolph, 185, 187.
Guilford Courthouse, N.C., 196.
Guire, Peter, 64.
Gwatkin, Rev. Thomas, 187, 188, 189.

Habersham, James, 231, 236.
Hackensack Valley, N.J., 122.
Hake, Samuel, 103.
Hale, Samuel, 6, 14.
Halifax, N.C., 199, 200.
Hall, Elihu, 61.
Halliburton, Dr., 50.
Hallowell, Benjamin, 32.
Hamilton, Alexander, 80, 81, 100, 101.
Hamilton, Col. John, 197, 198, 199.
Hamilton, Paul, 218
Hammond, Otis G., 6, 7, 9.
Hancock, Harold B., 157, 158, 159, 160.

Hancock, John, 20, 23, 26, 30.
Harassment of Loyalists by British, 111–13, 137–38, 241, 242–44, 251.
Harding, George, 135.
Harding, William, 235.
Hargreaves, William, 186.
Harper, Thomas, 276.
Harrell, Isaac, 189.
Harrington, Virginia D., 96
Harriott, James, 235.
Hart, Jacob, 54.
Hart, Moses, 47, 54.
Hartley, George, 223.
Harvard College, 26, 189.
Harvey, Alexander, 215–16, 223.
Hawley, Abijah, 84.
Henderson, James, 149.
Henley, Rev. Samuel, 189.
Henry, Elizabeth, 223.
Herkimer family, 94.
Heron, Isaac, 90.
Hessians, 89, 90, 111, 112, 169.
Hewett, Rev. Alexander, 228.
Hilding, Jane, 34.
Hilding, John, 34.
Hill, Joshua, 158, 160, 161.
Hill, Margaret Francis, 78.
Hill, William, 20, 37.
Hinchman, John, 116, 117.
Holland, Richard, 26.
Holland, Col. Stephen, 13.
Holmes, John, 237.
Honeyman, James, '54.
Hood, Zacharias, 132, 135.
Hopkins, Stephen, 53, 54.
Hopper, Thomas, 226.
Hopton, John, 226.
Horsmanden, Daniel, 95.
Houghton, William, 105.
Houseal, Rev. Bernard Michael, 85, 98.
Howard, Martin, Jr., 53, 55.
Howe, Gen. Sir William, 137, 138.
Hubbard, Isaac, 68.
Hubbard, James, 182–83.

Index

Index

Mein, John, 32.
Mennonites, 129, 142, 273.
Mercer, George, 183.
Merchants, 5, 22–23, 45, 51, 60, 68–
   69, 96–97, 147, 149–50, 165, 167,
   173–74, 180–81, 186–87, 198, 200–1,
   208–9, 219, 226–27, 261, 264, 282.
Mergath, Thomas, 226.
Meserve, George, 7.
Methodists, 161.
Micklejohn, Rev. George, 205.
Middleton, Austin, 8.
Miles, Samuel, 72.
Miller, Andrew, 201.
Miller, James, 180.
Miller, Jeremiah, Sr., 63.
Milner, Rev. John, 95, 98.
Milton, John, 283.
Moffat, Dr. Thomas, 53.
Mohawk River, 77, 81, 86.
Molesworth, James, 134.
Monmouth County, N.J., 112, 115,
   117.
Montgomery, Rev. John, 170.
Montgomery, Samuel, 234.
Moody, Lt. James, 123.
Moore, James, 227.
Moore, William, 138.
Moores Creek Bridge, N.C., 195,
   196, 197, 203, 205, 207.
Morris family, 94.
Morris, Roger, 94, 103, 104.
Morrison, Alexander, 206.
Morrison, Rev. John, 10.
Moseley, Isaac, 69.
Mosengeil, Anthony, 125, 278.
Motives of Loyalists, N.H., 13–15;
   Mass., 36–41; R.I., 55; Conn., 68–
   69; N.Y., 92, 96, 98–99, 105; N.J.,
   120–26; Pa., 149–53; Del., 159–60;
   Md., 173–74; Va., 186–91; N.C.,
   202–10; S.C., 222–23; Ga., 232–40,
   241.
Mount, George, 115.
Munro, Rev. Harry, 97.

Murray, Rev. Alexander, 144, 145.
Murray, John, of Georgia, 245, 246.
Murray, John, of Massachusetts, 31,
   39.

Napper, George, 149.
Nationality of Loyalists, 258–61,
   see also individual colonies.
Negroes, 79, 94, 190, 275–76, 282.
Neilson, Arthur, 124.
Nelson, William H., 281, 282.
Neutrals, 8–9, 71–72, 131, 137, 159,
   252, 268.
New Bern, N.C., 199, 200, 201, 202.
Newcomer, Lee N., 39.
New Hampshire, banishment of
   Loyalists, 3–4; geographical dis-
   tribution, 4–5; economic status,
   5; analysis of claimants, 5–6;
   Portsmouth Loyalists, 6; number
   of Loyalists, 6–7; persecution, 7;
   Stamp Act crisis, 7–8; neutralism
   and apathy, 8–9; Anglicans, 9–10;
   Congregationalists, 10; political
   leadership, 10–11; Governor John
   Wentworth, 11–12; Benjamin
   Thompson, 12; Robert Rogers,
   12–13; counterfeiters, 13; motives
   of Loyalists, 13–15; see also 256,
   257.
New Haven, Conn., 59, 67, 68, 72.
New Jersey, strength of Loyalists,
   111; British depredations, 111–13;
   political leadership, 113–14; College of New Jersey—Princeton,
   114–15; persecution, 115–17; geographical distribution, 117–18;
   analysis of claimants, 117–19;
   economic status, 118; Thomas B.
   Chandler and Jonathan Odell,
   119–20; William Franklin and
   General Cortlandt Skinner, 120;
   motives of Loyalists, 120–26;
   Anglicans, 121; Dutch, 121–23;
   Quakers, 123; James Moody, 123–

Index

24; British occupation, 125–26; see also 250, 256, 257.

New Jersey Volunteers, 111, 115, 117, 120.

Newport, R.I., 45, 46, 49, 50, 51, 52, 54, 55, 256, 257.

Newport Junto, 53, 55.

Newtown, Conn., 72.

New York, background, 77; number of claimants, 77–78; strength of Loyalists, 78, 80–81; persecution, 78–80; analysis of claimants, 81–87; geographical distribution, 81–85; economic status, 86; New York City, 86–87; British occupation, 87–90; Royal officials, 90–92; Chief Justice William Smith, 92; Henry Van Schaack, 92; intellectual Loyalists, 92–94; the Johnson family, 93; Peter Van Schaack, 93–94; social cleavage, 94; local politics, 94–96; merchants, 96–97; Anglicans, 97–99; King's College, 99–100; Samuel Seabury, Charles Inglis, Myles Cooper, 100–1; landlords, farmers, tenants, 101–4; Johnson tenants (Catholic Highlanders), 104–6; Indians—Joseph Brant, 106; conclusion, 106–7; see also 251, 256, 257, 258.

New York Chamber of Commerce, 96.

New York City, 77, 78, 81, 83, 84, 85, 86, 87, 88, 89, 90, 97, 98, 101, 106, 256, 257.

Nickolls, Robert B., 26.

Nicoll, John, 50.

Ninety-Six, S.C., 214, 217, 220, 221, 222, 223, 226, 227, 258.

Non-importation, 21.

Norfolk, Va., 179, 181, 182, 184, 185, 256, 257.

North Carolina, strength of Loyalists, 195–96; persecution, 196–98;

analysis of claimants, 198–202; economic status, 198–99; geographical distribution, 199–201; political leadership, 201–2; motives of Loyalists, 202–10; the Regulators, 202–4; Anglicans, 204–5; Scots, 205–8; merchants, 208–9; office-holders, 209; native-born claimants, 209–10; see also 256, 258.

North, Joshua, 281.

Norwalk, Conn., 60, 62, 68.

Number of Loyalists, N.H., 6–7; Mass., 33; R.I., 47; Conn., 59–60, 62, 63; N.Y., 77–78, 80–83; N.J., 111, 113; Pa., 138, 145–46; Del., 157–59; Md., 165–66, 167; Va., 181–83; N.C., 195–96; S.C., 213–14, 217; Ga., 240–41; see also 252–53, 256.

Oaths, 37, 206, 239–40, 282.

Occupations of Loyalists, N.H., 3, 4; Mass., 23; R.I., 45, 55; Conn., 60; N.Y., 86–87; N.J., 117; Pa., 141; Del., 161, 162; Md., 165, 166; Va., 180–81, 184; N.C., 198; S.C., 219; Ga., 231; see also 261–65.

Odell, Rev. Jonathan, 113, 115, 119, 120, 121.

Ogden, David, 114, 120, 124.

Ogden, Isaac, 112, 113, 121, 279.

Ogilvie, George, 218.

Oliver, Andrew, 28, 36.

Oliver family, 39.

Oliver, Chief Justice Peter, 29, 32, 37.

Oliver, Lt.-Gov. Thomas, 32.

Orange, William, 183.

Otis, James, 19, 33, 36.

Oxnard, Edward, 271.

Pacifist sects, 268, see also Quakers, Mennonites.

Page, Rev. Bernard, 144, 145.

Index

Page, William Byrd, 185, 186.
Paine family, 39.
Paine, Dr. William, 33.
Palmer, Robert, 203.
Palmer, Robert R., 249.
Panton, Rev. George, 121.
Parker, James, 114.
Parroch, John, 147.
Partridge family, 39.
Pastorious, Abraham, 142.
Patterson, Rev. John, 174.
Patriots, 219, 233, 239, 244.
Pemberton, James, 209.
Penn family, 130, 148-49.
Penn, Gov. John, 136, 148.
Penn, Richard, 148.
Pennsylvania, background, 129-31;
    Loyalist equivocation, 131-33;
    the Allen family, 132-33; Phineas
    Bond, 133; James Galloway and
    John Dickinson, 133-34; persecu-
    tion, 134-36; British depredations,
    137-38; number and analysis of
    claimants, 138-49; geographical
    distribution, 138-41; economic
    status, 141, 147; occupations, 141;
    Germans, 142; Quakers, 142-43;
    Anglicans, 143-45; Philadelphia,
    145-47; merchants, 147; political
    leadership, 147-48; the Penn fam-
    ily, 148-49; motives of Loyalists,
    149-53; James Allen, 151-52;
    summary, 153; see also 256, 257.
Pepperell, Sir William, 32.
Perkins, Dr. William Lee, 32.
Peronneau, Henry, 223, 227.
Persecution of Loyalists, N.H., 7;
    Mass., 34-36; R.I., 47-48; Conn.,
    63-66; N.Y., 78-80; N.J., 115-17;
    Pa., 134-36; Del., 158; Md., 168-
    69; Va., 183; N.C., 196-98; S.C.,
    214-16; Ga., 240, 245.
Perth Amboy, N.J., 117, 257.
Peters, Col. John, of New Hamp-
    shire, 9.

Peters, Judge John, of New York,
    91.
Peters, Rev. Samuel, 61, 62, 63, 64,
    70, 71, 73.
Philadelphia, 130, 132, 139, 140, 141,
    142, 143, 145-47, 149, 150, 159,
    256, 257.
Philipsburg, N.Y., 104.
Phillips, Rev. John Lott, 143.
Phillipse, Frederick, 100, 103, 104.
Pickett, David, 64.
Pickman, Benjamin, 279.
Piercy, Rev. William, 237.
Pitt, Floyd, 186.
Pittsburgh, 139, 140.
Political leadership and the Loyal-
    ists, N.H., 10-11; Mass., 25-26;
    R.I., 49, 54-55; Conn., 63; N.Y.,
    94-96; N.J., 113-14; Pa., 147-48;
    Del., 161-62; Md., 169-70; Va.,
    189-90; N.C., 201-2; S.C., 218-19;
    Ga., 241-42.
Poor Loyalists, 24, 60-61, 86, 101-3,
    141, 220, 221, 231-32, 234-35, 265.
Portsmouth, N.H., 4, 5, 6, 7, 9, 11,
    12, 13, 14, 15, 257.
Portsmouth, Va., 179, 181, 184, 185,
    257.
Portuguese, 239.
Potts, Judge John, 137, 148, 162.
Powell, William, 224.
Presbyterians, 10, 47, 94, 98, 99, 101,
    160, 205, 228, 237-38, 263, 268.
Preston, Capt. Thomas, 20, 28.
Price, Charles, 236.
Price, Thomas, 186.
Prince, Newton, 21.
Prince, William, 276.
Princeton, see College of New
    Jersey.
Pritchard, Azariah, 62.
Professional men as Loyalists, 23,
    45, 165, 261-65.
Proprietary officials, see royal offi-
    cials.

[407]

Index

Index

Schaw, Alexander, 207.
Schlesinger, A. M., Sr., 8, 22, 51, 167, 208, 279.
Scotch-Irish, 129, 140, 160, 219, 227–28, 237–38.
Scots, 21, 85, 104–5, 165, 180, 181, 187, 190, 195, 198, 199, 201, 202, 203, 205–8, 221, 232, 237, 259, 260–61, 282.
Seabury, Rev. Samuel, 72, 97, 100, 107.
Seely, Seth, 64.
Serle, Ambrose, 146, 158, 280.
Service with British, 5–6, 24–25, 61, 78, 111, 182, 195, 198–99, 249.
Seven Years War, 59, 90, 260, 268, 270.
Sewall, Atty.-Gen. Jonathan, 32, 38, 40.
Seymour, Rev. James, 237.
Sheafe, James, 6.
Shelton, Isaac Wells, 67.
Sheppard, James, 135.
Sherwood, Justus, 66.
Shippen, Edward, 136.
Shoemaker, Samuel, 132, 134, 143, 144, 148, 150, 153.
Silsby, Daniel, 21.
Simpson, James, 217, 227, 239, 278–79.
Simpson, John, 242.
Simsbury, Conn., 65, 66.
Skene, Lt.-Gov. Philip, 91, 103, 281.
Skenesborough, N.Y., 104.
Skingle, Samuel, 168.
Skinner, Gen. Cortlandt, 111, 118, 120.
Skinner, Stephen, 114.
Skinner, Thomas, 124.
Slocum, Charles, 48.
Slocum, Ebenezer, 48.
Smith, Rev. Haddon, 237.
Smith, Chief Justice William, of New York, 91, 92, 102, 107, 252, 268.

Smith, Rev. William, of Pennsylvania, 142, 144.
Smyth, Chief Justice Frederick, 89, 114, 117.
Snyder, Elias, 135.
Snyder, Peter, 135.
Society for the Propagation of Christian Knowledge, 239.
Society for the Propagation of the Gospel, 9, 24, 26, 70, 85–86, 98, 99, 121, 144, 145, 227.
Sommersett's case, 276.
South Carolina, background, 213; strength of Loyalists, 213–14; persecution, 214–16; British power, 216–18; political leadership, 218–19; analysis of claimants, 219–22; economic status, 219–20; geographical distribution, 220–22; motives of Loyalists, 222–23; timidity of claimants, 223–25; the Regulators, 225–26; Germans, 226; trade with the enemy, 226–27; Anglicans, 227; dissenters, 227–28; summary, 228; see also 242, 256, 257, 258.
Sower, Christopher, 153.
Sower, Christopher, Jr., 142.
Spangler, George, 134.
Sparhawk family, 32.
Spies, 268.
Sprowle, Andrew 186.
Stamford, Conn., 60, 62, 257.
Stamp Act, N.H., 7–8; Mass., 19–20, 28, 34; R.I., 46, 52, 53; Conn., 63, 71, 72; N.Y., 91, 92, 93, 94, 95, 102; N.J., 119, 120; Pa., 132; Md., 171, 172; Va., 183; N.C., 195; S.C., 213, 219.
Stansbury, Joseph, 153.
Stark, William, 14.
Starr, John, 240.
Startin, Charles, 150.
Staten Island, N.Y., 81, 82.
Stavers, Bartholomew, 7.

Index

Index

Wanton, Joseph, Jr., 46, 52, 54.
Wanton, William, 52.
Ward, Phebe, 79–80.
Ward, Samuel, 53, 54, 55.
Warden, William, 19.
Warville, Brissot de, 268.
Warwick, Anthony, 180, 183.
Washington, George, 88, 111, 113, 117, 185, 188.
"Watch Tower," 101.
Watson, John, 47.
Watson, Dr. John, 158.
Watts, Charles, 235.
Watts, John, 94, 103.
Wealth of Loyalists, 265–67, see also individual colonies.
Wealthy Loyalists, 5, 24, 45, 86, 87, 103–4, 147, 161, 165, 180, 184, 186, 220, 221, 231, 233, 266–67.
Weatherford, Martin, 234.
Weatherhead, John, 89.
Webster, John, 136.
Weeks, Rev. Joshua W., 28.
Wells, Robert, 228.
Wentworth, Benning, 12.
Wentworth, Gov. John, 8, 9, 11–12, 13, 271.
West, Benjamin, 106, 275.
Westchester County, N.Y., 81, 82, 83, 90, 95, 102, 258.
"A Westchester Farmer," see Samuel Seabury.
Wharton, Isaac, 147.
Whigs, see Patriots.
White, Alexander, 91.
White, Rev. Calvin, 67.
White, Philip, 116.

Whitecuff, Benjamin, 79, 94.
Whitney, Rev. Aaron, 39.
Wilkins, Isaac, 100, 101.
Willard, Abijah, 32, 37.
Williams family, 39.
Williams, Samuel, 204.
Williamsburg, Va., 181, 184, 185, 187, 257.
Williamson, Gen. Andrew, 217.
Wilmington, N.C., 199, 200, 203, 258.
Wilson, Richard, 203.
Winslow, Edward, 25, 32.
Winslow family, 23, 39.
Winslow, Isaac, 29.
Winthrop, John, 69.
Wiswall, Rev. John, 28.
Witherspoon, President John, 100, 114.
Worcester County, Mass., 31.
Wormington, John, 132, 135.
Wormley, Ralph, 186, 189.
Wragg, William, 217.
Wright, Esther Clark, 249, 250.
Wright, Gov. Sir James, 231, 239, 241, 242, 246.
Wright, Jermyn, 242–43.
Wylly, Alexander, 233, 245.

Yale, 63, 119.
Yonge, Henry, 233.
Yorktown, Va., 179, 190, 196.
Young family, 94.

Zubly, David, 114, 244.
Zubly, Rev. John Joachim, 244.

[411]